HarperCollins

ITALIAN

LANGUAGE SURVIVAL GUIDE

THE VISUAL PHRASE BOOK AND DICTIONARY

HarperResource

An Imprint of HarperCollins*Publishers*

HarperCollins books may be purchased for educational,
business, or sales promotional use. For information, please write:
Special Markets Department, HarperCollins Publishers Inc.,
10 East 53rd Street, New York, NY 10022.

First published in 2001 by HarperCollins Publishers in the
United Kingdom.

Photography: Miroslav Imbrisevic/Brighteye Productions

With additional photography/material from: Christine Bahr,
    Marianne Davidson & Gordon Noble, Hertie (Mainz),
    Hotel Dorint (Mainz), Opel-Bad (Wiesbaden)
    Artville (pp. 89, 90, 91, 92, 93, 94, 95, 96, 97, 98, 99, 101, 102, 103)
    Anthony Blake (pp. 75, 91[tl & mr], 92[tr], 93[mr], 95[br], 97[tr & br],
    98[bl], 99[tl], 101[tl], 102[tl, bl, mr], 103 [br], 105 [ml])
    Wine material: Andrea Gillies
    Map: Heather Moore

Layout: The Printer's Devil, Glasgow, UK

Other titles in the HarperCollins Language Survival Guide series:
    France (0-06-053692-6)
    Spain (0-06-053740-X)
    Italy (0-06-053693-4)
    Greece (0-06-057975-7)
    Portugal (0-06-057977-3)

ISBN 0–06–053693–4

04 05 06 07 08   10 9 8 7 6 5 4 3 2

Printed in Italy by Amadeus SpA

CONTENTS

TOURIST INFORMATION SITES

Currency Converters
www.oanda.com
www.x-rates.com

Foreign Office Advice
www.fco.gov.uk/travel/
countryadvice.asp

Passport Office
www.ukpa.gov.uk/

Health advice
www.thetraveldoctor.com
www.doh.gov.uk/traveladvice

Travel insurance
www.insurance.org.uk

Pets
www.defra.gov.uk/animalh/
quarantine

Weather
www.bbc.co.uk/weather

ITALIAN SITES

Hotel Listings
www.travel.it
www.italy-rome-hotel.com
www.italyhotel.com

Transport
www.fs-on-line.com (Italian railways)

Tourism
www.enit.it
www.initaly.com
www.italytour.com
www.romeguide.it
www.doge.it (Venice guide)
www.northernitaly.com
www.uffizi.firenze.it (Uffizi, Florence)

Internet Cafés
www.cybercafe.com
www.netcafes.com
www.ecs.net/cafe

Shopping
www.made-in-italy.com/index.html

Opera
www.operabase.com/en/

Newspapers
www.repubblica.it (La Repubblica online)
www.corriere.it (Corriere della Sera)
www.mega.it/mask (Florence's paper, La Maschera, with listings, maps, etc.)

INTRODUCTION

As technology sweeps across the world, travellers aren't just faced with the prospect of speaking a foreign language – they also have foreign machines to contend with. Machines for parking, for dispensing cash, for buying tickets and food. Often there is nobody about to ask how they work. *Collins Language Survival Guides* address this problem by showing photographically signs and situations you might come across.

The things that throw you are often the ones that look familiar – such as buses, trains or phones – but which operate slightly differently.

There are usually codes to how things operate, and though you might not think you are aware of them, you are probably using them every day: the colour-coding for roads (blue for motorways, green for major roads, yellow for temporary signs) or when buying milk (generally blue for whole milk, green for semi-skimmed and red for skimmed). It's when these familiar codes don't work in the same way, that you feel slightly at a loss and probably more unsure than you need be. By making a note of how these types of things work and knowing a few keywords, you will feel much more confident.

The unique combination of practical information, photos and phrases found in this book provides the key to hassle-free travel and the colour-coding below shows how information is presented and how to access it as quickly as possible.

General, practical information which will provide useful tips on getting the best out of your trip

keywords ◀

these are words that are useful to know both when you see them written down or you hear them spoken

keywords
destra
*des-*tra
right
sinistra
see-*nees*-tra
left

key talk ▶

short, simple phrases that you can change and adapt to suit your own situation

talking
excuse me!   **we're looking for...**
scusi!   cerchiamo...
skoo-zee   *cherk-ya*-mo...
do you know where...?
sa dov'è...?
sa do-**ve**...

The **Food Section** allows you to choose more easily from what is on offer, both for snacks and at restaurants.

The practical 5000-word, English-Italian and Italian-English **Dictionary** means that you will never be stuck for words.

SPEAKING ITALIAN

We've tried to make the pronunciation under the phrases as clear as possible. We've split up the words to make them easy to read, but don't pause too long between syllables. Italian isn't really hard to pronounce and once you learn a few basic rules, it shouldn't be too long before you can read straight from the Italian.

Longer words are usually stressed on the next to last syllable, but we show all stressed syllables in **heavy type**, so you won't be caught out by any exceptions.

The spellings **c** and **ch** might confuse you, because **c** is sometimes pronounced like English **ch** as in church, while the Italian **ch** is pronounced like the English **k**. (Look at the English for kilogram and the Italian **chilogramma**.) So **c'è** (there is) is pronounced like English check without the final **k** sound, while **che?** (what?) is pronounced **kay**. The rule to remember is that **c** followed by **e** or **i** makes it a soft **ch** sound. But **c** followed by **a**, **o** or **u** has a hard **k** sound. Try practising saying and reading the following words:

chiave *kee-a-vay* (key)   **cibo** *chee-bo* (food)
chiesa *kee-ay-za* (church)   **cena** *chay-na* (dinner)

The letter **g** behaves in a similar way. When followed by **a**, **o** or **u**, **g** will be hard. When followed by **e** or **i**, **g** will be soft. The word for lake is **lago**, for lakes the word is **laghi**. The **h** has been added to keep the **g** hard. So when you see a **ch** or **gh** combination in Italian, remember to make the **c** and **g** hard.

Sometimes Italian has two distinctive vowel sounds next to each other, in other words like **dei**, shown in the pronunciation as *day-ee*. These sounds merge with each other, so don't separate them with a long pause.

Finally, pronounce all **r**'s when you see them in Italian words.

Basic rules to remember are:

italian	sounds like	example	pronunciation
a	cat	**pasta**	*pas-ta*
e	bet/day	**letto/per**	*let-to/payr*
i	meet	**vino**	*vee-no*
o	got	**botta**	*bot-ta*
u	boot	**luna**	*loo-na*
gli	million	**figlio**	*feel-yo*
sc *(before e/i)*	shop	**sci**	*shee*
sc *(before a/o/u)*	scan	**scarpa**	*skar-pa*

EVERYDAY TALK

There are two forms of address in Italian, formal and informal. You should always stick with the formal until you are on a first-name basis. For the purposes of this book we will use the formal.

yes
sì
see

no
no
no

ok/that's fine
va bene
*va **be**-nay*

please
per favore
*payr fa-**vo**-ray*

thank you
grazie
***grats**-yay*

thanks very much
grazie mille
***grats**-yay **meel**-lay*

don't mention it
prego
***pray**-go*

that's very kind
molto gentile
***mol**-to jen-**tee**-lay*

hello
buon giorno
*bwon **jor**-no*

goodbye
arrivederci
*ar-ree-ve-**der**-chee*

hi/bye
ciao
chow

good evening
buona sera
***bwo**-na **say**-ra*

good night
buona notte
***bwo**-na **not**-tay*

see you later
a più tardi
*a pyoo **tar**-dee*

excuse me!
permesso!
*per-**mes**-so*

sorry!
scusi!
***skoo**-zee*

I am sorry
mi dispiace
*mee dees-**pya**-chay*

I don't understand
non capisco
*non ka-**pees**-ko*

I don't know
non lo so
non lo so

Addressing people

Italians are quite formal when addressing each other. When greeting someone in the street or shop you can simply say *buon giorno, Signora* (for a woman) and *buon giorno, Signore* (for a man). If you are not sure how formal to be, a good alternative for hello is *salve* which you can use with anyone. Among young people and friends, you will hear *ciao*.

how are you?
come sta?
***ko**-may sta*

fine thanks?
bene grazie
*be-nay **grat**-see-ay*

and you?
e lei?
e lay

hi, Michele
ciao Michele
*chow mee-**ke**-le*

bye, Luisa
ciao Luisa
*chow loo-**ee**-za*

piacere
nice to meet you
*pya-**cher**-ay*

*The simplest way to ask for something in a shop or bar is by naming what you want and adding **per favore**.*

keywords keywords keywords

1	**uno**
	oo-no
2	**due**
	doo-ay
3	**tre**
	tray
4	**quattro**
	kwat-ro
5	**cinque**
	cheen-kway
6	**sei**
	say
7	**sette**
	set-tay
8	**otto**
	ot-to
9	**nove**
	no-vay
10	**dieci**
	dee-ay-chee

a ... please
un/una ... per favore
oon/oo-na ... payr fa-vo-ray

a coffee please
un caffè per favore
oon kaf-fe payr fa-vo-ray

a beer please
una birra per favore
oo-na beer-ra payr fa-vo-ray

an ice cream and 2 beers please
un gelato e due birre per favore
oon jay-la-to ay doo-ay beer-ray payr fa-vo-ray

the (singular)
il/la
eel/la

the (plural)
i/le
ee/lay

the menu please
il menù per favore
eel me-noo payr fa-vo-ray

the bill please
il conto per favore
eel kon-to payr fa-vo-ray

another...
un altro/un' altra...
oon al-tro/oon al-tra...

more...
ancora...
an-ko-ra...

another beer
un'altra birra
oon al-tra beer-ra

another tea
un altro tè
oon al-tro te

2 more beers
ancora due birre
an-ko-ra doo-ay beer-ray

2 more coffees
ancora due caffè
an-ko-ra doo-ay kaf-fe

3 tickets
tre biglietti
tray beel-yet-tee

4 ice creams
quattro gelati
kwat-tro jay-la-tee

To catch someone's attention

The easiest way to catch someone's attention is by using *scusi*. If it is an older man or woman, it is polite to add *Signore* (for the man) and *Signora* (for the woman). If you are trying to get through a crowd, use *permesso*.

excuse me!
scusi, Signore/Signora!
skoo-zee seen-yo-ray/seen-yo-ra

can you help me?
può aiutarmi?
pwo a-yoo-tar-mee

do you know where... is?
sa dov'è...?
sa do-ve...

do you know how I get to...?
sa come si va a...?
sa ko-may see va a...

By combining key words and phrases you can build up your language and adapt the phrases to suit your own situation.

avete...?
do you have...?

do you have a map?
avete una cartina?
a-vay-tay oo-na kar-tee-na

do you have a room?
avete una camera?
a-vay-tay oo-na ka-may-ra

quanto costa?
how much?

how much is the wine?
quanto costa il vino?
kwan-ta kos-ta eel vee-no

how much is the trip?
quanto costa il viaggio?
kwan-ta kos-ta eel vee-ad-jo

vorrei...
I'd like...

I'd like a red wine
vorrei un vino rosso
vor-ray oon vee-no ros-so

I'd like an ice cream
vorrei un gelato
vor-ray oon jay-la-to

ho bisogno di...
I need...

I need a taxi
ho bisogno di un taxi
o bee-zon-yo dee oon tak-see

I need to go
ho bisogno di andare
o bee-zon-yo dee an-da-ray

quando?
when?

when does it open?
quando apre?
kwan-do a-pray

when does it close?
quando chiude?
kwan-do kee-oo-day

when does it leave?
quando parte?
kwan-do par-tay

when does it arrive?
quando arriva?
kwan-do ar-ree-va

dove?
where?

where is the bank?
dov'è la banca?
do-ve la ban-ka

where is the hotel?
dov'è l'albergo?
do-ve lal-ber-go

c'è...?
is there...?

is there a market?
c'è un mercato?
che oon mer-ka-to

where is there a market?
dove c'è un mercato?
do-vay che oon mer-ka-to

non c'è...
there is no...

there is no bread
non c'è pane
non che pa-nay

is there no train?
non c'è un treno?
non che oon tray-no

posso...?
can I...?

can I go by train?
posso andare in treno?
pos-so an-da-ray een tray-no

can I smoke?
posso fumare?
pos-so foo-ma-ray

where can I buy milk?
dove posso comprare del latte?
do-vay pos-so kom-pra-ray del lat-tay

è...?
is it...?

is it near?
è vicino?
e vee-chee-no

is it far?
è lontano?
e lon-ta-no

mi piace...
I like...

I like wine
mi piace il vino
mee pee-a-chay eel vee-no

I don't like dancing
non mi piace ballare
non mee pya-chay bal-la-ray

These are a selection of small but very useful words to know.

keywords · keywords · keywords · keywords · keywords

grande
gran-day
large

piccolo
pee-ko-lo
small

un poco
oon *po*-ko
a little

basta
bas-ta
enough

più vicino
pyoo vee-*chee*-no
nearest

lontano
lon-*ta*-no
far

troppo caro
trop-po *ka*-ro
too expensive

pieno
pee-*ay*-no
full

libero
lee-bay-ro
free

e
ay
and

con/senza
kon/*sent*-sa
with/without

questo/quello
kwes-to/*kwel*-lo
this one/that one

subito
soo-bee-to
straightaway

più tardi
pyoo *tar*-dee
later

a large car
una macchina grande
oo-na *mak*-kee-na *gran*-day

a small house
una casa piccola
oo-na *ka*-za *peek*-ko-la

a little please
un poco per favore
oon *po*-ko payr fa-*vo*-ray

that's enough thanks
basta così grazie
bas-ta ko-*zee* grats-yay

where is the nearest chemist?
dov'è la farmacia più vicina?
do-*ve* la far-ma-*chee*-a pyoo vee-*chee*-na

is it far?
è lontano?
e lon-*ta*-no

it is too expensive
è troppo caro
e *trop*-po *ka*-ro

it is too small
è troppo piccolo
e *trop*-po *peek*-ko-lo

is it full?
e pieno?
e pee-*ay*-no

is it free (unoccupied)**?**
è libero?
e *lee*-bay-ro

a tea and 2 beers
un tè e due birre
oon te e *doo*-ay *beer*-ray

with sugar
con zucchero
kon *tsook*-kay-ro

with milk
col latte
kol *lat*-tay

without sugar
senza zucchero
sent-sa *tsook*-kay-ro

without milk
senza latte
sent-sa *lat*-tay

for me
per me
payr me

for her/for him
per lei/per lui
payr lay/per *loo*-ee

my passport
il mio passaporto
eel *mee*-o pas-sa-*por*-to

my keys
le mie chiavi
lay *mee*-ay kee-a-vee

I'd like this one
vorrei questo
vor-*ray kwes*-to

I'd like that one
vorrei quello
vor-*ray kwel*-lo

I need a taxi straightaway
ho bisogno di un taxi subito
o bee-*zon*-yo dee oon *tak*-see *soo*-bee-to

I'll call again later
richiamo più tardi
reek-*ya*-mo pyoo *tar*-dee

It is always good to be able to say a few words about yourself to break the ice, even if you won't be able to tell your life story.

my name is...
mi chiamo...
mee kee-a-mo...

I am from...
sono di...
so-no dee...

I'm here on holiday
sono qui in vacanza
so-no kwee een va-kan-za

I'm here on business
sono qui per lavoro
so-no kwee payr la-vo-ro

I'm not married
non sono sposato/a
non so-no spo-za-to/a

I am married
sono sposato/a
so-no spo-za-to/a

I have a boyfriend
ho un ragazzo
o oon rag-at-so

I have a girlfriend
ho una ragazza
o oo-na rag-at-sa

I am a widow
sono vedova
so-no vay-do-va

I am a widower
sono vedovo
so-no vay-do-vo

I am divorced
sono divorziato/a
so-no dee-vorts-ya-to/a

I am separated
sono separato/a
so-no sep-a-ra-to/a

I have a son/daughter
ho un figlio/una figlia
o oon feel-yo/oo-na feel-ya

I have ... children
ho ... figli
o ... feel-yee

I work
lavoro
la-vo-ro

I am retired
sono in pensione
so-no een pens-yo-nay

I am a student
sono studente
so-no stoo-den-tay

Italy is very beautiful
l'Italia è molto bella
lee-tal-ya e mol-to bel-la

I love Italian food
mi piace molto la cucina italiana
mee pee-a-chay mol-to la koo-chee-na ee-tal-ya-na

Italian people are very kind
gli Italiani sono molto gentili
lee ee-tal-ya-nee so-no mol-to jen-tee-lee

I'd like to come back
vorrei ritornare
vor-ray ree-tor-na-ray

thank you very much for your kindness
grazie mille per la sua gentilezza
grats-yay meel-lay payr la soo-a jen-tee-let-sa

you are very kind
lei è molto gentile
lay e mol-to jen-tee-lay

I have enjoyed myself very much
mi sono divertito/a moltissimo
mee so-no dee-ver-tee-to/a mol-tees-see-mo

we will be back next year
ritorniamo l'anno prossimo
ree-torn-ya-mo lan-no pros-see-mo

can I have your address?
potrei avere il suo indirizzo?
po-tray a-vay-ray eel soo-o een-dee-reet-so

see you next year!
all'anno prossimo!
al-lan-no pros-see-mo

Although problems are not something anyone wants, you might come across the odd difficulty, and it is best to be armed with a few phrases to cope with the situation.

excuse me!
scusi!
skoo-zee

can you help me
può aiutarmi?
pwo a-yoo-tar-mee

I don't speak...
non parlo...
non par-lo...

I am sorry, I did not know
mi scusi, non lo sapevo
mee skoo-zee non lo sa-pay-vo

I am lost
mi sono smarrito/a
mee so-no smar-ree-to/a

we are lost
ci siamo persi
chee see-a-mo per-see

I have lost...
ho perso...
ho payr-so...

my money
i soldi
ee sol-dee

my tickets
i biglietti
ee beel-yet-tee

my passport
il mio passaporto
eel mee-o pas-sa-por-to

I have left...
ho lasciato...
o la-sha-to...

in the restaurant
nel ristorante
nel rees-to-ran-tay

on the train
sul treno
sool tray-no

I have missed...
ho perso...
ho per-so...

my flight
il volo
eel vo-lo

the train
il treno
eel tray-no

the coach
il pullman
eel pool-man

I need to get to...
devo andare a...
day-vo an-da-ray...

how can I get there today?
come ci posso arrivare oggi?
ko-may chee pos-so ar-ree-va-ray od-jee

my luggage hasn't arrived
il mio bagaglio non è arrivato
eel mee-o ba-gal-yo non e ar-ree-va-to

my case has been damaged
la mia valigia è stata danneggiata
la mee-a va-lee-ja e sta-ta dan-nay-ja-ta

my bag
la mia borsa
la mee-a bor-sa

my purse
il mio portafoglio
eel mee-o por-ta-fol-yo

my camera
la mia macchina fotografica
la mee-a mak-kee-na fo-to-gra-fee-ka

... has been stolen
... è stato rubato/a
... e sta-to roo-ba-to/a

you can get me at this address
mi trova a questo indirizzo
mee tro-va a kwes-to een-dee-reet-so

I have to go to hospital
devo andare in ospedale
day-vo an-da-ray een os-pay-da-lay

I have no money
non ho soldi
non o sol-dee

I can't find my son
non trovo mio figlio
non tro-vo mee-yo feel-yo

I can't find my daughter
non trovo mia figlia
non tro-vo mee-a feel-ya

go away!
se ne vada!
say nay va-da

that man is following me
quell'uomo mi sta seguendo
kwel wo-mo mee sta seg-wen-do

Italians expect to receive good service and quality. They will complain when things are not to their liking.

there is no...
non c'è...
non che...

there is no soap
non c'è sapone
non che sa-po-nay

it is dirty
è sporco
e spor-ko

they are dirty
sono sporchi
so-no spor-kee

it is broken
è rotto
e rot-to

they are broken
sono rotti
so-no rot-tee

the ... does not work
il/la ... non funziona
eel/la ... non foonts-yo-na

the ... do not work
i/le ... non funzionano
ee/lay ... non foonts-yo-na-no

the window doesn't open
la finestra non apre
la fee-nes-tra non ap-ray

the window doesn't close
la finestra non chiude
la fee-nes-tra non kee-oo-day

there is too much noise
c'è troppo rumore
che trop-po roo-mor-ay

the room is too small
la camera è troppo piccola
la ka-may-ra e trop-po peek-ko-la

the room is too hot
la camera è troppo calda
la ka-may-ra e trop-po kal-da

the room is too cold
la camera è troppo fredda
la ka-may-ra e trop-po fred-da

it is too expensive
è troppo caro
e trop-po ka-ro

you are charging too much
lei mi chiede troppo
lay mee kyay-dee trop-po

I want to complain
voglio fare un reclamo
vol-yo fa-ray oon rek-la-mo

I want to speak to the manager
voglio parlare con il gerente
vol-yo par-la-ray kon eel jay-ren-tay

we'd like to order
vorremmo ordinare
vor-rem-mo or-dee-na-ray

the service is bad
il servizio è impossibile
eel ser-veets-yo e eem-pos-see-bee-lay

this food is cold
il cibo è freddo
eel chee-bo e fred-do

this cappuccino is cold
questo cappuccino è freddo
kwes-to kap-poo-chee-no e fred-do

there is a mistake
c'è un errore
che oon er-ro-ray

can we check the bill?
possiamo controllare il conto?
poss-ya-mo kon-trol-la-ray eel kon-to

I didn't order this
non ho ordinato questo
non o or-dee-na-to kwes-to

please take it off the bill
può toglierlo dal conto?
pwo tol-yer-lo dal kon-to

The next four pages should give you an idea of the type of things you will come across in Italy.

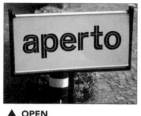

▲ OPEN

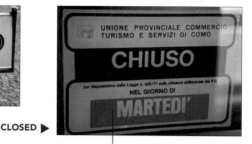

CLOSED ▶

closing day Tuesday

▼ OPENING HOURS

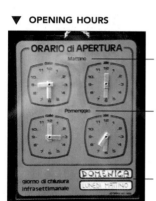

mattino
morning

pomeriggio
afternoon

giorno di chiusura
day closed Sun. & Mon. afternoon

L'orario estivo is the summer timetable. Shops close on Sat afternoon and stay open on Mon mornings. In winter shops are generally closed on Mon mornings but open in the afternoon. From Tue to Sat opening hours are generally 8.30 am to 1 pm and from about 4 pm to 7 pm. Shops are shut on Sun except those in tourist areas which may open to sell holiday items.

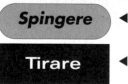

Spingere ◀ PUSH

Tirare ◀ PULL

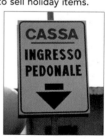

PAY HERE
pedestrian entrance ▶

talking

do you have...?	**stamps**	**phonecards**
avete...?	francobolli	schede telefoniche
a-vay-tay...	*fran-ko-**bol**-lee*	***skay**-day te-le-**fo**-nee-kay*
where can I get...?	**a newspaper**	**postcards**
dove posso comprare...?	un giornale	cartoline
***do**-vay **pos**-so komp-**ra**-ray...*	*oon jor-**na**-lay*	*kar-to-**lee**-nay*

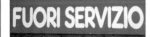

▲ IN SERVICE

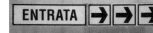

▲ OUT OF SERVICE

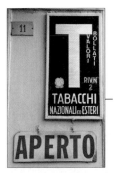

— TOBACCONIST

These are often attached to a bar and sell cigarettes, stamps, bus tickets, etc. You can also buy salt here – a legacy of the days when salt was a state monopoly.

ENTRATA →→→

▲ ENTRANCE

▼ EMERGENCY EXIT

USCITA DI SICUREZZA

You will also see the word *uscita* used for exit on the motorway.

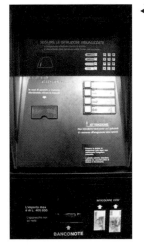

◀ There is an increasing number of automated machines. Instructions are often given in different languages.

Post boxes are red. The blue post box is for priority mail abroad.

▼

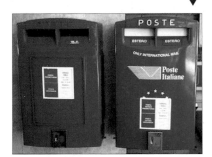

excuse me...
scusi...
skoo-zee...

what do I have to do?
cosa devo fare?
ko-za day-vo fa-ray

how does this work?
come funziona?
ko-may foonts-yo-na

what does this mean?
cosa significa?
ko-za seen-yee-fee-ka

talking

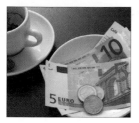

◀ Service is usually included in a restaurant bill so tipping is discretionary. However, it is usual to leave a small tip. In busy bars, there will often be a saucer to leave coins.

NO FISHING
divieto means forbidden

from 1 April to 30 September

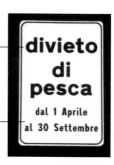

divieto di pesca
dal 1 Aprile al 30 Settembre

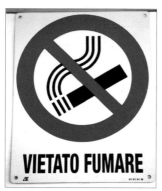

▲ **NO SMOKING**

Smoking is still pretty popular in Italy and you are unlikely to find non-smoking areas in restaurants and bars. If people are smoking in a restaurant, they are also likely to light up in between courses (whether or not you have finished eating).

no entry for unauthorised persons

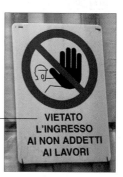

VIETATO L'INGRESSO AI NON ADDETTI AI LAVORI

▲ *Vietato* is another word that means forbidden.

can I smoke?
posso fumare?
pos-so foo-*ma*-ray

do you mind if I smoke?
le dà fastidio se fumo?
lay da fas-*teed*-yo say *foo*-mo

I don't smoke
non fumo
non *foo*-mo

please don't smoke
le dispiace non fumare
lay deesp-*ya*-chay non foo-*ma*-ray

an ashtray
un portacenere
oon por-ta-*chen*-nay-ray

a smoking seat
un posto fumatore
oon *pos*-to foo-ma-*tor*-ay

talking

There are toilets at railway stations, often with an attendant. Although you do not have to pay, you may see a plate for coins. The attendant may even hand out toilet paper. If you do come across a public toilet, it is unlikely to have toilet paper, so remember always to carry tissues. Bars and restaurants have toilets, but they will not look at you kindly if you use their facilities without buying something. Remember it is cheapest to buy a drink standing at the bar. Toilets are sometimes locked and you will have to ask for the key.

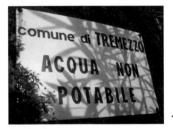

◀ Toilets are usually indicated with a pictogram.

▼ MEN

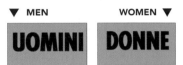

UOMINI   DONNE

WOMEN ▼

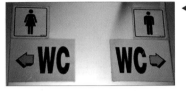

Don't be fooled: ▶
caldo means hot,
freddo means cold.

Caldo

Freddo

NON-DRINKING
◀ WATER

excuse me! where is the toilet?
scusi! dov'è la toilette?
skoo-zee do-ve la twa-let

excuse me! may I use the bathroom?
scusi! posso usare il bagno?
skoo-zee pos-so oo-za-ray eel ban-yo

do you have the key for the toilet?
avete la chiave per la toilette?
a-vay-tay la kee-a-vay payr la twa-let

is there a disabled toilet?
ci sono le toilette per i disabili?
chee so-no lay twa-let payr ee dee-za-bee-lee

is there somewhere to change the baby?
c'è un posto per cambiare il bambino?
che oon pos-to payr kamb-ya-ray eel bam-bee-no

talking talking

ASKING THE WAY

Tourist offices provide free maps, usually with an English version.
They are usually well-stocked with brochures and leaflets about
attractions in the area. They can also help finding somewhere to stay.

Newer signs
▼ often carry pictograms.

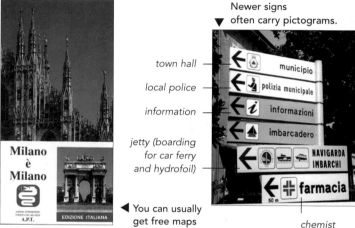

town hall — municipio

local police — polizia municipale

information — informazioni

jetty (boarding
for car ferry
and hydrofoil) — imbarcadero

NAVIGARDA IMBARCHI

farmacia — chemist

◀ You can usually
get free maps
(in English) from tourist offices.

Milano è Milano
EDIZIONE ITALIANA
A.P.T.

---

talking talking talking

excuse me!
scusi!
skoo-zee

do you know where...?
sa dov'è...?
sa do-ve...

how do I get to...?
per andare a...?
payr an-da-ray a...

is this the right way to...?
è la strada giusta per...?
e la stra-da joos-ta payr...

do you have a map of the town?
avete una piantina della città?
a-vay-tay oo-na pyan-tee-na del-la cheet-ta

can you show me on the map?
mi può indicare sulla piantina?
mee pwo een-dee-ka-ray sool-la pyan-tee-na

we're looking for...
cerchiamo...
cherk-ya-mo...

where is the tourist office?
dov'è l'ufficio turistico?
do-ve loof-fee-cho too-rees-tee-ko

is it far?
è lontano?
e lon-ta-no

a street directory
uno stradario
oo-no stra-dar-ee-o

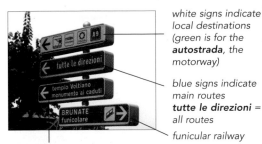

white signs indicate local destinations (green is for the **autostrada**, the motorway)

blue signs indicate main routes
tutte le direzioni = all routes

funicular railway

brown signs indicate places of interest;
monumento ai caduti is a war memorial.

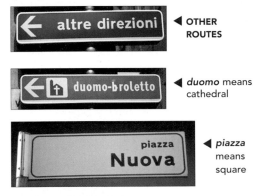

◀ OTHER ROUTES

◀ **duomo** means cathedral

◀ **piazza** means square

name of the road

indicates one-way street

centre

parking

Church of the Crucifix

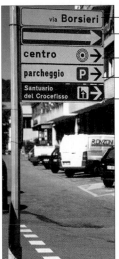

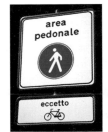

◀ PEDESTRIAN AREA
bicycles allowed

a destra
a des-tra
to the right

a sinistra
a see-nees-tra
to the left

va
va
go

giri
jee-ree
turn

via
vee-a
road

piazza
pee-at-sa
square

semaforo
se-ma-fo-ro
traffic lights

chiesa
kee-ay-za
church

primo
pree-mo
first

secondo
se-kon-do
second

lontano
lon-ta-no
far

vicino a
vee-chee-no a
near to

accanto a
ak-kan-to a
next to

in faccia a
een fat-cha a
opposite

fino a
fee-no a
until

keywords keywords keywords keywords keywords

BANKS & MONEY

Banks offer the best rate of exchange, though changing traveller's cheques can sometimes be quite lengthy. Remember to take your passport with you and don't expect cashiers to speak English. In smaller places banks tend to be shut in the afternoon, so it is best to go in the mornings, when you can be sure that they are open. Banking hours are generally 8.30 am to1.30 pm Monday to Friday and in the afternoon for an hour from 2.45 to 3.45. But check when you are there, as times vary from place to place. Credit cards and switch payments are widely accepted.

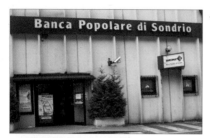

◀ Italy has many regional banks such as *Banco Popolare di Sondrio*; nationwide banks include *Credito Italiano* and *Banca Nazionale del Lavoro*.

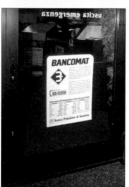

Some cash-points are located inside the bank. Look out for the *Bancomat* sign. ◀

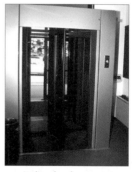

▲ Italian banks operate a double-door or revolving-door system with metal detectors to check you aren't armed. To enter you press a button and wait for a green light to show and let you through.

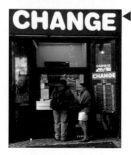

◀ Bureaus de Change are usually open longer, but tend not to offer as good rates as banks.

◀ Symbol for the euro. It is also abbreviated to EUR. A comma is used between euro and cent and a full stop for thousands, i.e. € 6,50 or EUR 6.500,05.

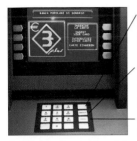

Press the yellow button (**cancella**) to delete last part of the transaction and return to previous menu.

Press the red button (**annulla**) to delete the whole transaction and get your card back.

Press the green button (**esegui**) to go ahead.

▲ Most cash machines let you select the language for your transaction.

keywords keywords keywords

carta di credito
kar-ta dee
kray-dee-to
credit card

bancomat
ban-ko-*mat*
cashpoint

numero pin
noo-may-ro peen
pin number

spiccioli
speech-cho-lee
change

inserire
een-ser-*ee*-ray
insert

cambio
kamb-yo
exchange rate

contanti
kon-*tan*-tee
cash

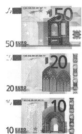

The euro is the currency of Italy. It breaks down into 100 euro cents.

◀ Notes: 5, 10, 20, 50, 100, 200 and 500 euro.

Euro notes are the same throughout Europe. The backs of coins carry different designs from each of the member European countries.

◀ Coins: 2 euro, 1 euro, 50 cent, 20 cent, 10 cent, 5 cent, 2 cent, 1 cent. You find that Italians refer to them as **centesimi** (chen-*tes*-ee-mee), a more familiar term for them.

talking

where can I change money?
dove posso cambiare dei soldi?
do-vay *pos*-so kamb-*ya*-ray day *sol*-dee

where is there a bureau de change
dove c'è un cambio
do-vay che oon **kamb**-yo

I want to change these traveller's cheques
vorrei cambiare questi travellers cheque
vor-**ray** kamb-**ya**-ray **kwes**-tee travellers cheques

the cashpoint has swallowed my card
il bancomat ha mangiato la mia carta
eel **ban**-ko-mat a man-**ja**-to la **mee**-a **kar**-ta

where is the nearest cashpoint?
dov'è il bancomat più vicino?
do-**ve** eel **ban**-ko-mat pyoo vee-**chee**-no

where is the bank?
dov'è la banca?
do-**ve** la **ban**-ka

small notes
biglietti piccoli
beel-**yet**-tee **pee**-ko-lee

Italy is one hour ahead of Great Britain apart from the last week of September when they have the same time.

keywords keywords keywords keywords

mattina
mat-**tee**-na
morning

pomeriggio
po-may-**reed**-jo
afternoon

stasera
sta-**say**-ra
this evening

oggi
od-jee
today

domani
do-**ma**-nee
tomorrow

ieri
yer-ee
yesterday

più tardi
pyoo **tar**-dee
later

subito
soo-bee-to
straightaway

adesso
a-**des**-so
now

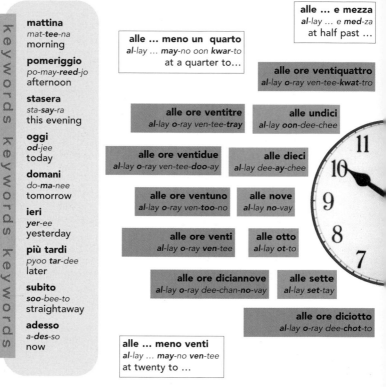

alle ... e mezza
al-lay ... e **med**-za
at half past ...

alle ... meno un quarto
al-lay ... **may**-no oon **kwar**-to
at a quarter to...

alle ore ventiquattro
al-lay o-ray ven-tee-**kwat**-tro

alle ore ventitre
al-lay o-ray ven-tee-**tray**

alle undici
al-lay oon-dee-chee

alle ore ventidue
al-lay o-ray ven-tee-**doo**-ay

alle dieci
al-lay dee-**ay**-chee

alle ore ventuno
al-lay o-ray ven-**too**-no

alle nove
al-lay **no**-vay

alle ore venti
al-lay o-ray **ven**-tee

alle otto
al-lay ot-to

alle ore diciannove
al-lay o-ray dee-chan-**no**-vay

alle sette
al-lay **set**-tay

alle ore diciotto
al-lay o-ray dee-**chot**-to

alle ... meno venti
al-lay ... **may**-no **ven**-tee
at twenty to ...

talking

when is the next...?
quando c'è il prossimo...?
kwan-do che eel **pros**-see-mo...

train
treno
tray-no

boat
battello
bat-**tel**-lo

what time is...?
a che ora è...?
a kay **o**-ra e...

breakfast
la prima colazione
la **pree**-ma ko-**lats**-yo-nay

dinner
la cena
la **chay**-na

when does it leave?
quando parte?
kwan-do **par**-tay

when does it arrive?
quando arriva?
kwan-do ar-**ree**-va

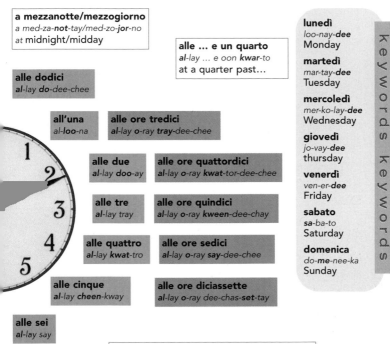

a mezzanotte/mezzogiorno
*a med-za-**not**-tay/med-zo-**jor**-no*
at midnight/midday

alle ... e un quarto
*al-lay ... e oon **kwar**-to*
at a quarter past...

alle dodici
*al-lay **do**-dee-chee*

all'una
*al-**loo**-na*

alle ore tredici
*al-lay o-ray **tray**-dee-chee*

alle due
*al-lay **doo**-ay*

alle ore quattordici
*al-lay o-ray **kwat**-tor-dee-chee*

alle tre
al-lay tray

alle ore quindici
*al-lay o-ray **kween**-dee-chay*

alle quattro
*al-lay **kwat**-tro*

alle ore sedici
*al-lay o-ray **say**-dee-chee*

alle cinque
*al-lay **cheen**-kway*

alle ore diciassette
*al-lay o-ray dee-chas-**set**-tay*

alle sei
al-lay say

alle ore diciotto e quarantacinque
*al-lay o-ray dee-**chot**-to ay kwa-ran-ta-**cheen**-kway*
at 18.45

keywords keywords keywords

lunedì
*loo-nay-**dee***
Monday

martedì
*mar-tay-**dee***
Tuesday

mercoledì
*mer-ko-lay-**dee***
Wednesday

giovedì
*jo-vay-**dee***
thursday

venerdì
*ven-er-**dee***
Friday

sabato
sa-ba-to
Saturday

domenica
*do-**me**-nee-ka*
Sunday

what is the date?
qual è la data?
*kwal e la **da**-ta*

it is the 8th May
è l'otto maggio
*e **lot**-to **mad**-jo*

16 September 2002
il sedici settembre duemilaedue
*eel **say**-dee-chee set-**tem**-bray doo-ay-mee-la-ay-**doo**-ay*

which day?
quale giorno?
*kwa-lay **jor**-no*

which month?
quale mese?
*kwa-lay **may**-zay*

talking

TIMETABLES

 Timetables use the 24 hour clock. The Italian for timetable is **orario***. There are winter (***invernale***) and summer (***estivo***) timetables.*

Train timetable ▶

Fer = feriale weekdays Mon-Sat

operates until 23/12 from 7/1

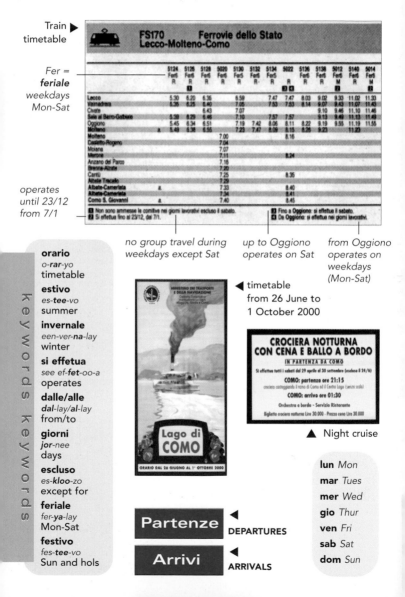

FS170   Ferrovie dello Stato
Lecco-Molteno-Como

	5124 Fer5 R	5126 Fer5 R	5128 Fer5 R ❶	5020 Fer5 R	5130 Fer5 R	5132 Fer5 R	5134 Fer5 R	5022 Fer5 R ❸❹	5136 Fer5 R	5138 Fer5 R	5012 Fer5 M	5140 Fer5 R	5014 Fer5 M
Lecco	5.30	6.20	6.35		6.59		7.47	7.47	8.03	9.02	9.30	11.02	11.33
Valmadrera	5.35	6.25	6.40		7.05		7.53	7.53	8.14	9.07	9.43	11.07	11.43
Civate			6.43		7.07					9.10	9.46	11.10	11.46
Sala al Barro-Galbiate	5.39	6.29	6.46		7.10		7.57	7.57		9.13	9.49	11.13	11.49
Oggiono	5.45	6.34	6.51		7.19	7.42	8.04		8.22	9.19	9.55	11.19	11.55
Molteno	a 5.49	6.38	6.55		7.23	7.47	8.09		8.15	8.26	9.23		11.23
Molteno				7.00				8.16					
Castello-Rogeno				7.04									
Molana				7.07									
Merone				7.11				8.24					
Anzano del Parco				7.16									
Brenna-Alzate				7.20									
Cantù				7.25				8.35					
Albate Trecallo				7.29									
Albate-Camerlata	a			7.33				8.40					
Albate-Camerlata				7.34				8.41					
Como S. Giovanni	a			7.40				8.45					

❶ Non sono ammesse le comitive nei giorni lavorativi escluso il sabato.
❷ Si effettua fino al 23/12, dal 7/1.
❸ Fino a Oggiono: si effettua il sabato.
❹ Da Oggiono: si effettua nei giorni lavorativi.

no group travel during weekdays except Sat

up to Oggiono operates on Sat

from Oggiono operates on weekdays (Mon-Sat)

orario
o-rar-yo
timetable

estivo
es-tee-vo
summer

invernale
een-ver-na-lay
winter

si effetua
see ef-fet-oo-a
operates

dalle/alle
dal-lay/al-lay
from/to

giorni
jor-nee
days

escluso
es-kloo-zo
except for

feriale
fer-ya-lay
Mon-Sat

festivo
fes-tee-vo
Sun and hols

◀ *timetable from 26 June to 1 October 2000*

CROCIERA NOTTURNA CON CENA E BALLO A BORDO
IN PARTENZA DA COMO
Si effettua tutti i sabati dal 29 aprile al 30 settembre (escluso il 24/6)
COMO: partenza ore 21:15
crociera costeggiando il ramo di Como ed il Centro Lago (senza scalo)
COMO: arrivo ore 01:30
Orchestra a bordo - Servizio Ristorante
Biglietto crociera notturna Lire 30.000 - Prezzo cena Lire 30.000

▲ Night cruise

ORARIO DAL 26 GIUGNO AL 1° OTTOBRE 2000
Lago di COMO

Partenze ◀ DEPARTURES

Arrivi ◀ ARRIVALS

lun *Mon*
mar *Tues*
mer *Wed*
gio *Thur*
ven *Fri*
sab *Sat*
dom *Sun*

keywords

Bus timetable ▼

SPT (bus company)

number of bus service

Fes = **festivo** Sun & hols

Fer = **feriale** weekdays Mon-Sat

services operating from there

Scol = **scolastici** school term

p = square

v = street

uff. PT = post office

monum. caduti = war memorial

tickets must be bought on the ground (i.e. before boarding)

operates on school days except Sat

C13   SPT
Menaggio-Plesio

Barna (km 1.7)

Menaggio   Plesio (km 9.1)

C10 C12 C14 C250   (km 6.3)
C827 CA1 CB1 CT1

	1302 Scol ①	1304 Fer6	1306 Fest ①	1308 Fer6 ①	1310 Fer6 ②	1314 Fer6	1320 Fer6 ②	1330 Fer6	1334 Fer6	1336 Fer6 ⑩ ②	1340 ①	1344 Fer6 ②
Menaggio p. Garibaldi a)	5.50	7.10	7.20	8.32	9.30	10.50	12.10	13.50	14.40	16.10	17.32	18.32
Menaggio v. Como	5.52	7.12	7.22	8.33	9.32	10.52	12.12	13.52	14.42	16.12	17.34	18.34
Menaggio l. Fossati	5.55	7.15	7.25	8.35	9.35	10.55	12.15	13.54	14.45	16.15	17.37	18.37
Loveno Inferiore bv. Grona	5.58	7.18	7.28	8.38	9.38	10.58	12.18	13.57	14.48	16.18	17.40	18.40
Loveno Superiore Cappella	5.59	7.19	7.29	8.39	9.39	10.59	12.19	13.58	14.49	16.19	17.41	18.41
Piazzo v. provinciale	6.03	7.23	7.33	8.43	9.43	11.03	12.23	14.02	14.53	16.23	17.45	18.45
Loggo v. provinciale 12	6.06	7.26	7.36	8.46	9.46	11.06	12.26	14.05	14.56	16.26	17.48	18.48
Ligomena bv. Barna	6.08	7.28	7.38	8.48	9.48	11.08	12.30	14.07	14.58	16.30	17.50	18.50
Barna v. provinciale 1									14.10			
Ligomena bv. Barna	6.08	7.28	7.38	8.48	9.48	11.08	12.30	14.13	14.58	16.30	17.50	18.50
Calvasino v. uff. PT	6.09	7.29	7.39	8.49	9.49	11.09	12.31	14.14	14.59	16.31	17.51	18.51
Plesio paese-piazza	6.10	7.30	7.40	8.50	9.50	11.10	12.32	14.15	15.00	16.32	17.52	18.52
Plesio mulino Spinzi	6.12	7.32	7.42	8.52	9.52		12.34	14.17	15.02	16.34	17.54	18.54
Plesio Breglia-monum. caduti a.	6.15	7.35	7.45	8.55	9.55		12.37	14.20	15.05	16.37	17.57	18.57

I BIGLIETTI DEVONO ESSERE ACQUISTATI A TERRA.
L'ESERCIZIO DELL'AUTOLINEA È SOSPESO IL 25 DICEMBRE E L'1 GENNAIO.
① Si effettua nei giorni scolastici escluso il sabato.
a) Nei festivi la fermata si effettua in via Mazzini n. 1 (CARIPLO).

⑩ Parte da p. Roma (deposito SPT).
② Effettua deviazione per Barna a richiesta.

on holidays the bus stops in Via Mazzini

service suspended from 25 Dec to 1 Jan

departs from Piazza Roma

will go to Barna if requested

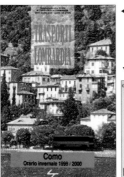

Como
Orario invernale 1999 / 2000

TRASPORTI LOMBARDIA

◀ Winter timetable

▼ Summer timetable

ORARIO ESTIVO 2000

Como città del Lago di Volta della Seta ...e della S.P.T. ⑥

TRASPORTI REGIONE LOMBARDIA   COMO

gennaio *Jan*
febbraio *Feb*
marzo *Mar*
aprile *Apr*
maggio *May*
giugno *Jun*
luglio *Jul*
agosto *Aug*
settembre *Sep*
ottobre *Oct*
novembre *Nov*
dicembre *Dec*

do you have a timetable?
avete un orario?
a-**vay**-tay oon o-**rar**-yo

can you explain the timetable?
mi può spiegare l'orario?
mee pwo spyay-**ga**-ray lo-**rar**-yo

talk

TICKETS

Tickets for bus, metro and trains need to be validated, otherwise you can be fined. Bus tickets are validated on board the bus. Train and metro tickets are validated at the special orange machines in the stations.

There is an increasing number of self-service ticket machines. You can choose the language for ▼ your transaction.

Bus ticket ▶ listing all the stops en route. The destination is punched.

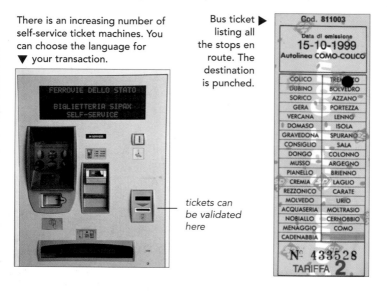

tickets can be validated here

Cod. 811003	
Data di emissione	
15-10-1999	
Autolinea COMO-COLICO	
COLICO	TREMEZZO
DUBINO	BOLVEDRO
SORICO	AZZANO
GERA	PORTEZZA
VERCANA	LENNO
DOMASO	ISOLA
GRAVEDONA	SPURANO
CONSIGLIO	SALA
DONGO	COLONNO
MUSSO	ARGEGNO
PIANELLO	BRIENNO
CREMIA	LAGLIO
REZZONICO	CARATE
MOLVEDO	URIO
ACQUASERIA	MOLTRASIO
NOBIALLO	CERNOBBIO
MENAGGIO	COMO
CADENABBIA	

N° 433528
TARIFFA **2**

Train ticket ▼

valid for 6 hours from validating

ticket valid for 2 months from date of issue

2nd class

Adulti adults

Ragazzi children

Da From

A To

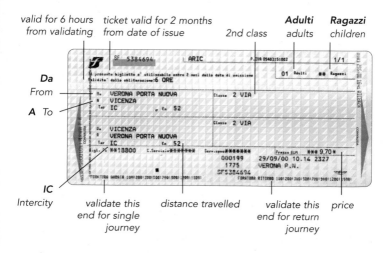

IC Intercity

validate this end for single journey

distance travelled

validate this end for return journey

price

Boat ticket ▼

retain ticket until end of journey

valid on all motorboats

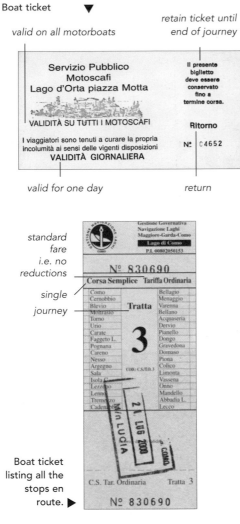

Servizio Pubblico Motoscafi
Lago d'Orta piazza Motta

Il presente biglietto deve essere conservato fino a termine corsa.

VALIDITÀ SU TUTTI I MOTOSCAFI

Ritorno

I viaggiatori sono tenuti a curare la propria incolumità ai sensi delle vigenti disposizioni
VALIDITÀ GIORNALIERA

N° C4652

valid for one day   *return*

standard fare i.e. no reductions

single

journey

Gestione Governativa
Navigazione Laghi
Maggiore-Garda-Como
Lago di Como
P.I. 00802050153

N° 830690

Corsa Semplice Tariffa Ordinaria

Tratta 3

Boat ticket listing all the stops en route. ▶

C.S. Tar. Ordinaria   Tratta 3

N° 830690

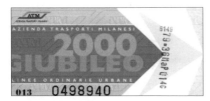

City transport ticket ◀ which has been stamped

keywords keywords keywords keywords keywords

carnet da 10 biglietti *kar-nay dee-ay-chee beel-yet-tee* book of 10 tickets

biglietto *beel-yet-to* ticket

riduzione *ree-doots-yo-nay* reduction

andata *an-da-ta* single

andata e ritorno *an-da-ta ay ree-tor-no* return

adulto *a-dool-to* adult

ragazzo *ra-gat-so* child

studente *stoo-den-tay* student

terza età *terl-za ay-ta* over 60s

disabile *dee-za-bee-lay* disabled

famiglia *fa-meel-ya* family

Most Italian cities operate an integrated transport system, which means that all the different kinds of transport are part of one network, and you can use any of them with your ticket. Bus tickets must be bought in advance and you can buy them at newsagents/kiosks and at tobacconists. In smaller places they will be sold at the shop or bar near to the bus stop. Look out for a sign stating that bus tickets are on sale. You validate the ticket in the machine at the back of the bus, or on long-distance buses there will be a conductor to check your ticket, not to sell you one.

◀ Tickets for Milan's integrated transport system

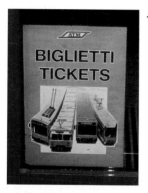

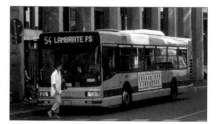

▲ City buses are generally orange. You enter from the back and validate your ticket at the machine as you enter.

Tram ▼

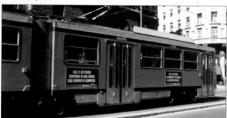

Sign showing bus tickets for sale – here, at the local butcher's. Shops like this shut from 12.30-3.30 pm, so you should buy tickets well in advance. ▼

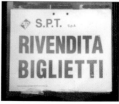

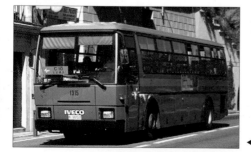

Rural buses usually have a conductor. This does not mean you can buy a ticket on board – you still must buy it in advance. ◀

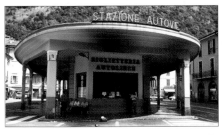

◀ Bus station are generally located near train stations. It is the most likely place to find a public toilet.

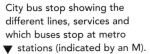

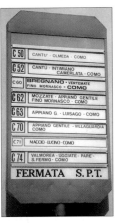

City bus stop showing the different lines, services and which buses stop at metro ▼ stations (indicated by an M).

▶ Long-distance bus stop showing the different services and routes.

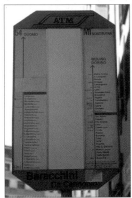

Italian airports are well served by buses. Tourist offices will have information. ▼

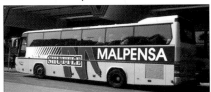

where does the bus to ... leave from?
da dove parte l'autobus per...?
da do-vay par-tay low-to-boos payr...

is there a bus to...?
c'è un autobus per...?
che oon ow-to-boos payr...

which bus goes to the centre?
quale autobus va al centro?
kwa-lay ow-to-boos va al chen-tro

which number goes to...?
quale linea va a...?
kwa-lay lee-nay-a va a...

does this bus go to...?
questo autobus va a...?
kwes-to ow-to-boos va a...

when is the next bus to...?
quando c'è il prossimo autobus per...?
kwan-do che eel pros-see-mo ow-to-boos payr...

can you tell me when it is my stop
mi può dire quando è la mia fermata
mee pwo deer-mee kwan-do e la mee-a fer-ma-ta

I want to get off!
voglio scendere!
vol-yo shen-day-ray

talking talking talking

Milan and Rome are the only two Italian cities to have metro systems. You can buy a carnet of 10 tickets which is cheaper than buying tickets individually. Tickets must be validated before you get on the train. You can also buy weekly tickets valid for 2 journeys per day 6 days a week. These are geared to commuters. There are also 24 and 48 hour tickets, which are ideal for tourists.

▲ Metro sign

Metro station ▶

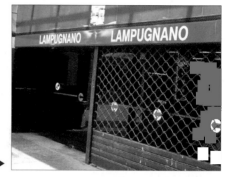

Ticket machine ▶
A single ticket is valid for 75 minutes from validating and can be used for one metro ride and any number of bus and tram journeys within that time limit.

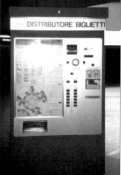

tickets on sale at kiosk or from ticket machines

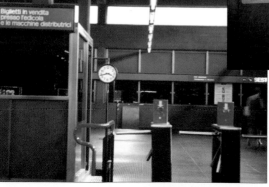

Kiosk selling metro tickets ▶
and parking tickets

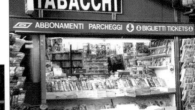

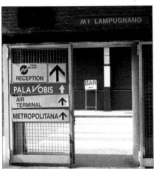

The Milan underground has three colour-coded lines: MI is red, M2 is green and M3 yellow. There is also a fourth, blue line called the *passante ferroviario* ◀ linking with the main train stations.

a single ticket
un biglietto singolo
oon beel-yet-to seen-go-lo

a 24-hour ticket
un biglietto da ventiquattro ore
oon beel-yet-to da ven-tee-kwat-tro o-ray

a carnet of tickets
un carnet di biglietti
oon kar-nay dee beel-yet-tee

a 48-hour ticket
un biglietto da quarantotto ore
oon beel-yet-to da kwa-rant-ot-to o-ray

have you a map of the underground?
avete una piantina della metro?
a-vay-tay oo-na pyan-tee-na del-la met-ro

where is the nearest metro station?
dov'è la stazione della metropolitana più vicina?
do-ve la stats-yo-nay del-la met-ro-po-lee-ta-na pyoo vee-chee-na

I want to go to...
voglio andare a...
vol-yo an-da-ray a...

do I have to change?
devo cambiare?
day-vo kamb-ya-ray

where?
dove?
do-vay

which line do I take?
quale linea prendo?
kwa-lay lee-nay-a pren-do

in which direction?
per quale direzione?
payr kwa-lay dee-rets-yo-nay

which station is it for...?
qual è la stazione per...?
kwa-le la stats-yo-nay payr...

what is the next stop?
qual è la prossima fermata?
kwa-le la pros-see-ma fer-ma-ta

excuse me! I want to get off
permesso! voglio scendere
payr-mes-so vol-yo shen-day-ray

talking talking talking talking

Italian trains are good value. Fares are charged according to the distance travelled, so buying a return does not make it any cheaper. Return tickets are valid only within 48 hours of outward journey, so it is not worth buying one if you are staying for a longer period. On Intercity trains you must pay a supplement when you purchase your ticket. If you do not, the train conductor can ask you to pay a surcharge that is more expensive than the supplement. On both Eurocity and Intercity trains, reservations are obligatory. Remember to validate your ticket before boarding the train.

DEPARTURES ▼

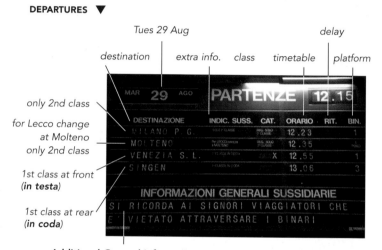

Tues 29 Aug

delay

destination extra info. class timetable platform

only 2nd class

for Lecco change at Molteno

only 2nd class

1st class at front (**in testa**)

1st class at rear (**in coda**)

Additional General Information
Passengers are reminded that it is forbidden to walk across the tracks

2 singles to...
due andate per...
doo-ay an-da-tay payr...

2 returns to...
due andate e ritorno per...
doo-ay an-da-tay ay ree-tor-no payr...

I want to book...
voglio prenotare...
vol-yo pray-no-ta-ray...

2 seats
due posti
doo-ay pos-tee

a couchette
una cuccetta
oo-na koo-chet-ta

what time is the next train to...?
a che ora c'è il prossimo treno per...?
a kay o-ra che eel pros-see-mo tray-no payr...

which platform?
quale binario?
kwa-lay bee-nar-yo

is there a supplement to pay?
c'e un supplemento da pagare?
che oon soop-lay-men-to da pa-ga-ray

do I have to change?
devo cambiare?
day-vo kam-bee-a-ray

talking

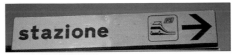

▲ Station with rail logo

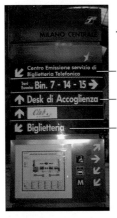

◀ Milan Central station information board

telephone booking collection

information desk

ticket office

Automated ticket ▼ machine

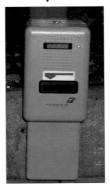

Validating machines are usually situated at platform entrances and can easily be missed. ▼

corsa semplice
kor-sa sem-plee-chay
one-way

andata e ritorno
an-da-ta ay ree-tor-no
return

prima classe
pree-ma klas-say
first class

seconda classe
se-kon-da klas-say
second class

prezzo ridotto
pret-so ree-dot-to
reduced fare

prenotazione
pray-no-tats-yo-nay
reservation

carta d'argento
kar-ta dar-jen-to
over 60s pass

sportello
spor-tel-lo
ticket counter

tessera
tes-say-ra
pass

corridoio
ko-ree-doy-o
aisle

finestra
fee-nes-tra
window

fumatori
foo-ma-tor-ee
smoking

non fumatori
non foo-ma-tor-ee
non-smoking

does this train stop at...?
questo treno si ferma a...?
kwes-to tray-no see fer-ma a...

is this the train for...?
è questo il treno per...?
e kwes-to eel tray-no payr...

how long does the train stop for?
quanto tempo si ferma il treno?
kwan-to tem-po see fer-ma eel tray-no

this is my seat
questo è il mio posto
kwes-to e eel mee-o pos-to

TAXI

The easiest place to find a taxi is at a railway station. Be sure
to take an official taxi, yellow in Rome and white in most
other places. In smaller places you can ask at the tourist office
for the number of the local taxi. Tipping is normally 10-15% of the
fare and you may be charged extra to go to or from the airport.
Watch out for pirate cab operators as they are more likely to overcharge. Try and establish in advance how much the fare will be.

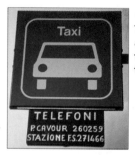

◀ Taxi sign
Two phone numbers
are given, one for the
town centre and one
for the station.

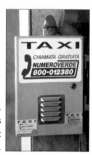

▶

You can phone for a taxi.
Numero Verde means
free phone so you don't
need any money to call.

Taxis are generally white (except in Rome).

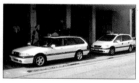

This is a
taxi stand
at the
railway
station.

◀

▼ Roman taxis are yellow.

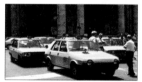

where is the nearest taxi stand?
dov'è il posteggio dei taxi più vicino
*do-**ve** eel pos-**ted**-jo day **tak**-see pyoo vee-**chee**-no*

to ... please
a ... per favore
*a ... payr fa-**vo**-ray*

how much is it to go to...?
quanto costa per andare a...?
*kwan-to **kos**-ta payr an-**da**-ray a...*

please order me a taxi
per favore, mi chiami un taxi
*payr fa-**vo**-ray mee kee-a-mee oon **tak**-see*

now
subito
soo-bee-to

for... o'clock
per le...
payr lay...

I need a receipt
ho bisogno di una ricevuta
*o bee-**zon**-yo dee **oo**-na ree-chay-**voo**-ta*

keep the change
tenga il resto
***ten**-ga eel **res**-to*

is there a special rate for the airport?
c'è una tariffa speciale per l'aeroporto?
*che **oo**-na ta-**reef**-fa spay-**cha**-lay payr lay-ro-**por**-to*

talking talking talking

CAR HIRE

You will find all the big car hire firms in Italy, but hiring a car on the spot can prove more expensive than arranging it before your trip. You have to be at least 21 and to have held a driving licence for over a year to hire a car. Drivers under 23 will be charged a daily surcharge.

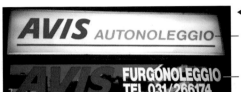

◄ Most of the big hire firms operate in Italy

— car hire

— van hire

I want to hire a car
vorrei noleggiare una macchina
vor-ray nol-ed-ja-ray oo-na mak-kee-na

for one day
per un giorno
payr oon jor-no

for ... days
per ... giorni
payr ... jor-nee

I want...
vorrei...
vor-ray...

a small car
una macchina piccola
oo-na mak-kee-na peek-ko-la

a large car
una macchina grande
oo-na mak-kee-na gran-day

a people carrier
un monovolume
oon mo-no-vo-loo-may

an automatic car
un macchina con cambio automatico
oo-na mak-kee-na kon kam-bee-o ow-to-ma-teek-ko

how much is it?
quanto costa?
kwan-to kos-ta

is there a kilometre charge?
si paga per chilometro?
see pa-ga payr kee-lo-may-tro

I am ... old
ho ... anni
o ... an-nee

here is my driving licence
ecco la mia patente
ek-ko la mee-a pa-ten-tay

what is included in the insurance?
cos'è compreso nell'assicurazione?
ko-ze kom-pray-zo nel-las-see-koo-rats-yo-nay

how do the controls work?
come funzionano i comandi?
ko-may foonts-yo-na-no ee ko-man-dee

where are the documents?
dove sono i documenti?
do-vay so-no ee do-koo-men-tee

what do we do if...?
cosa si deve fare se...?
ko-za see day-vay fa-ray say...

when there is a breakdown
quando c'è un guasto
kwan-do che oon gwas-to

can we have a babyseat?
si può avere un seggiolino per il bambino?
see pwo a-vay-ray oon sed-jo-lee-no payr eel bam-bee-no

how is it fitted?
come si monta?
ko-may see mon-ta

talking talking talking talking talking

DRIVING

*The minimum age for driving in Italy is 18. Italian drivers can sometimes be impatient and will often overtake dangerously. Zebra crossings show where you can cross the road but don't expect cars to stop for you. The **Polizia Stradale** look after the roads and their cars are equipped with speed-monitoring machines. You must carry your passport and car documents with you at all times and it is likely that the police will ask to look at these. Non EU-members need to have an international driving licence. If you are caught speeding they will fine you on the spot. If you break down, call 116 (ACI, the Italian equivalent to the AA). They operate 24 hours a day and have multilingual staff. They will need to know where you are, the type of car and the registration number.*

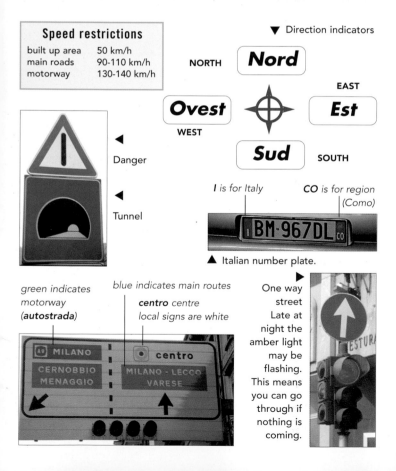

Speed restrictions

built up area	50 km/h
main roads	90-110 km/h
motorway	130-140 km/h

▼ Direction indicators

NORTH **Nord**

Ovest WEST

EAST **Est**

Sud SOUTH

◄ Danger

◄ Tunnel

I is for Italy

CO is for region (Como)

BM·967DL

▲ Italian number plate.

*green indicates motorway (**autostrada**)*

blue indicates main routes

***centro** centre*
local signs are white

MILANO
CERNOBBIO
MENAGGIO

centro
MILANO - LECCO
VARESE

► One way street Late at night the amber light may be flashing. This means you can go through if nothing is coming.

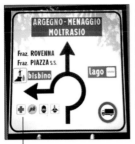

pictograms on road signs indicate services available: Hospital, Post Office and police

◀ Take extra care at roundabouts. Remember, you are driving on the right and traffic from the right has priority unless otherwise indicated. Even on roundabouts where traffic **on** the roundabout has to give way to traffic joining it. Stopping to give way instead of hurtling straight on may cause an angry rebuke from behind.

◀ **CAUTION ELECTRONIC SPEED CONTROL**

No sounding ▶ horn

◀ **CAUTION LORRY EXIT**

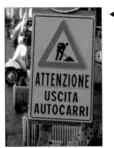

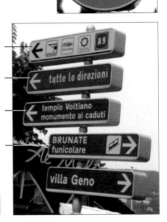

local sites and route to the motorway (A9)

all routes, follow this sign if you are passing through

Voltiano temple & war memorial

funicular railway

▼ **SWITCH ON LIGHTS**

You must have your headlights on at all times on the motorways and SS roads.

ACCENDERE I FARI

we are going to...
andiamo a...
and-ya-mo a...

is it a good road?
è una buona strada?
e oo-na bwo-na stra-da

is the pass open?
il passo è aperto?
eel pas-so e a-payr-to

which is the best route?
qual è la strada migliore?
kwa-le la stra-da meel-yo-ray

can you show me on the map?
mi può indicare sulla cartina?
mee pwo een-dee-ka-ray sool-la kar-tee-na

do we need snow chains?
c'è bisogno delle catene per le gomme?
che bee-zon-yo del-lay ka-tay-nay payr lay gom-may

talking

*Italian motorways (**autostrada**) are often two-laned and cars can come up very fast in the outside lane. Italian drivers are apt to come up very close behind you and to flash their lights if they want you to get out of the way. The speed limit on 3-lane Italian motorways (in good weather) has been raised to 140km/h. But take care, 3-lane sections are not widespread. And in bad weather, you must reduce speed to 110km/h. You must also keep your headlights on all the time on motorways and SS roads. On most motorways you pay a toll.*

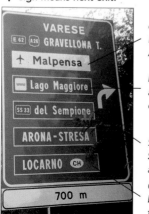

◀ Entrance to motorway
Italian motorway signs are green.

no hitch-hiking

toll to pay.

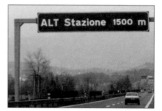

PAY STATION COMING UP ▲

Motorway exit sign
Prossima Uscita on a motorway
▼ sign means next exit.

You must stop and pay unless you have a ***Telepass***. This device, installed in the car, allows you to go through the automatic barrier.
▼

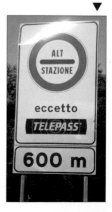

exit for Malpensa Airport

brown signs are for places of interest

*SS 33 indicates a **Strada Statale**, a main road*

CH indicates border crossing to Switzerland.

Viacards can be bought at newsagents and are useful if you use the motorway frequently.

Telepass, the in-car device

Pay with cash or by credit card. The amount will be lit up on the screen in front of you (on the passenger side if you are driving a right-hand drive).

There are ▶ different lanes for different methods of payment.

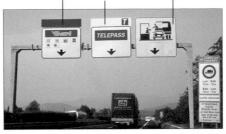

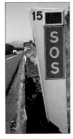

◀ SOS phones are every 2km on the motorway.

Service station ▶ in 500 m with facilities for the disabled and a cash point. Italian service stations offer hot and cold food.

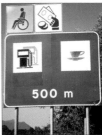

If you break down on the motorway

If you break down on the motorway, first you should put on your warning lights and place the warning triangle about 30 m behind the car. There are SOS points every 2km. They are simple to use and instructions are in four languages. Simply press either the red cross button for ambulance assistance or the spanner button if you need breakdown recovery. The confirmation light (**lampada da conferma**) should light when your call has been acknowledged. You should then return to the car and wait for help to arrive.

my car has broken down
la mia macchina è in panne
la **mee**-a **mak**-kee-na e een **pan**-nay

what should I do?
cosa devo fare?
ko-za **day**-vo **fa**-ray

I'm a female on my own
sono da sola
so-no da **so**-la

my children are in the car
i miei figli sono nella macchina
ee mee-**yay feel**-yee **so**-no **nel**-la **mak**-kee-na

the car is...
la macchina è...
la **mak**-kee-na e...

after exit...
dopo l'uscita...
do-po loo-**shee**-ta...

before exit...
prima dell'uscita...
pree-ma del-loo-**shee**-ta...

it's a red Nissan
è una Nissan rossa
e **oo**-na **nees**-san **ros**-sa

registration number...
il numero di targa...
eel **noo**-may-ro dee **tar**-ga ...

*There are a number of different systems used for parking. More and more automated machines are being used and you will need coins. Some machines will take banknotes but they must be in good condition. Some parking is with a parking disk (**disco orario**) and you can get these from petrol stations. Don't park in a **zona di rimozione** or you will be towed away.*

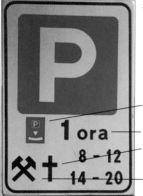

◀ Parking sign. More and more pictograms are being used on signs. It often makes them more baffling.

parking disk required
1 hour

cross = Sundays

crossed mallets = work day Mon-Sat

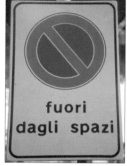

▲ No parking outside authorised spaces

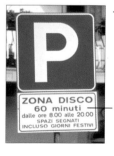

◀ Parking disk required. You must display it on the dash-board where it is visible.

maximum 60 minutes from 8 am–8 pm, holidays included

▶ You will be towed away if you park here

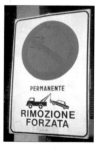

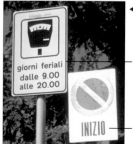

◀ Pay at the meter

Giorni feriali means Mon-Sat from 9 am–8 pm

Inizio means begins (i.e. parking restriction begins here).

▶ No parking at any time of the day (you will be towed away)

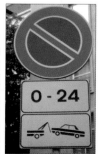

Parking ticket machine
Instructions on the right are
also in English.

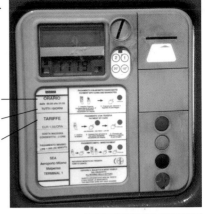

orario (when payment applies)
00.00 to 24.00 (i.e. all the time)

tutti i giorni means every day

tariffe tariff
maximum stay allowed 3 hours
minimum payment for 30 minutes

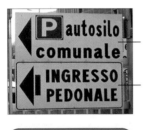

municipal
parking

pedestrian
entrance

Be careful: *libero*
means there are
spaces, not that
parking is free.

libero

completo

completo
means
no spaces

P Parcheggio gratuito ◀ Free parking

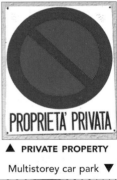

▲ PRIVATE PROPERTY

Multistorey car park ▼

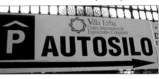

where is there a car park?
dove c'è un parcheggio?
do-vay che oon par-ked-jo

where's the best place to park?
dov'è il posto migliore per parcheggiare?
do-ve eel pos-to meel-yo-ray payr par-ked-ja-ray

I don't have a parking disc
non ho un disco orario
non o oon deesk o-rar-yo

can I park here?
posso parcheggiare qui?
pos-so par-ked-ja-ray kwee

how long for?
per quanto tempo?
payr kwan-to tem-po

the ticket machine doesn't work
il parchimetro non funziona
eel par-kee-may-tro non foonts-yo-na

talking

Petrol stations generally follow shop hours and are closed between 12.30 and 3.30 pm. They stay open until 7.30 pm and are shut on Sundays. However, they usually have automatic pumps which accept banknotes.

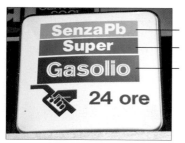

Senza Pb unleaded

Super 4-star

Gasolio diesel

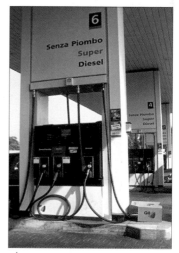

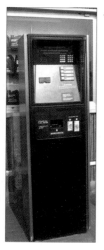

◀ Many petrol stations have machines where you can select and pay for the petrol you want. Select the petrol, pay in advance and then the pump will release the petrol.

▲ Pumps in large petrol stations are generally numbered and you just need to tell the attendant the pump number.

where is the nearest petrol station?
dov'è la stazione di servizio più vicina?
*do-**ve** la stats-**yo**-nay dee ser-**veets**-yo pyoo vee-**chee**-na*

... worth of unleaded petrol
... di benzina senza piombo
*... dee bent-**see**-na **sent**-sa pee-**om**-bo*

can I get the car washed?
si può lavare la macchina?
*see pwo la-**va**-ray la **mak**-kee-na*

fill it up
il pieno
*eel pee-**ay**-no*

pump number
pompa numero
***pom**-pa **noo**-may-ro*

*If you break down, phone 116 for assistance. Garages that do repairs are known as **Autofficina**.*

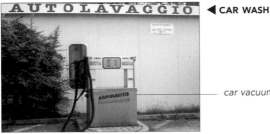

◀ CAR WASH

car vacuum

I have broken down
sono in panne
*so-no een **pan**-nay*

the car won't start
la macchina non parte
*la **mak**-kee-na non **par**-tay*

the battery is flat
la batteria è scarica
*la bat-tay-**ree**-a e **ska**-ree-ka*

I have a flat tyre
ho una foratura
*o **oo**-na fo-ra-**too**-ra*

I need new tyres
ho bisogno delle gomme
*o bee-**zon**-yo **del**-lay **gom**-may*

where is the nearest garage?
dov'è l'autorimessa più vicina?
*do-**ve** low-to-ree-**mes**-sa pyoo vee-**chee**-na*

I have run out of petrol
non ho più benzina
*non o pyoo bent-**see**-na*

there is something wrong with...
c'è qualcosa che non va con...
*che kwal-**ko**-za kay non va kon...*

the ... is not working
il/la ... non funziona
*eel/la ... non foonts-**yo**-na*

have you the parts?
avete i pezzi di ricambio?
*a-**vay**-tay ee **pet**-see dee ree-**kamb**-yo*

can you repair it?
può ripararlo?
*pwo ree-par-**ar**-lo*

how long will it take?
quanto ci vuole?
***kwan**-to chee **vwo**-lay*

when will it be ready?
quando sarà pronta?
***kwan**-do sa-ra **pron**-ta*

how much will it cost?
quanto costerà?
kwan**-to kos-tay-**ra

can you replace the windscreen?
può cambiare il parabrezza?
*pwo kamb-**ya**-ray eel pa-ra-**bret**-sa*

can you change...	**the oil**	**the water**	**the tyres**
mi può cambiare...	l'olio	l'acqua	le gomme
*mee pwo kamb-**ya**-ray...*	***lol**-yo*	***lak**-wa*	*lay **gom**-may*

talking talking talking talking talking talking

SHOPPING

Shops are generally shut on Monday mornings (except during the summer when they close on Saturday afternoons but open on Monday mornings). Other days they are open in the mornings from 9 am to 1 pm and in the afternoons from 4 pm to 7.30 pm. Shops are shut on Sundays except for food shops selling bread which open in the mornings and cake shops. You may notice that shop assistants are very insistent in handing you a receipt. You must take it with you: if you are stopped by the finance police within 100 m of the shop without it, both you and the shopkeeper will be fined. This measure was brought in to avoid tax evasion.

keywords keywords keywords

panificio
pa-nee-**fee**-cho
baker's

macelleria
ma-chel-lay-**ree**-a
butcher's

fruttivendola
froot-tee-**ven**-do-la
fruit shop

alimentari
a-lee-men-**ta**-ree
grocer's

pasticceria
pas-tee-cher-**ee**-a
cake shop

supermercato
soo-per-mer-**ka**-to
supermarket

pescheria
pes-kay-**ree**-a
fishmonger's

giornalaio
jor-nal-**a**-yo
newsagent's

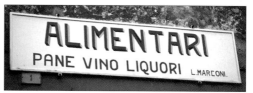

▲ *Alimentari* is the grocer's, selling fresh bread, milk and other food. People will generally shop here daily for bread and milk. It tends to open early, about 8 am.

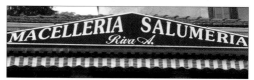

▲ Butcher & Pork products (e.g. ham, salami, sausage)

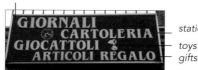

newspapers

stationery

toys

gifts

An *enoteca* sells wine. ▶
Look out for local specialities.

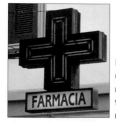

◀

Pharmacies sell baby products such as nappies and baby food, but they cost more than in supermarkets.

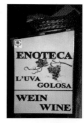

45

Supermarkets are generally open all day (until 8 pm) from Monday to Saturdays. They are generally shut on Sundays. You can find other services within supermarkets such as dry-cleaning and shoe repairs as well as a café serving fast food.

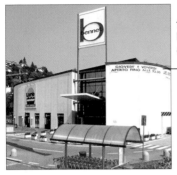

◀ Although Italians will still shop daily for bread, milk and other foods such as ham and cheese, they are now likely to do a large shop in a supermarket.

Giovedì e Venerdì aperto fino alle 22.00
Thu and Fri open until 10 pm

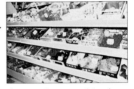

Fruit ▶ and veg must be weighed and stickered (the weighing machine has pictures so you can identify the produce) before getting to the checkout. The checkout assistant does not do this. You will also have to ask for and pay for plastic bags.

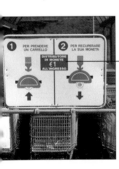

change machine at entrance

You need a coin for ◀ the trolley.

pay for 2 —— **paghi 2**
take 3 —— **prendi 3**

---

where can I buy...?
dove posso comprare...?
*do-vay **pos**-so komp-**ra**-ray...*

do you have...?
avete...?
*a-**vay**-tay...*

I am looking for...
cerco...
***cher**-ko...*

can I pay with this card?
posso pagare con questa carta?
***pos**-so pa-**ga**-ray kon **kwes**-ta **kar**-ta*

batteries
pile
pee-lay

how much is it?
quanto costa?
***kwan**-to **kos**-ta*

a present
un regalo
*oon ray-**ga**-lo*

a tin-opener
un apriscatole
*oon ap-ree-**ska**-to-lay*

a good wine
un buon vino
*oon bwon **vee**-no*

4 plastic bags
quattro borse di plastica
***kwat**-tro **bor**-say dee **plas**-tee-ka*

talking

*Quantities are expressed in kilos and grams. For those who are more used to pounds and ounces, 1 kilo is roughly equivalent to 2 lb, half a kilo is equivalent to 1 lb, 250 g is equivalent to a half pound and an ounce is equivalent to about 30 g. You will also hear the word **etto** used, which is 100 g. So 250 g could be expressed either **due cento cinquanta grammi** or **due etti e mezzo**, i.e. two and a half **etti**.*

Bread is sold by weight, or if you are buying ▶ rolls (*panini*) by number. Large wholemeal loaves are cut up and you can ask for a piece. Bread is bought fresh each day and eaten with meals. Italians don't usually put butter on their bread, so you won't find it on the dinner table. Italian butter is unsalted.

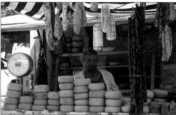

▲ Markets are held in the morning, either daily in large towns or weekly in smaller places. They generally have a great variety of stalls: cheese, bread, meat and fish. It is the best place to buy your fruit and vegetables. Markets will also have stalls selling hardware, clothes, shoes, etc. If you feel confident, in markets you can ask for a discount on anything other than food.

Ham is either cured, such as Parma ham, and known as *prosciutto crudo*. Cooked ham is *prosciutto cotto*. When you ask for *prosciutto*, you may hear the shop assistant asking whether you want *crudo* or *cotto*. It is sliced very finely. *Un etto di prosciutto* should generously fill a couple of bread rolls. ▼

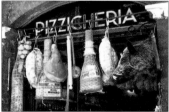

talking

is there a market?
c'è un mercato?
che oon mer-ka-to

it's a bit too much
è un pò troppo caro
e oon po trop-po ka-ro

which day?
quale giorno?
kwa-lay jor-no

would you give me a discount?
mi fà uno sconto?
mee fa oo-no skon-to

da consumarsi entro
to be consumed by

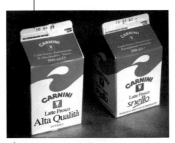

▲ Milk is generally colour-coded. Here blue is for whole milk (*intero*), pink for semi-skimmed (*parzialmente scremato*). It is sold by the half litre (*mezzo litro*) or litre (*litro*).

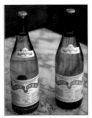

Mineral water is sparkling (*frizzante*) or still (*naturale*). Look out for the colour coding: red for sparkling and blue/grey for still.

frozen foods ▶
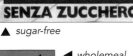
surgelati

SENZA COLORANTI ◀ *free of colouring*

SENZA ZUCCHERO

▲ *sugar-free*

◀ *wholemeal*
integrale

biologico

organic ▲

---

a piece of that cheese
un pezzo di quel formaggio
*oon **pet**-so dee kwel for-**mad**-jo*

a little more   **a little less**
ancora un po'   un po' meno
*an-**ko**-ra oon po*   *oon po **may**-no*

that's fine thanks
basta così grazie
***bas**-ta ko-**zee grats**-yay*

8 slices of ham
otto fette di prosciutto
***ot**-to **fet**-tay dee pro-**shoot**-to*

a litre of milk
un litro di latte
*oon **leet**-ro dee **lat**-tay*

a bottle of...
una bottiglia di...
***oo**-na bot-**teel**-ya dee...*

mineral water
acqua minerale
***ak**-wa mee-nay-**ra**-lay*

still   **fizzy**
naturale   gassata
*na-too-**ra**-lay*   *ga-**za**-ta*

a tin of...
una scatola di...
***oo**-na **ska**-to-la dee...*

a jar of...
un vaso di...
*oon **va**-zo dee...*

a packet of...
un pacchetto di...
*oon pak-**ket**-to dee...*

that's everything thanks
è tutto grazie
*e **toot**-to **grats**-yay*

▼ Typical nutritional info per 100 g

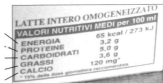

LATTE INTERO OMOGENEIZZATO
VALORI NUTRITIVI MEDI per 100 ml

	65 kcal / 273 kJ
energy — ENERGIA	3,2 g
protein — PROTEINE	5,0 g
carbohydrates — CARBOIDRATI	3,6 g
fat — GRASSI	120 mg*
calcium — CALCIO	

* 15% della dose giornaliera raccomandata

Here is a list of basic foodstuffs you might need.

Everyday Foods alimentari a-lee-men-ta-ree

biscuits	i biscotti *bees-kot-tee*
bread	il pane *pa-nay*
bread roll	il panino *pa-nee-no*
bread (sliced)	il pancarrè *pan-kar-ray*
butter	il burro *boor-ro*
cereal	i cereali *chay-ray-a-lee*
cheese	il formaggio *for-mad-jo*
chicken	il pollo *pol-lo*
coffee	il caffè *kaf-fe*
cream	la panna *pan-na*
crisps	le patatine *pat-a-tee-nay*
eggs	le uova *wov-a*
fish	il pesce *pay-shay*
flour	la farina *fa-ree-na*
fruit juice	il succo di frutta *sook-ko dee froot-ta*
ham (cooked)	il prosciutto cotto *pro-shoot-to kot-to*
ham (cured	il prosciutto crudo *pro-shoot-to kroo-do*
herbal tea	la tisana *tee-za-na*
honey	il miele *myay-lay*
jam	la marmellata *mar-mel-la-ta*
margarine	la margarina *mar-ga-ree-na*
marmalade	la marmellata d'arance *mar-mel-la-ta da-ran-chay*
meat	la carne *kar-nay*
milk	il latte *lat-tay*
mustard	la senape *sen-a-pay*
oil	l'olio *ol-yo*
orange juice	il succo d'arancia *sook-ko da-ran-cha*
pasta	la pasta *pas-ta*
pepper	il pepe *pep-ay*
rice	il riso *ree-zo*
salt	il sale *sa-lay*
sausage	la salsiccia *sal-see-cha*
sugar	lo zucchero *tsook-kay-ro*
stock cube	i dadi da brodo *da-dee da bro-do*
tea	il tè *te*
tomatoes (tin)	i pelati *pay-la-tee*
tuna (tin)	il tonno *ton-no*
vinegar	l'aceto *a-chay-to*
yoghurt	lo yogurt *yo-goort*

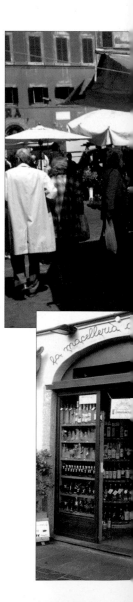

The market is the best place to buy fresh fruit and vegetables.
*A greengrocer's is called **il fruttivendolo**.*

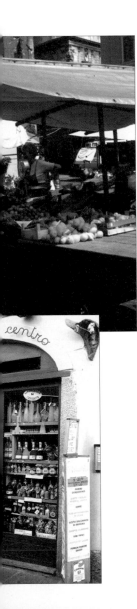

Fruit	frutta *froot*-ta
apples	le mele *may*-lay
apricots	le albicocche *al-bee-***kok***-kay*
bananas	le banane *ba-na-nay*
cherries	le ciliegie *cheel-***yay***-jay*
figs	i fichi *fee*-kee
grapefruit	il pompelmo *pom-***pel***-mo*
grapes	l'uva *oo*-va
lemon	il limone *lee-***mo***-nay*
melon	il melone *may-lo-nay*
nectarines	le peschenoci *pes-kay-***no***-chee*
oranges	le arance *a-***ran***-chay*
peaches	le pesche *pes*-kay
pears	le pere *pay*-ray
pineapple	l'ananas *a*-na-nas
plums	le prugne *proon*-yay
raspberries	i lamponi *lam-po-nee*
strawberries	le fragole *fra*-go-lay
watermelon	l'anguria *an-***goo***-ree-a*
Vegetables	verdura *ver-***doo***-ra*
artichokes	i carciofi *kar-***cho***-fee*
aubergines	le melanzane *may-lant-***sa***-nay*
asparagus	gli asparagi *as-***pa***-ra-jee*
carrots	le carote *ka-ro-tay*
cauliflower	il cavolfiore *ka-volf-***yor***-ay*
celery	il sedano *sed*-a-no
courgettes	le zucchine *tsook-***kee***-nay*
cucumber	il cetriolo *chay-tree-***yo***-lo*
french beans	i fagiolini *fa-jo-***lee***-nee*
garlic	l'aglio *al*-yo
leeks	i porri *por*-ree
lettuce	la lattuga *lat-***too***-ga*
mushrooms	i funghi *foong*-ee
onions	le cipolle *chee-***pol***-lay*
peas	i piselli *pee-***zel***-lee*
peppers	i peperoni *pay-pay-***ro***-nee*
potatoes	le patate *pa-***ta***-tay*
radishes	i ravanelli *ra-va-***nel***-lee*
spinach	gli spinaci *spee-***na***-chee*
spring onions	le cipolline *chee-pol-***lee***-nay*
tomatoes	i pomodori *po-mo-***do***-ree*
turnip	la rapa *ra*-pa

Look out for **Upim** and **Standa**, Italy's two main chains of department stores. In Milan there is **la Rinascente**. The stores are generally not open on Sundays.

keywords

negozio
nay-gots-yo
shop

seminterrato
say-meen-ter-ra-to
basement

pianterreno
pee-an-ter-ray-no
ground floor

primo piano
pree-mo pee-a-no
first floor

reparto
ray-par-to
department

giocattoli
jo-kat-to-lee
toys

gioielleria
jo-yel-lay-ree-a
jewellery

donne
don-nay
ladies'

uomini
wo-mee-nee
men's

bambini
bam-bee-nee
children's

Italy is the land of style and you can find lots of small boutiques. ▼

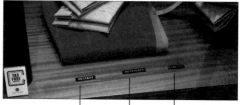

sciarpe scarves   **pantaloni** trousers   **camicie** shirts

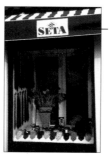

silk

Italians take their seasons very seriously. You may get a boiling-hot day in April, but this does not mean that you will see people stripping off into shorts and bare legs. Summer clothes won't be worn until the end of May.

You can get good ▶ bargains at the end of season sales (Aug/Sep for summer and March for winter).

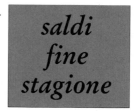

saldi fine stagione

talking

on which floor can I find...?
a che piano si trova...?
a kay pee-a-no see tro-va...

lingerie
la biancheria intima
la bee-an-kay-ree-a een-tee-ma

swimsuits
costume da bagno
kos-too-may da ban-yo

shoes
le scarpe
lay skar-pay

Women's clothes sizes

UK/Australia	8	10	12	14	16	18	20	22
Europe	36	38	40	42	44	46	48	50
US/Canada	6	8	10	12	14	16	18	20

Men's clothes sizes (suits)

UK/US/Canada	36	38	40	42	44	46
Europe	46	48	50	52	54	56
Australia	92	97	102	107	112	117

Shoes

UK/Australia	2	3	4	5	6	7	8	9	10	11
Europe	35	36	37	38	39	41	42	43	45	46
US/Canada women	4	5	6	7	8	9	10	11	12	-
US/Canada men	3	4	5	6	7	8	9	10	11	12

Children's Shoes

UK/US/Canada	0	1	2	3	4	5	6	7	8	9	10	11
Europe	15	17	18	19	20	22	23	24	26	27	28	29

do you have this in my size?
c'è nella mia taglia?
che **nel**-la **mee**-a **tal**-ya

where are the changing rooms?
dove sono gli spogliatoi?
do-vay so-no lee spol-ya-**toy**-ee

it is too big
è troppo grande
e **trop**-po **gran**-day

I need a larger/smaller size
ho bisogno di una taglia più grande/più piccola
o bee-**zon**-yo dee **oo**-na **tal**-ya pyoo **gran**-day/pyoo **peek**-ko-la

I take shoe size 39
io porto il numero trentanove
ee-yo **por**-to eel **noo**-may-ro tren-ta-**no**-vay

can I try this on?
posso provarlo?
po-so pro-**var**-lo

I take size 44
la mia taglia è quarantaquattro
la mee-a **tal**-ya è kwa-ran-ta-**kwat**-tro

it is too small
è troppo piccolo
e **trop**-po **peek**-ko-lo

do you have this in...?
c'è in...?
che een...

black/brown
nero/marrone
nay-ro/mar-**ro**-nay

other colours
altri colori
al-tree ko-**lo**-ree

talking talking talking

i *Post offices are open 8.30 am–2 pm Monday to Friday. Main post offices in large towns will stay open all day until 7pm. On Saturdays they are open until 12 pm. Stamps can also be bought at **tabbacchi** or shops selling postcards.*

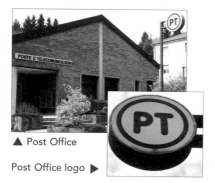

▲ Post Office

Post Office logo ▶

To ▶ 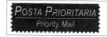 ensure a fast, reliable delivery, you can pay extra and send your cards or letters *posta prioritaria*. Post letters and cards stamped *prioritaria* in the postbox with the blue sticker.

ultimo ritiro

▲ **LAST COLLECTION**

The blue sticker indicates ▶ priority mail. In theory letters take 2 days to be delivered within Italy and 3 days for abroad. However, the Italian mail can sometimes be erratic.

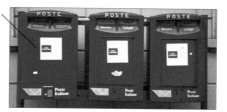

where is the post office?
dov'è la posta?
*do-**ve** la **pos**-ta*

do you have stamps?
avete dei francobolli?
*a-**vay**-tay day fran-ko-**bol**-lee*

10 stamps
dieci francobolli
*dee-**ay**-chee fran-ko-**bol**-lee*

for postcards
per cartoline
*payr kar-to-lee-**nay***

for letters
per lettere
*payr **let**-tay-ray*

to Europe
per l'Europa
*payr lay-oo-**ro**-pa*

to America
per gli Stati Uniti
*payr lee **sta**-tee oo-**nee**-tee*

to Australia
per l'Australia
*payr low-**stra**-lee-a*

I want to send this registered
voglio spedire questo raccomandato
***vol**-yo spay-**dee**-ray **kwes**-to rak-ko-man-**da**-to*

priority
posta prioritaria
***pos**-ta pree-o-ree-**tar**-ya*

I want to send this parcel
voglio spedire questo pacco
*· **vol**-yo spay-**dee**-ray **kwes**-to **pak**-ko*

surface
via normale
***vee**-a nor-**ma**-lay*

airmail
via aerea
***vee**-a a-**ay**-ree-a*

You can find photobooths at photo shops and stations. If you want to buy film, look out for 3 for 2 offers.

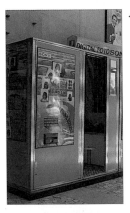

◀ You can find photo-booths in train stations.

your photos ready in 30 minutes

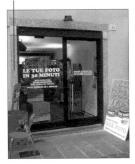

VIETATO FOTOGRAFARE

◀ NO PHOTOGRAPHY

Photography is not allowed in art galleries, museums and churches.

SERVIZI FOTOGRAFICI

◀ PHOTOGRAPHIC SERVICES AVAILABLE

rullino
rool-lee-no
film

pile
pee-lay
battery

opache
o-pa-kay
mat

lucide
loo-chee-day
glossy

videocamera
vee-day-o-ka-may-ra
camcorder

fuoco
fwo-ko
focus

where can I buy tapes for a videocamera?
dove posso comprare le cassette per la videocamera?
do-vay pos-so komp-ra-ray lay kas-set-tay payr la vee-day-o-ka-may-ra

a colour film	**24**	**36**	**exposures**
un rullino a colori	ventiquattro	trentasei	pose
oon rool-lee-no a ko-lo-ree	*ven-tee-kwat-tro*	*tren-ta-say*	*po-zay*

can you develop this film?
può svilupparmi questo rullino?
pwo svee-loop-par-mee kwes-to rool-lee-no

can we take pictures?
si può fare delle foto?
see pwo fa-ray del-lay fo-to

can you take a picture of us?
ci può fare una foto?
chee pwo fa-ray oo-na fo-to

talking

PHONES

*There is no shortage of public phones in Italy taking coins and phonecards (**scheda telefonica**) available from **tabacchi** and newsagents. Cheaper times to phone are between 10 pm and 8 am Monday-Saturday and all day Sunday. Italy is awash with mobile phones. If you take your own, ensure that you contact your service provider to enable you to use it abroad.*

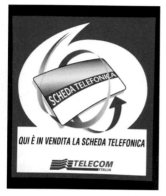

▶ There are also machines selling phonecards.

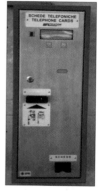

◀ Phonecards will be on sale where you see the words *scheda telefonica*.

talking talking talking talking

do you have phonecards?
avete delle schede telefoniche?
*a-**vay**-tay **del**-lay **skay**-day te-le-**fo**-nee-kay*

a phonecard
una scheda telefonica
*oo-na **skay**-da te-le-**fo**-nee-ka*

a 5-euro card
una scheda da cinque euro
*oo-na **skay**-da da **cheen**-kway ay-**oo**-ro*

can I make a phone call?
posso fare una chiamata?
*pos-so fa-ray oo-na kee-a-**ma**-ta*

Signor Grandi please
Signor Grandi per favore
*seen-**yor gran**-dee payr fa-**vo**-ray*

extension number...
interno numero...
*een-**ter**-no **noo**-may-ro...*

can I speak to Paul?
posso parlare con Paul?
*pos-so par-**la**-ray kon paul*

this is Caroline
qui è Caroline
kwee e caroline

it's Anna
sono Anna
*so-no **An**-na*

can I have an outside line please?
posso avere la linea per favore
*pos-so a-**vay**-ray la **lee**-nay-a payr fa-**vo**-ray*

hello
pronto
pron-to

I'd like to make a reverse-charge call
vorrei fare una chiamata a carico del destinatario
*vor-**ray** fa-ray oo-na kee-a-**ma**-ta a ka-**ree**-ko del des-tee-na-**tar**-yo*

what is you phone number?
qual è il suo numero di telefono?
*kwal e eel **soo**-o **noo**-may-ro dee te-**le**-fo-no*

my phone number is...
il mio numero è...
*eel **mee**-o **noo**-may-ro e...*

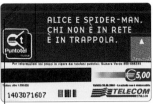

◀ Phonecards come in 5-euro units (*da cinque euro* da *cheen*-kway ay-*oo*-ro) and 10-euro units (*da dieci euro* da dee-*ay*-chee ay-*oo*-ro)

To use phonecards you must tear off the perforated corner.
Strappare = *tear off*

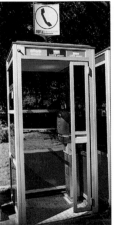

◀ Note the pictogram across the top of the phonebox. It takes
monete - coins
schede - phonecards
carte - credit cards.

UK	00 44
USA	00 11
Australia	00 61

▲ International dialling codes from Italy

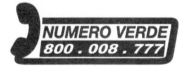

NUMERO VERDE
800 . 008 . 777

◀
Numero verde literally means green number. It is freephone, so no money is needed.

I'll call back...
richiamo...
reek-ya-mo...

later
più tardi
pyoo tar-dee

tomorrow
domani
do-ma-nee

do you have a mobile phone?
ha un telefonino?
a oon te-le-fo-nee-no

is it switched on?
è acceso
e ach-ay-zo

what is your mobile number?
qual è il suo numero di cellulare
kwal e eel soo-o noo-may-ro dee che-loo-la-ray

talking

E-MAIL, INTERNET, FAX

> *If you want to check your e-mail messages, internet cafés are becoming more and more widespread. If you know where you are going to be staying in Italy, check in advance at www.cyberfafe.com if there is a local internet café nearby. The suffix for Italian websites is .it.*

Internet ▶
café

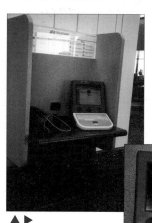

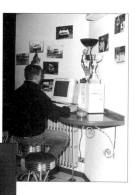

▲ ▶
There are internet access points at airports. You insert your credit card to pay for time online.

what is your e-mail address?
qual è il suo indirizzo e-mail?
kwal e eel soo-o een-dee-reet-so ee-mail

my e-mail address is...
il mio indirizzo e-mail è...
eel mee-o een-dee-reet-so ee-mail e...

caroline.smith@anycompany.co.uk
caroline punto smith chiocciola anycompany punto co punto uk
caroline poon-to smith chee-och-lo-la anycompany poon-to co poon-to uk

can I send an e-mail?
posso mandare un'e-mail?
po-so man-da-ray oon ee-mail

did you get my e-mail?
ha ricevuto la mia e-mail?
a ree-chay-voo-to la mee-a ee-mail

can you send it by e-mail?
può mandarlo via e-mail?
pwo man-dar-lo vee-a ee-mail

as an attachment
allegato
al-lay-ga-to

how much does an hour of netsurfing cost?
quanto costa un'ora in internet
kwan-to kos-ta oon o-ra een een-ter-net

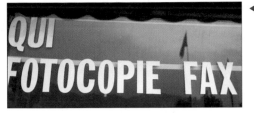

◀ Here you can photocopy and send faxes.

National and local tourist and what's-on information can be accessed via the internet.

▼

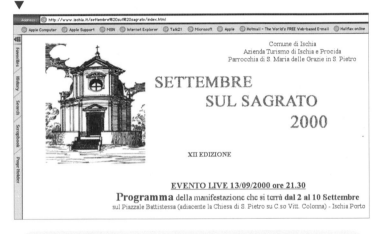

I want to send a fax
voglio mandare un fax
vol-yo man-da-ray oon faks

can I send a fax from here?
posso mandare un fax da qui?
pos-so man-da-ray oon faks da kwee

how much is it to send a fax?
quanto costa per mandare un fax?
kwan-to kos-ta payr man-da-ray oon faks

what is your fax number?
qual è il suo numero di fax?
kwal e eel soo-o noo-may-ro dee faks

did you get my fax?
ha ricevuto il mio fax?
a ree-chay-voo-to eel mee-o faks

do you have a fax?
avete un fax?
a-vay-tay oon faks

can I receive a fax here?
posso ricevere un fax qui?
pos-so ree-chev-ay-ray oon faks kwee

it has ... pages
ha ... pagine
a ... pa-jee-nay

can you confirm the number
può confirmare il numero
pwo kon-feer-ma-ray eel noo-may-ro

talking talking talking

OUT & ABOUT

Local tourist offices have free maps and brochures. They can generally help with booking accommodation and advise on local attractions and excursions. Museum opening hours are very variable so it is best to check before you visit. If you are visiting churches or religious sites you should remember that these are primarily places of worship, so dress appropriately: no shorts or bare shoulders.

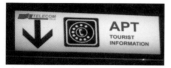

▲ Most Italian cities, towns and small villages have a tourist information office, known officially as *l'Azienda di Promozione Turistica*, but they can usually be identified with the *i* sign. ▼

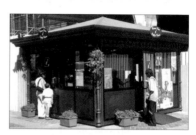

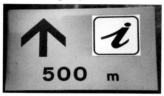

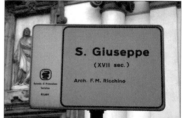

Places of interest such as museums and art galleries are ▼ signposted in brown.

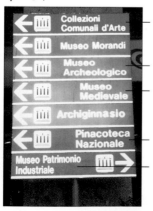

Muncipal art collection

Archeological museum

Medieval museum

National Art Gallery

Industrial Heritage Museum

▲ Churches are signposted in yellow. Opening hours can vary, particularly in smaller places. Churches are places of worship and visitors should take care to dress appropriately. If a Mass is taking place, you should disturb worshippers as little as possible.

Piazza means square, *Duomo* means cathedral. ▼

DUOMO

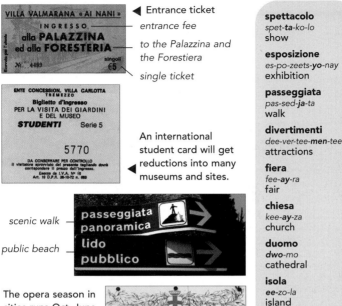

◀ Entrance ticket

— *entrance fee*

to the Palazzina and the Forestiera

— *single ticket*

An international student card will get reductions into many museums and sites.

scenic walk —

public beach —

The opera season in cities runs Oct–June (though the season at *La Scala* starts in Dec). Theatre performances in Italy generally start at 9 pm. Concert tickets are sold in music stores, kiosks or at the place of performance, prior to it.

keywords keywords keywords

spettacolo
spet-ta-ko-lo
show

esposizione
es-po-zeets-yo-nay
exhibition

passeggiata
pas-sed-ja-ta
walk

divertimenti
dee-ver-tee-men-tee
attractions

fiera
fee-ay-ra
fair

chiesa
kee-ay-za
church

duomo
dwo-mo
cathedral

isola
ee-zo-la
island

municipio
moo-nee-cheep-yo
town hall

excuse me, where is the tourist office?
scusi, dov'è l'ufficio turistico?
skoo-zee do-ve loof-fee-cho too-rees-tee-ko

do you have...?	**a town guide**	**leaflets**
avete...?	una guida della città	degli opuscoli
a-vay-tay...	*oo-na gwee-da del-la cheet-ta*	*del-yee o-poos-ko-lee*

we want to visit...
vogliamo visitare...
vol-ya-mo vee-zee-ta-ray...

are there any excursions?
ci sono delle gite?
chee so-no del-lay jee-tay

when can we visit the...?
quando si può visitare...?
kwan-do see pwo vee-zee-ta-ray...

when does it close?
quando chiude?
kwan-do kee-oo-day

how much is it to get in?
quanto costa l'ingresso?
kwan-to kos-ta leen-gres-so

is there a guided tour?
c'è una visita guidata?
che oo-na vee-zee-ta gwee-da-ta

talking talking talking

Many beaches in Italy are private or attached to a hotel and you will have to pay to hire a sunbed and sunshade.

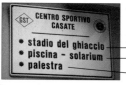

sports centre

swimming pool

▲ It is obligatory to wear a swimming cap in pools. Check locally for pool times.

◀ SPORTS CENTRE

CENTRO SPORTIVO CASATE
* stadio del ghiaccio — ice rink
* piscina – solarium — pool – solarium
* palestra — gym

The local tourist office will have brochures on many sporting and leisure activities. If you are interested in hiking, ask for brochures on any local hikes. ▶

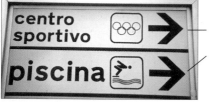

HIKING ON THE
VIA DEI MONTI LARIANI

1	CERNOBBIO - VAL D'INTELVI
2	VAL D'INTELVI - VAL MENAGGIO
3	VAL MENAGGIO - VALLE ALBANO
4	VALLE ALBANO - SORICO

talking talking talking

where can we...?
dove si può...?
do-vay see pwo...

how much is it...?
quanto costa...?
kwan-to kos-ta...

go riding
andare a cavallo
an-da-ray a ka-val-lo

is there a swimming pool?
c'è una piscina?
che oo-na pee-shee-na

where can we go...?
dove si può...?
do-vay see pwo...

play tennis
giocare a tennis
jo-ka-ray a ten-nees

to hire bikes
noleggiare le bici
no-led-ja-ray lay bee-chee

per hour/day
all'ora/al giorno
al-lo-ra/al jor-no

is dangerous to swim here?
è pericoloso nuotare qui?
e pay-ree-ko-lo-zo nwo-ta-ray kwee

windsurfing
fare del windsurf
fa-ray del windsurf

play golf
giocare a golf
jo-ka-ray a golf

to fish
pescare
pes-ka-ray

waterskiing
fare lo sci nautico
fa-ray lo shee now-tee-ko

how do we hire a beach umbrella?
come si noleggia un ombrellone?
ko-may see no-led-ja oon om-brel-lo-nay

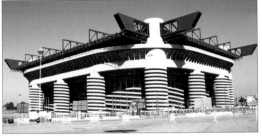

◀ The football season in Italy runs from end Aug to early June. Games are usually played on Sun afternoons. Italians are passionate about the game.

STADIUM ▶
If you do go to a match, be prepared for fireworks being set off (it may be worth worth wearing a scarf to cover your mouth).

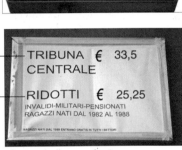

main stand seats ——

reductions ——
disabled-military-retired
children born from 1982 to 1988

Tickets to football matches can be bought at the stadiums. ▼

▲ Football ground prices

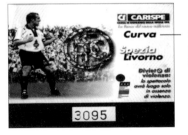

Curva seats are at each end of the ground. The most expensive tickets are *Tribuna* in the main stand.

we'd like to see a football match
ci piacerebbe vedere una partita di calcio
*chee pee-a-chay-**reb**-bay ved-**ay**-ray **oo**-na par-**tee**-ta dee **kal**-cho*

where can we get tickets?
dove si prendono i biglietti?
***do**-vay see **pren**-do-no ee beel-**yet**-tee*

how much are they?
quanto costano?
***kwan**-to **kos**-ta-no*

how do we get to the stadium?
come si arriva allo stadio?
***ko**-may see ar-**ree**-va **al**-lo **stad**-yo*

what time is the match?
quando comincia la partita?
***kwan**-do ko-**meen**-cha la par-**tee**-ta*

talking

ACCOMMODATION

Hotels are classified one to five stars. One star is generally quite basic, with shared facilities. Two star might have en suite facilities. Three star will have en suite facilities and perhaps a pool. Four star will probably be down to the location. And five star is luxury, either because its location or the type of building it occupies.

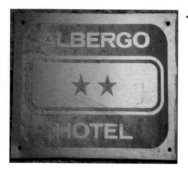

◀ Italian hotels are star rated

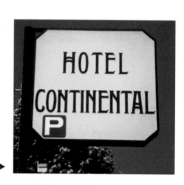

The Italian word for hotel is *albergo*, but you will often find the word hotel. ▶

Booking in advance

You can phone up the hotel of your choice and book a room. They generally require a fax to confirm the booking and your credit card number. Smaller places generally don't take bookings very far in advance, particularly if there is perhaps a trade fair on, when they are likely to be busy.

I would like to book a room
vorrei prenotare una camera
vor-**ray** pray-no-**ta**-ray oo-na **ka**-may-ra

single/double
singola/doppia
seen-go-la/**dop**-pya

for ... nights
per ... notti
payr ... **not**-tee

from ... to ...
dal ... al ...
dal ... al ...

my name is...
il mio nome è...
eel **mee**-o **no**-may e...

I'll fax to confirm
confermo con un fax
kon-**fer**-mo kon oon faks

my credit card number is ...
il numero della mia carta di credito è...
eel **noo**-may-ro **del**-la **mee**-a **kar**-ta dee **kray**-dee-to e...

expiry date...
data di scadenza...
da-ta dee ska-**dent**-sa...

Hotels are generally signposted. ▶
The busiest time outside the
cities is August, particularly the
weekend nearest 15 August,
known as **ferragosto**.

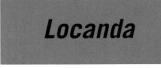

There is little difference
between a **pensione** and a 1-
or 2-star hotel. Many retired
Italians spend the winter
months in hotels or **pensioni**
by the seaside. ▼

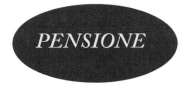

PENSIONE

Locanda

▲ A **locanda** is a basic guesthouse,
generally with shared facilities, though
there will be a sink in the room. No
food is provided. Smaller city estab-
lishments may shut in August.

do you have a room?
avete una camera?
a-**vay**-tay **oo**-na **ka**-may-ra

a single/double room
una camera singola/doppia
oo-na **ka**-may-ra **seen**-go-la/**dop**-pya

a family room
una camera per una famiglia
oo-na **ka**-may-ra payr **oo**-na fa-**meel**-ya

with ensuite bath
con bagno
kon **ban**-yo

with shower
con doccia
kon **doch**-cha

for tonight
per stanotte
payr sta-**not**-tay

for just one night
per una notte sola
payr **oo**-na **not**-tay **so**-la

for ... nights
per ... notti
payr ... **not**-tee

how much is it?
quanto costa?
kwan-to **kos**-ta

is breakfast included?
comprende la colazione?
com-**pren**-day la ko-lats-**yo**-nay

how much is half board?
quanto costa mezza pensione?
kwan-to **kos**-ta **med**-za pens-**yo**-nay

full board
la pensione completa
la pens-**yo**-nay kom-**play**-ta

I would like to see the room
vorrei vedere la camera
vor-**ray** ved-**ay**-ray la **ka**-may-ra

talking talking talking talking

To stay at a youth hostel in Italy you generally have to be a member of the International Youth Hostelling Association. You can join on the spot or simply pay a supplement. In the summer you will have to book in advance as they are often full.

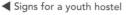
◀ Signs for a youth hostel ▼

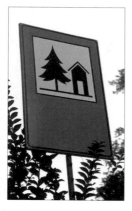

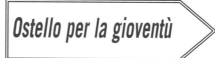

Ostello per la gioventù

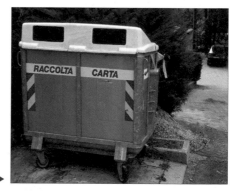

Paper recycling bank
You will also come across bottle banks. In smaller villages there is a refuse point where you leave your rubbish. The times of the collection will be posted next to it. ▶

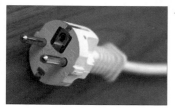

◀ Italian plugs are two-pin and you should take an adapter with you if you are taking any of your own electrical appliances such as hair-dryer or iron. The electric current is 220 v.

how do we get to the youth hostel?
come si arriva all'ostello per la gioventù
ko-may see ar-ree-va al-los-tel-lo payr la jov-en-too

how much is it to become a member?
quanto costa diventare socio?
kwan-to kos-ta dee-ven-ta-ray so-cho

talking

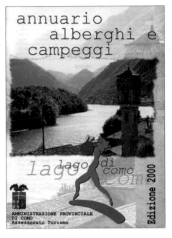

annuario
alberghi e
campeggi

lago di como

Edizione 2000

AMMINISTRAZIONE PROVINCIALE
DI COMO
Assessorato Turismo

◀ Local tourist offices provide annual guides to self-catering, hotel and and camping accommodation in their area. They should also be able to assist you with booking.

Camere   ◀ ROOMS

FULL UP ▶   **COMPLETO**

keywords keywords keywords

detersivo per i piatti
day-ter-see-vo payr ee pee-a-tee
washing-up liquid

carta igienica
kar-ta ee-jay-nee-ka
toilet paper

sapone
sa-po-nay
soap

apriscatole
ap-ree-ska-to-lay
tin-opener

candele
kan-day-lay
candles

fiammiferi
fee-am-mee-fay-ree
matches

bombola del gas
bom-bo-la del gaz
gas cylinder

talking talking talking

there is/are no...
non c'è/non ci sono...
non che/chee so-no...

how does ... work?
come funziona...
ko-may foonts-yo-na...

can you show us how it works?
può farci vedere come funziona?
pwo far-chee ved-ay-ray ko-may foonts-yo-na

the cooker
la cucina
la koo-chee-na

the dishwasher
la lavastoviglia
la la-va-sto-veel-ya

the washing machine
la lavatrice
la la-va-tree-chay

the microwave
il forno a microonde
eel for-no a mee-kro-on-day

who do I contact if there is a problem?
con chi parlo se c'è un problema?
kon kee par-lo say che oon prob-lay-ma

when is the rubbish collected?
quando passano gli spazzini?
kwan-do pas-sa-no lee spats-see-nee

where do we leave the rubbish?
dove mettiamo la spazzatura?
do-vay met-ya-mo la spats-sa-too-ra

can we have another key?
possiamo avere un'altra chiave?
poss-ya-mo a-vay-ray oon-alt-ra kee-a-vay

The local tourist office will provide information about local campsites. Off-site camping is only allowed in Italy provided you have the permission of the landowner on whose land you are camping – otherwise it is illegal. Official campsites are open mainly from April to September and are well equipped.

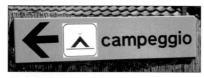

◀ CAMPSITE
The local tourist information office will provide a list of sites.

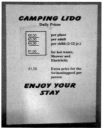

no parking from 1 Jun to 30 Sep for lorries and camping vans —

◀ Campsites display

their prices. You generally pay per person, per place plus extra for hot water and electricity.

A car towing a caravan or trailer must not exceed 50 kph in built-up areas, 70 kph outside built-up areas and 80 kph on motorways.

is there a campsite near here?
c'è un campeggio qui vicino?
*che oon kam-**ped**-jo kwee vee-**chee**-no*

have you any vacancies?
avete dei posti?
*a-**vay**-tay day **pos**-tee*

we want to stay for ... nights
vogliamo restare per ... notti
*vol-**ya**-mo res-**ta**-ray payr ... **not**-tee*

how much is it...?
quanto costa...
*kwan-to **kos**-ta...*

per tent
per tenda
*payr **ten**-da*

per caravan
per roulotte
*payr roo-**lot***

where are...?
dove sono...?
do-vay so-no...

the showers
le doccie
*lay **doch**-chay*

the toilets
le toilette
*lay twa-**let***

is there a restaurant on the campsite?
c'è un ristorante nel campeggio?
*che oon rees-to-**ran**-tay nel kam-**ped**-jo*

is there a more sheltered site?
c'è un posto più riparato?
*che oon **pos**-to pyoo ree-pa-**ra**-to*

DRY-CLEANERS ▶

trousers
skirts
jackets
coats
jumpers

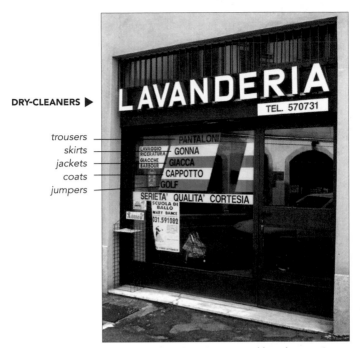

There are not many coin-operated launderettes in
Italy. Large supermarkets have cleaning services
which take 1 to 2 hours and are good value. At the
dry-cleaners it will take a day, but it is generally
better value and service.

is there a launderette?
c'è una lavanderia automatica?
*che oon la-van-day-**ree**-a ow-to-**ma**-tee-ka*

where can I do some washing?
dove posso lavare questi panni?
***do**-vay **pos**-so la-**va**-ray **kwes**-tee **pan**-nee*

is there an iron
c'è un ferro da stiro?
*che oon **fer**-ro da **stee**-ro*

is there a laundry service?
c'è il servizio lavanderia?
*che eel ser-**veets**-yo la-van-day-**ree**-a*

when will my things be ready?
quando saranno pronti?
***kwan**-do sa-**ran**-no **pron**-tee*

where is the nearest dry-cleaner's?
dov'è la tintoria più vicina?
*do-**ve** la teen-to-**ree**-a pyoo vee-**chee**-na*

talking talking talking

SPECIAL NEEDS

Disabled facilities are gradually improving in Italy with some museums and churches providing wheelchair-accessible entrances.

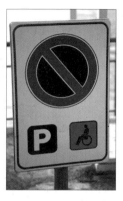

◀ Disabled parking is usually available and indicated by the yellow wheelchair sign. The space is reserved for disabled parking only.

Some service ▶ stations offer facilities for the disabled.

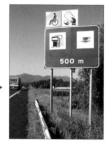

◀ Trains marked with this blue disabled badge are equipped to carry wheelchairs. These are mainly the newer intercity trains.

---

are there any toilets for the disabled?
ci sono le toilette per i disabili?
chee so-no lay twa-let payr ee dee-za-bee-lee

is there an entrance for wheelchairs?
c'è l'accesso per la sedia a rotelle?
che la-ches-so payr la sed-ya a ro-tel-lay

is it possible to visit ... with a wheelchair?
si può visitare ... con la sedie a rotelle?
see pwo vee-zee-ta-ray ... kon la sed-ya a ro-tel-lay

is there a reduction for the disabled?
c'è una riduzione per i disabili?
che oo-na ree-doots-yo-nay payr ee dee-za-bee-lee

I need a bedroom on the ground floor
ho bisogno di una camera al pian terreno
o bee-zon-yo dee oo-na ka-may-ra al pee-an ter-ray-no

can I take the train to ... with a wheelchair?
si può prendere il treno per ... con la sedia a rotelle?
see pwo pren-day-ray eel tray-no payr ... kon la sed-ya a ro-tel-lay

I'm a wheelchair
sono in una sedia a rotelle
so-no een oo-na sed-ya a ro-tel-lay

is there a lift?
c'è un ascensore?
che oon a-shen-so-ray

talking talking talking talking

WITH KIDS

Despite Italy's reputed love of children, northern Italy has the lowest birth rate in Europe. In some restaurants you might find it quite difficult to find a highchair.

GESTIONE

12363 / 106

ONE GOVERNATIVA NAVIGAZIONE LAGHI

```
Navigazione Lago di Como
P.IVA 00802050153

Biglietteria di Menaggio

21-07-00   17:35   36841   22/ 1

Da MENAGGIO      a TREMEZZO

A -->

1 - ORDINARIO BATTELLO
Vale giorni 1

Euro 6,09

Adulti 2  Ragazzi 1

Non sono ammesse fermate intermedie
```

◀

On most public transport children under 5 travel free. Between 5 and 12 years old they can get a 50% discount on their ticket.

2 adults, 1 child

keywords keywords keywords

bambino/a
bam-bee-no/a
child

seggiolino
sed-jo-lee-no
baby seat

seggiolone
sed-jo-lo-nay
high chair

lettino
let-tee-no
cot

parco giochi
par-ko jo-kee
play park

panolini
pa-no-lee-nee
nappies

---

talking talking talking

what is there for children to do?
cosa c'è da fare per i bambini?
ko-za che da fa-ray payr ee bam-bee-nee

where can I change the baby?
dove posso cambiare il bambino?
do-vay pos-so kamb-ya-ray eel bam-bee-no

do you have...?	**a high chair**	**a cot**
avete...?	un seggiolone	un lettino
a-vay-tay...	*oon sed-jo-lo-nay*	*oon let-tee-no*

nappies	**baby wipes**	**baby food**
panolini	salviettine	alimenti per bambini
pa-no-lee-nee	*sal-vyet-tee-nay*	*a-lee-men-tee payr bam-bee-nee*

is there a children's menu?	**a half portion**
c'è un menù per bambini?	una mezza porzione
che oon me-noo payr bam-bee-nee	*oo-na med-za ports-yo-nay*

is there a play park near here?
c'è un parco giochi qui vicino?
che oon par-ko jo-kee kwee vee-chee-no

HEALTH

i

You should fill in an E111 form before you leave. They are available from post offices and should be stamped by them. The form entitles you to free medical emergency treatment. If you have to have treatment, take the form to any Italian USL office and obtain a certicate of entitlement. Ask for the list of practitioners you can visit and then take the certificate to one of them, who will charge you a fee which you can claim on your return (you will have to send your E11 form and original bills, prescriptions and receipts to the address listed in the Health Advice Brochure which you get with the form). For prescribed medicines you will be charged a standard fee which is not refundable.

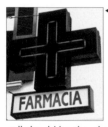

◀ Pharmacies are open during shopping hours. If you are feeling unwell (and it is not an emergency), your first point of call should be the pharmacy, especially if you have an idea of what is wrong. They are usually helpful and know which products would suit.

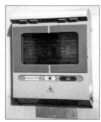

Each pharmacy must display the list of duty chemists open at night ◀ or on Sunday.

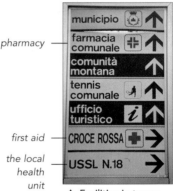

pharmacy —

first aid —

the local health unit —

▲ Facilities in towns are usually well sign-posted.

where is there a chemist?
dove c'è una farmacia?
do-vay che oo-na far-ma-chee-a

have you something for...?
avete qualcosa per...?
a-vay-tay kwal-ko-za payr...

indigestion
l'indigestione
leen-dee-jest-yo-nay

sunburn
la scottatura solare
la skot-ta-too-ra so-la-ray

diarrhoea
la diarrea
la dee-a-ray-a

a cough
la tosse
la tos-say

I need...
ho bisogno di...
o bee-zon-yo dee...

a painkiller
un analgesico
oon a-nal-jay-zee-ko

antibiotics
antibiotici
an-tee-bee-o-tee-chee

OSPEDALE di MENAGGIO →

▲ Sign to local hospital

▶
You are entering a hospital zone in 150 m

zona ospedaliera 150 m

I am not well
mi sento male
*mee **sen**-to **ma**-lay*

... doesn't feel well
... si sente male
*... see **sen**-tay **ma**-lay*

I need a doctor
ho bisogno di un dottore
*o bee-**zon**-yo dee oon dot-**to**-ray*

please call the doctor
mi chiami il dottore
*mee kee-**a**-mee eel dot-**to**-ray*

my son/my daughter is ill
mio figlio/mai figlia sta male
***mee**-o **feel**-yo/**mee**-a **feel**-ya sta **ma**-lay*

I have a pain here
ho un dolore qui
*o oon do-**lor**-ay kwee*

I am on this medication
sto prendendo queste medicine
*sto pren-**den**-do **kwes**-tay may-dee-**chee**-nay*

I'm pregnant
sono incinta
*so-no een-**cheen**-ta*

I am on the pill
prendo la pillola
***pren**-do la **peel**-lo-la*

I'm breastfeeding
sto allattando al seno
*sto al-lat-**tan**-do al **say**-no*

I have cystitis
ho la cistite
*o la chees-**tee**-tay*

I'm diabetic
sono diabetico/a
*so-no dee-a-**bet**-ee-ko*

I am allergic to...
sono allergico/a a...
*so-no al-**ler**-jee-ko/a a...*

I have high blood pressure
ho la pressione alta
*o la pres-**yo**-nay **al**-ta*

my blood group is...
il mio gruppo sanguigno è...
*eel **mee**-yo **groop**-po san-**gween**-yo e...*

can I have a receipt for my insurance
mi dà una ricevuta per l'assicurazione
*mee da **oo**-na ree-chay-**voo**-ta payr las-see-koo-rats-**yo**-nay*

I need a dentist
ho bisogno di un dentista
*o bee-**zon**-yo dee oon den-**tees**-ta*

I have toothache
ho mal di denti
*o mal dee **den**-tee*

I need a temporary filling
ho bisogno di un'otturazione provvisoria
*o bee-**zon**-yo dee oon ot-too-rats-**yo**-nay prov-vee-**sor**-ya*

can your repair my dentures?
può riparare la mia dentiera?
*pwo ree-pa-**ra**-ray la **mee**-a dent-**yer**-a*

my filling has come out
è uscita l'otturazione
*e oo-**shee**-ta lot-too-rats-**yo**-nay*

talking talking talking talking talking talking talking

If you need emergency treatment, you should go directly to the **Pronto Soccorso** (A & E) in the nearest hospital. You should present them with your E111 form and your passport.

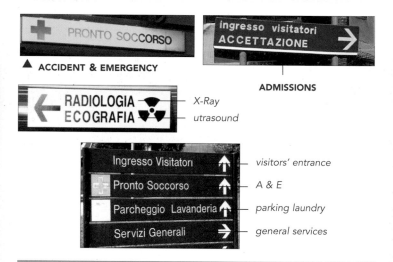

PRONTO SOCCORSO

▲ **ACCIDENT & EMERGENCY**

ingresso visitatori
ACCETTAZIONE →

ADMISSIONS

← RADIOLOGIA ☢
ECOGRAFIA ☢

— X-Ray
— utrasound

Ingresso Visitatori	↑	— visitors' entrance
Pronto Soccorso	↑	— A & E
Parcheggio Lavanderia	↑	— parking laundry
Servizi Generali	→	— general services

If you need to go to hospital

will he/she have to go to hospital?
deve andare all'ospedale?
day-vay an-da-ray al-los-ped-a-lay

where is the nearest A & E department?
dov'è il pronto soccorso più vicino?
do-ve eel pron-to sok-kor-so pyoo vee-chee-no

please take me to the hospital
per favore mi porti all'ospedale
payr fa-vo-ray mee por-tee al-los-ped-a-lay

I need to go to casualty
devo andare al pronto soccorso
day-vo an-da-ray al pron-to sok-kor-so

when are visiting hours?
quando sono le ore di visite?
kwan-do so-no lay o-ray dee vee-zee-tay

can you explain what is the matter?
può spiegare cos'è il problema?
pwo spyay-ga-ray ko-ze eel prob-lay-ma

where is the hospital?
dov'è l'ospedale
do-ve los-ped-a-lay

which ward?
quale reparto?
kwa-lay ray-par-to

EMERGENCY

*If you are robbed or suffer a crime, you should make a report to the police (either **Polizia** or **Carabinieri**, both perform more or less the same function) at the police station, **Questura**. You will need a copy of the report to present to your insurance company if you want to make a claim. All the emergency services can be called on 113 though each has its own number: Police, 112; Medical emergency 118; Fire brigade 115.*

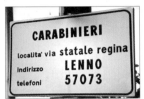

◀ Address of the local police

Police car ▶

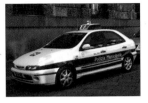

help!	**can you help me?**	
aiuto!	può aiutarmi?	
*a-**yoo**-to*	*pwo a-yoo-**tar**-mee*	

please call...	**the police**	**an ambulance**
per favore chiamate...	la polizia	un'ambulanza
*payr fa-**vo**-ray kee-a-**ma**-tay...*	*la po-leet-**see**-a*	*oon am-boo-**lant**-sa*

help! Fire!	**please call the fire brigade!**
aiuto! Fuoco!	per favore chiamate i vigili del fuoco!
*a-**yoo**-to fwo-ko*	*payr fa-**vo**-ray kee-a-**ma**-tay ee **vee**-jee-lee del **fwo**-ko*

my ... has been stolen	**I want to report a theft**
mi hanno rubato...	voglio denunciare un furto
*mee **an**-no roo-**ba**-to...*	*vol-yo den-oon-**cha**-ray oon **foor**-to*

here are my insurance details
ecco i dati della mia assicurazione
*ek-ko ee **da**-tee **del**-la **mee**-a as-see-koo-rats-**yo**-nay*

please give me your insurance details
mi dia i vostri dati di assicurazione
*mee **dee**-a ee **vos**-tree **da**-tee dee as-see-koo-rats-**yo**-nay*

where is the police station?
dov'è la questura?
*do-**ve** la kwes-**too**-ra*

I would like to phone...	**my car has been broken into**
vorrei telefonare...	hanno svaligiato la mia macchina
*vor-**ray** te-le-fo-**na**-ray...*	*an-no sva-lee-**ja**-to la **mee**-a **mak**-kee-na*

I need a report for my insurance
ho bisogno di un verbalè per la mia assicurazione
*o bee-**zon**-yo dee oon ver-**ba**-lay payr la **mee**-a as-see-koo-rats-**yo**-nay*

talking talking talking talking talking

FOOD AND DRINK

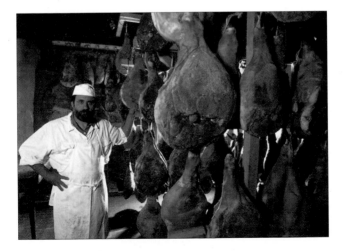

Italians enjoy good food and to do this they make sure that they cook with the best ingredients available.

In the north of Italy traditionally the main meal of the day is lunch, **il pranzo**. In the south of Italy, because of the heat, it is dinner, **la cena**. However with working habits changing and people working further away from their homes, a large lunch is not always possible except at weekends.

La prima colazione (breakfast) is often eaten standing at a bar and is usually an **espresso** (small strong black coffee) or **cappuccino** and **brioche** (sweet bun). Otherwise at home it is generally milky coffee and biscuits. However, cereals are becoming more common.

A traditional full Italian meal consists of **antipasto** (often finely sliced ham, salami, and other cold meats), **primo** (pasta or risotto) and **secondo** (meat or fish) served with a salad or French fries or vegetables. Cheese and a dessert normally follow.

Many bars and **caffès** ▶ serve food: generally salads, sandwiches, pasta dishes and pizzas. Check where the bar is situated: if it is in a very touristy area, it may be expensive. It is worth checking side streets to see if you can find a quieter bar. If Italians are eating there, take that as a recommendation.

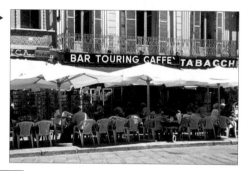

MENÙ TURISTICO

▲ Many restaurants offer set price meals (sometimes including wine). Although generally good value, the food is aimed mainly at the tourist market.

As well as a tobacconist, a **tabbacaio** is often a bar and may serve meals. There are no frills, but the food will be good. ▼

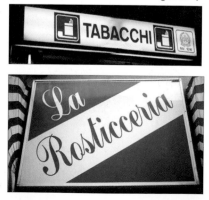

A *rosticceria* sells spit-roasted chicken and food to be eaten there (generally standing) or to take away. The food should be good and well-worth sampling. ▶

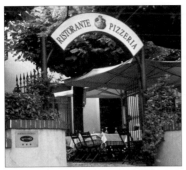

▲ Italians are more interested in their food than the decor, so most restaurants are quite similar, with crisp linen tablecloths and unfussy surroundings.

Traditionally, a *trattoria* is a family-run restaurant, usually with less choice than a restaurant. There may be no menu and you will be told what is available that day. Again, it is somewhere well worth trying. ▼

Trattoria

Hamburger chains are appearing in Italy, but with a slight Italian flavour in that Italians don't like queuing, so you may find them trying to sneak ahead! ▼

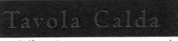

▲ Self-service type restaurant; good for a quick meal.

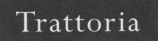

◀ HOME COOKING

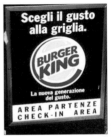

where can we get a snack?
dove possiamo trovare uno spuntino?
do-vay pos-ya-mo tro-va-ray oo-no spoon-tee-no

can you recommend a good restaurant?
ci può consigliare un buon ristorante?
chee pwo kon-seel-ya-ray oon bwon rees-to-ran-tay

are there any vegetarian restaurants?
ci sono dei ristoranti vegetariani?
chee so-no day rees-to-ran-tee vay-jay-tar-ya-nee

do we need to book a table?
dobbiamo prenotare un tavolo?
dob-ya-mo pray-no-ta-ray oon ta-vo-lo

what do you recommend?
che cosa ci consiglia?
kay ko-za chee kon-seel-ya

how do we get to the restaurant?
come ci si arriva a questo ristorante?
ko-may chee see ar-ree-va a kwes-to rees-to-ran-tay

talking talking talking

*If you want a snack rather than a full meal, bars generally have things such as **pizza**, **toast** (toasted sandwiches) and **panini** (sandwiches). They may also serve pasta dishes such as **spaghetti**, **lasagne**, etc.*

keywords

formaggio
for-**mad**-jo
cheese

prosciutto
pro-**shoot**-to
ham

pomodoro
po-mo-**do**-ro
tomato

farcito
far-**chee**-to
stuffed with titbits

liscio
lee-sho
plain

FOOD ON OFFER ▶

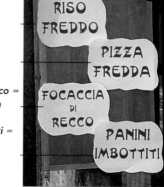

riso freddo =
cold rice dish

pizza freddo =
cold pizza

focaccia di recco =
cheese focaccia

panini imbottiti =
filled rolls/
sandwiches

RISO FREDDO

PIZZA FREDDA

FOCACCIA DI RECCO

PANINI IMBOTTITI

tramezzini

◀ These are sandwiches made with soft white bread.

talking talking

I'd like ... please
vorrei ... per favore
*vor-**ray** ... payr fa-**vo**-ray*

we'd like...
vorremmo...
*vor-**rem**-mo*

a cappuccino
un cappuccino
*oon kap-poo-**chee**-no*

a large black coffee
un caffè americano
*oon kaf-**fe** a-mer-ee-**ka**-no*

decaffeinated
decaffeinato
*day-kaf-fay-**na**-to*

a hot chocolate
una cioccolata calda
*oo-na chok-ko-**la**-ta **kal**-da*

a tea with milk
un tè al latte
*oon te al **lat**-tay*

an orange juice
un succo d'arancia
*oon **sook**-ko da-**ran**-cha*

an peach juice
un succo di pesca
*oon **sook**-ko dee **pes**-ka*

a red wine
un vino rosso
*oon **vee**-no **ros**-so*

a white wine
un vino bianco
*oon **vee**-no bee-**an**-ko*

a lager
una birra
*oo-na **beer**-ra*

a bottle of mineral water
una bottiglia di acqua minerale
*oo-na bot-**teel**-ya dee **ak**-wa mee-nay-**ra**-lay*

fizzy
gassata
*gas-**sa**-ta*

still
naturale
*na-too-**ra**-lay*

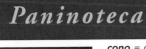

Paninoteca ◀ ICE CREAM

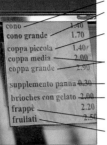

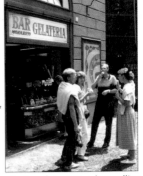

cono	1.40
cono grande	1.70
coppa piccola	1.40
coppa media	2.00
coppa grande	2.50
supplemento panna	0.30
brioches con gelato	2.00
frappè	2.20
frullati	2.50

cono = cone
cono grande = large cone
coppa piccola = small tub
coppa media/grande = medium/ large tub
supplemento panna = extra cost for cream
brioches con gelato = bun with ice cream
frappè = milkshake
frullati = freshly squeezed juice

▲ A *gelateria* is a bar selling ice cream where you can also get drinks. Italy has a mouth-watering variety of ice creams which can be almost a meal in themselves.

bibite

▲ SOFT DRINKS

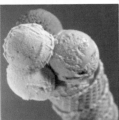

▲ If you buy a cone, *un cono*, you will be asked what flavours you want (*che gusti?*). If you want all chocolate, say *tutto cioccolato*, if you want lemon and chocolate, say *limone e cioccolato* If you prefer it in a tub, ask for *una coppa*.

Ice-creams ▶

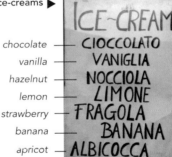

chocolate	CIOCCOLATO
vanilla	VANIGLIA
hazelnut	NOCCIOLA
lemon	LIMONE
strawberry	FRAGOLA
banana	BANANA
apricot	ALBICOCCA

can we eat here?
si può mangiare qui?
see pwo man-ja-ray kwee

what can we eat?
cosa si può mangiare?
ko-za see pwo man-ja-ray

is there a dish of the day?
c'è un piatto del giorno?
che oon pee-at-to del jor-no

what is the dish of the day?
qual è il piatto del giorno?
kwal e eel pee-at-to del jor-no

what sandwiches do you have?
quali panini avete?
kwa-lee pa-nee-nee a-vay-tay

I'd like an ice-cream
vorrei un gelato
vor-ray oon jay-la-to

what flavours do you have?
che gusti ci sono?
kay goos-tee chee so-no

talking

Italy is the home of the pizza. They are thin based and cooked in wood-fired ovens. You won't find the wide range of deep-pan options that originated in America. Nor will you find combinations such as ham and pineapple, though new additions are gradually finding their way into the classic pizza repertoire.

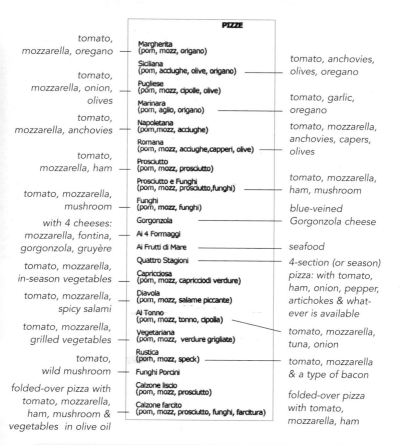

PIZZE

tomato, mozzarella, oregano —
Margherita
(pom, mozz, origano)

Siciliana
(pom, acciughe, olive, origano) — tomato, anchovies, olives, oregano

tomato, mozzarella, onion, olives —
Pugliese
(pom, mozz, cipolle, olive)

Marinara
(pom, aglio, origano) — tomato, garlic, oregano

tomato, mozzarella, anchovies —
Napoletana
(pom, mozz, acciughe) — tomato, mozzarella, anchovies, capers, olives

Romana
(pom, mozz, acciughe, capperi, olive)

tomato, mozzarella, ham —
Prosciutto
(pom, mozz, prosciutto)

Prosciutto e Funghi
(pom, mozz, prosciutto, funghi) — tomato, mozzarella, ham, mushroom

tomato, mozzarella, mushroom —
Funghi
(pom, mozz, funghi)

Gorgonzola — blue-veined Gorgonzola cheese

with 4 cheeses: mozzarella, fontina, gorgonzola, gruyère —
Ai 4 Formaggi

Ai Frutti di Mare — seafood

Quattro Stagioni — 4-section (or season) pizza: with tomato, ham, onion, pepper, artichokes & whatever is available

tomato, mozzarella, in-season vegetables —
Capricciosa
(pom, mozz, capriccio di verdure)

Diavola
(pom, mozz, salame piccante) — tomato, mozzarella, spicy salami

Al Tonno
(pom, mozz, tonno, cipolla)

tomato, mozzarella, grilled vegetables —
Vegetariana
(pom, mozz, verdure grigliate) — tomato, mozzarella, tuna, onion

Rustica
(pom, mozz, speck) — tomato, mozzarella & a type of bacon

tomato, wild mushroom —
Funghi Porcini

folded-over pizza with tomato, mozzarella, ham, mushroom & vegetables in olive oil —
Calzone liscio
(pom, mozz, prosciutto)

Calzone farcito
(pom, mozz, prosciutto, funghi, farcitura) — folded-over pizza with tomato, mozzarella, ham

one pizza please
una pizza per favore
*oo-na **peet**-sa payr fa-**vo**-ray*

2 pizzas please
due pizze per favore
*doo-ay **peet**-say payr fa-**vo**-ray*

I'd like a pizza
vorrei una pizza
*vor-**ray** oo-na **peet**-sa*

what is there to drink?
cosa c'è da bere?
*ko-za che da **ber**-ay*

*When you ask for a **birra** in Italy, you will be served lager. If you want an ale or bitter, you should ask for **birra scura** or **birra rossa**. Draught beer will come either **piccola** (half pint approx.) or **media** (just under a pint). If you want to drink beer, look out for bars which call themselves pubs. They may be quite expensive.*

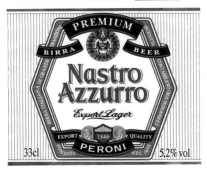

half a pint of lager
una birra piccola
oo-na beer-ra peek-ko-la

a pint of lager
una birra media
oo-na beer-ra med-ya

draught
alla spina
al-la spee-na

an Italian lager
una birra nazionale
oo-na beer-ra nats-yo-na-lay

do you have any ales?
avete delle birre rosse?
a-vay-tay del-lay beer-ray ros-say

Restaurants tend to shut one day a week. As a rule, eating places (including restaurants) have a menu with prices outside, so you will be prepared for the cost before going in.

Pizzeria, Ristorante Cinese
"La Vecchia Giostra"

Via Statale Regina, 63
Cadenabbia, Griante (CO) Tel. 0344-41278
Giorno di chiusura <u>Mercoledì</u>
In estate siamo aperti **tutti i giorni!**
<u>Gastronomia d'asporto</u>

◀ Menu of combined pizzeria and Chinese restaurant
Italians are conservative in their eating habits so you will not find a great variety of foreign restaurants as you do in London, for instance. However, Chinese and Indian restaurants are gradually appearing.

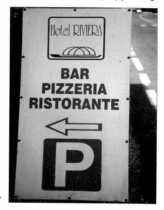

A pizza is often a cheaper option than a full meal. ▶

I would like to book a table
vorrei prenotare un tavolo
vor-**ray** pray-no-**ta**-ray oon **ta**-vo-lo

for 4 people
per quattro persone
payr **kwat**-tro per-**so**-nay

for tonight
per stasera
payr sta-**say**-ra

for tomorrow night
per domani sera
payr do-**ma**-nee **say**-ra

for lunch
per pranzo
payr **prant**-so

for 12.30
per le dodici e mezza
payr lay **do**-dee-chee e **med**-za

for 7.30
per le sette e mezza
payr lay **set**-tay ay **med**-za

for 8 o'clock
per le otto
payr lay **ot**-to

a non-smoking area
un posto non fumatori
oon **pos**-to non foo-mat-**or**-ee

in the name of...
a nome di...
a **no**-may dee...

In the countryside there is a type of rustic restaurant known as a *crotto*. These serve the real traditional food of the region, often homegrown and prepared. At harvest time (around the start of September) there are festivals, *sagre*, where you can sample the produce of the harvest.

▼

Crotto del Merlo

The typical Italian dining table will have a basket of bread rolls, *grissini* (breadsticks), salt and pepper, toothpicks, oil and vinegar to dress your salad, a jug or
◀ bottle of wine and mineral water.

OUR OWN CHEESE ▶

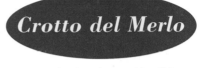

formaggio nostrano

the menu please
il menù per favore
*eel me-**noo** payr fa-**vo**-ray*

the wine list please
la lista dei vini per favore
*la **lees**-ta day **vee**-nee payr fa-**vo**-ray*

is there a set-price menu?
c'è un menù turistico?
*che oon me-**noo** too-**rees**-tee-ko*

for a starter I will have...
per antipasto prendo...
*payr an-tee-**pas**-to **pren**-do...*

for a main dish I will have...
per secondo prendo...
*payr se-**kon**-do **pren**-do...*

do you have any vegetarian dishes?
avete dei piatti vegetariani?
*a-**vay**-tay day **pyat**-tee ve-jay-ta-ree-**a**-nee*

what desserts do you have?
cosa c'è per dolce?
***ko**-za che payr **dol**-chay*

I'll have this
prendo questo
***pren**-do **kwes**-to*

a glass of water
un bicchiere di acqua semplice
*oon beek-**yer**-ay dee **ak**-wa **semp**-lee-chay*

some more bread
ancora un pò di pane
*an-**ko**-ra oon po dee **pa**-nay*

the bill please
il conto per favore
*eel **kon**-to payr fa-**vo**-ray*

we'd like separate bills
ci fà il conto separato
*chee fa eel **kon**-to sep-a-**ra**-to*

talking talking talking talking

*Most restaurants charge **pane e coperto** (cover charge).
Service is generally 10% and is often automatically charged.
If not, tipping of 10% is an acceptable amount.*

Restaurant bill listing ▶
exactly what has
been consumed.

RICEVUTA FISCALE - FATTURA (Legge 30 Dicembre 19991 n. 413)

Taverna antico agnello s.r.l.
ristorante
via olina n. 18
28016 Orta S. Giulio (no)
tel. 0322 90259
partita i.v.a. 01130970039

receipt for fiscal purposes —
☐ RICEVUTA FISCALE

bill/invoice —
☐ FATTURA - RICEVUTA FISCALE   N. ATTRIBUTO

DATA
02.03.00   **XNR № 04079** /2000

information about client —
Dati identificativi del Cliente

firm —
DITTA

residence or home address —
Residenza o domicilio

VAT —
P. IVA

number of people —	Per N. ___1___ pasti . . . .
bread & cover charge —	Pane - Coperto . . . .
wine —	Vino . . . .
other drinks —	Altre bevande . . . .
starter —	Antipasti . . . .
first course —	Primi . . . .
main course —	Secondi . . . .
vegetables —	Contorni . . . .
cheeses —	Formaggi . . . .
sweet —	Dolce . . . .
fruit —	Frutta . . . .
coffee —	Caffè . . . .
liqueurs —	Liquori . . . .

ALIQ. IVA	IMPONIBILE	IMPOSTA	CORRISPETTIVO PAGATO
%			CORRISPETTIVO NON PAGATO
%			
TOTALE			TOTALE DOCUMENTO

☐ PAGATO   A TITOLO DI: ☐ ANTICIPO ☐ ACCONTO
☐ R.F. EMESSA ALL'ATTO DELLA PRESTAZIONE O CONSEGNA (CORRISPETTIVO GIÀ SALDATO ANTICIPATAMENTE)
☐ SALDO DI R.F. GIÀ EMESSA ☐ RIFERIM. PREC DOCUM. R.F. _____ DEL

Tipolitografia Espana snc - Novara - Autorizzazione del Ministero delle Finanze VI-12-1095/94 del 31-01-94

▲ You must take your bill with you because
the law states that if you are found within
100 m of a bar, restaurant or shop without the
receipt, both you and the owner will be fined.

**Menù a prezzo fisso
(solo pranzo)
€9,50**

◀ FIXED PRICE MENU
(LUNCH ONLY)

*You don't have to have all the courses, you could skip **antipasto** and just have the first and second courses. Or you could have **antipasto** and the second course. Or you can just have one course.*

MENU *menu*

ANTIPASTI *starters*
antipasto misto *sliced ham, salami and other sliced meats*
prosciutto e melone *Parma ham and melon*

PRIMI *first courses*
pasta *different types of pasta dishes*
  al pomodoro *with a tomato sauce*
  al ragù *with a Bolognese sauce*
  all'arrabbiata *with a tomato and chilli pepper sauce*
  alla carbonara *with a bacon and egg sauce*
  alla puttanesca *with a tomato, chilli pepper and anchovy sauce*
  al pesto *with a basil, pine nut and pecorino sauce*
  in brodo *in broth (generally ravioli or other stuffed pasta)*
risotto *rice cooked in stock*
minestra *vegetable and pasta soup*

SECONDI *main dishes*
carne *meat*
  vitello *veal*
  manzo *beef*
  maiale *pork*
  pollo *chicken*
  agnello *lamb*
pesce *fish*

CONTORNI *vegetables*

FORMAGGI *cheeses*

DOLCI *sweets*

FRUTTA *fruit*

enjoy your meal!
buon appetito!
*bwon ap-pay-**tee**-to*

thanks, and you too!
grazie, e altrettanto!
***grats**-yay ay al-tret-**tan**-to*

talk

*The classic Italian wine is a red, made for food, light,
cherryish, dry, sharp. But things are changing. Not only are
better, richer white wines emerging now, but fruitier, deeper-
flavoured, more international reds. The best of them still retain that
signature Italian twist, a hint of cherrystone and of herb dryness
perhaps, rather than conforming to dull New World prototype.*

Italian classification of wine is a rough
guide to quality but there are bad and
▼ good wines in every grade.

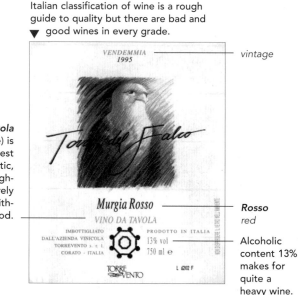

vintage

Vino da Tavola
(table wine) is
the lowest
class; rustic,
usually rough-
edged, rarely
quaffable with-
out food.

Rosso
red

Alcoholic
content 13%
makes for
quite a
heavy wine.

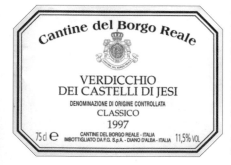

◄ DOC (*Denominazione di
Origine Controllata*) operates
like AC in France, with tight
controls on wine production.
The higher classification of
DOCG does not necessarily
promise a better wine, despite
its adding of *Garantita* (guaran-
teed). Some DOC quality wines
can also appear as IGT (*Indicazione Geograficha Tipica*;
see p. 87).

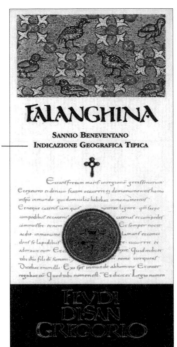

Indicazione Geograficha Tipica is the equivalent of French *vin de pays*; it can be rustic, can be superb.

bianco
bee-an-ko
white

rosso
ros-so
red

rosato
ro-za-to
rosé

secco
sek-ko
dry

dolce
dol-chay
sweet

un quarto
oon kwar-to
a quarter litre

un mezzo
oon med-so
half a litre

un litro
oon leet-ro
a litre

the wine list please
la lista dei vini per favore
la lees-ta day vee-nee payr fa-vo-ray

what wines do you have?
quali vini avete?
kwa-lee vee-nee a-vay-tay

is there a local wine?
c'è un vino locale?
che oon vee-no lo-ka-lay

can you recommend a good wine?
ci può consigliare un buon vino?
chee pwo kon-seel-ya-ray oon bwon vee-no

a glass of red wine
un bicchiere di vino rosso
oon beek-yer-ay dee vee-no ros-so

a quarter litre of white wine
un quarto di vino bianco
oon kwar-to dee vee-no bee-an-ko

a bottle of wine
una bottiglia di vino
oo-na bot-teel-ya dee vee-no

red	white
rosso	bianco
ros-so	*bee-an-ko*

a half litre of wine
un mezzo litro di vino
oon med-zo leet-ro dee vee-no

a litre of wine
un litro di vino
oon leet-ro dee vee-no

FLAVOURS OF ITALY

burrida
famous Genoese fish soup
pesto
sauce made from basil, olive oil, pecorino and pine-nuts
focaccia
flat bread brushed with garlic, salt and olive oil
cappon magro
cold seafood and vegetable salad

baccalà alla milanese
Milanese salt cod fritters, served with lemo
· **cotoletta alla milanese**
fried veal cutlet dressed in breadcrumbs
risotto alla milanese
rich saffron-coloured risotto
ossobucco
shin of veal cooked in tomato sauce
wines: Sassella, Grumello, Inferno

acqua cotta
traditional soup made from onions, peppers, celery and tomato. Beaten eggs and parmesan are added on serving.
bistecca alla fiorentina
large thick grilled T-bone steak
stracotto
braised beef cooked in red wine
trippa
tripe with tomatoes and onions
fagioli all'uccelletto
haricot beans in tomato, garlic and sage   .
wines: Chianti, Vernaccia, Brunello di Montalcino

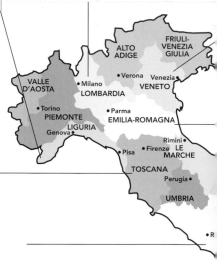

abbacchio
suckling pig
coda alla vaccinara
oxtail stewed with tomatoes and herbs
spaghetti all'amatriciana
spaghetti in a tomato and bacon sauce
gnocchi alla romana
oven-baked dumplings made from semolina, butter and parmesan
carciofi alla Giudia
flattened, deep-fried globe artichokes
saltimbocca alla romana
finely sliced veal with ham and sage
wines: frascati, Est! Est! Est!

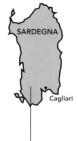

bottarga
preserved tuna or mullet roes, served in thin slices as a starter
cinghiale
wild boar
porceddu
suckling pig

apples
risi e bisati
rice cooked with eel
risotto alle seppie
risotto cooked with squid
fegato alla veneziana
calf's liver slices fried in butter with onions
baccalà alla vicentina
salt cod simmered in milk
polenta
corn or maize meal porridge
wines: Soave, Valpolicella, Bardolino

pasta
fresh pasta: tagliatelle, pappardelle, ravioli, etc
bolognese sauce
finely minced steak and tomato sauce served with pasta and in lasagne and cannelloni
parmigiano
parmesan cheese, grated over pasta dishes
parma ham
cured ham which is finely sliced
cotechino
spicy pork sausage often served with lentils
wines: Sangiovese, Trebbiano

agnello
lamb is a main ingredient

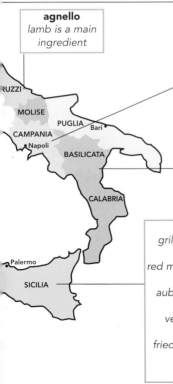

ABRUZZI
MOLISE
PUGLIA   Bari
CAMPANIA
Napoli
BASILICATA
CALABRIA
Palermo
SICILIA

pizza
Naples is the home of the pizza
parmigiana di melanzane
layers of finely sliced aubergines cooked in the oven with olive oil, tomato and parmesan
wines: Greco di Tufo, Taurasi, Limoncello
(lemon liqueur served as an aperitif)

CAMPANIA, BASILICATA & CALABRIA
mozzarella di bufala
mozzarella made from buffalo milk and stored in a buttermilk bath

pescespada
grilled mozzarella and herb-stuffed swordfish
triglie alla siciliana
red mullet cooked in white wine and orange peel
caponata
aubergines cooked in a sweet and sour sauce
farsu magru
veal stuffed and rolled up, cooked in wine
cannoli
fried pastries stuffed with ricotta, candied fruits and dark chocolate
wines: Marsala *(dark dessert wine)*

There are times when you cannot eat some things. It is as well to warn the waiter before making your choice.

talking talking talking talking talking talking

I'm vegetarian
sono vegetariano/a
so-no ve-jay-ta-ree-ya-no/a

I don't eat meat/pork
non mangio carne/carne di maiale
non man-jo kar-nay/kar-nay dee ma-ya-lay

I don't eat fish/shellfish
non mangio pesce/i frutti di mare
non man-jo pay-shay/ee froot-tee dee ma-ray

I'm allergic to shellfish
sono allergico/a ai frutti di mare
so-no al-ler-jee-ko/a a-ee froot-tee dee ma-ray

I am allergic to peanuts
sono allergico/a alle arachidi
so-no al-ler-jee-ko/a al-lay a-ra-kee-dee

I can't eat raw eggs
non posso mangiare le uova non cotte
non pos-so man-ja-ray lay wo-va non kot-tay

I can't eat liver
non posso mangiare il fegato
non pos-so man-ja-ray eel fay-ga-to

I am on a diet
sono a dieta
so-no a dee-ay-ta

I don't drink alcohol
non bevo l'alcool
non bay-vo lal-kol

what is in this?
cosa c'è dentro?
ko-za che den-tro

is it raw?
è crudo?
e kroo-do

is it made with unpasteurised milk?
è fatto con latte non pastorizzato?
e fat-to kon lat-tay non pas-to-reed-za-to

fritto
freet-to
fried

bollito
bol-lee-to
boiled

alla brace
al-la bra-chay
barbecued

arrosto
ar-ros-to
roast

allo spiedo
al-lo spyay-do
on a spit

ripieno
ree-pyay-no
stuffed

alla griglia
al-la greel-ya
grilled

affumicato
af-foo-mee-ka-to
smoked

al sangue
al sang-way
rare

cotto
kot-to
cooked

crudo
kroo-do
raw

al dente
al den-tay
firm

al forno
al for-no
baked

brasato
bra-za-to
cooked in wine

MENU READER

A

abbacchio suckling or milk-fed lamb, usually eaten at Easter. Roasted with garlic and rosemary
  abbacchio alla cacciatora lamb cooked in olive oil, garlic and rosemary

acciughe anchovies: fresh, salted or in olive oil
  acciughe ripiene fresh anchovies filled with fillets of salted anchovies and cream cheese and fried in oil

aceto vinegar
  aceto balsamico balsamic vinegar, the best comes from Modena

acqua brillante tonic water

acqua cotta literally 'cooked water', a traditional Tuscan soup made from onions, peppers, celery and tomato. Beaten eggs and parmesan are added just before serving

acqua minerale mineral water; this can be still (*naturale*), with gas (*effervescente*), or with artificial gas (*gassata*)

affettato misto selection of cold meats: ham, salami, mortadella, etc

affogato poached
  affogato al caffè vanilla ice cream with hot espresso coffee poured over it

affumicato smoked

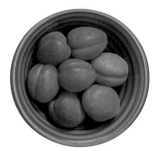

albicocche

aglio garlic
  aglio, olio e peperoncino garlic, olive oil and hot chilli sauce

agnello lamb
  agnello al forno roast lamb with vegetables
  agnello all'arrabbiata lamb cooked in a tomato and chilli sauce
  agnello arrosto roast lamb

agnollotti pasta squares filled with white meat and cheese, usually served with bolognese sauce

agoni small fish from Italian lakes, usually marinated in vinegar and herbs

agrodolce sweet and sour sauce made from sugar, water, vinegar, wine, pine-nuts and sultanas, often served with vegetables or meat such as rabbit or duck

ai ferri grilled

a, al, alla etc means with, or in the style of: eg *pasta al sugo* is pasta with tomato sauce, and *pollo alla cacciatora* is chicken hunter-style

albicocche apricots
  albicocche ripiene stuffed apricots

alici anchovies, often served dipped in flour and fried

alloro bayleaf

amarene dark morello cherries

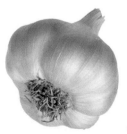

aglio

amaretti macaroons, biscuits with a strong almond flavour

Amaretto di Saronno almond liqueur

amaro bitter liqueur drunk as a *digestivo* (to aid digestion)

amatriciana, ...all' bacon, tomato and onion sauce

analcolico non-alcoholic, slightly bitter drink served as an aperitif

ananas pineapple

anatra duck
  anatra di Palmina duck cooked in wine
  anatra in porchetta roast duck stuffed with its liver and ham

anguille eel
  anguille alla comácchio stewed eel
  anguille carpionate fried eels
  anguille in umido eel stewed in tomato sauce

anguria watermelon

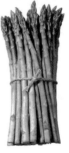

anguria

anice aniseed liqueur

anisetta powerful aniseed liqueur

annelletti baked squid or cuttle-fish rings

antipasto starters/appetizers
  antipasto misto selection of cold starters such as ham, salami, russian salad and pickles

aperitivo aperitif

Aperol aperitif made with the essence of various plants

aragosta crayfish
  aragosta allo spiedo crayfish cooked kebab-style

arance oranges

aranciata orangeade

arancini di riso rice croquettes filled with minced veal and peas

arrabbiata, ...all' tomato sauce with bacon, tomatoes, onion and hot chillies

arrosto roast meat, usually cooked in casserole with wine and herbs
  arrosto di maiale roast pork
  arrosto di manzo roast beef
  arrosto di vitello roast veal

asparagi asparagus
  asparagi alla parmigiana lightly

asparagi

boiled asparagus baked with parmesan

astice lobster

B

baccalà salt cod, popular in Italy
  baccalà alla fiorentina salt cod cooked in tomato sauce
  baccalà alla vicentina salt cod cooked in milk with anchovies, onion, garlic, parsley and herbs
  baccalà alla livornese salt cod cooked in a tomato sauce
  baccalà alla milanese Milanese salt cod fritters, served with lemon

bagna cauda hot garlic and anchovy dip. Literally it means 'hot bath' because raw vegetables such as pepper, celery and artichokes are dipped into it

banana banana

basilico basil

Bel Paese soft creamy mild cheese

baccalà alla fiorentina

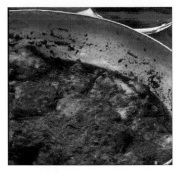

ben cotto well done

besciamella béchamel sauce

bianco, in literally it means white, pasta or rice served with melted butter, garlic, sage and parmesan

bietola beetroot

birra lager-type beer; draught beer is *birra alla spina*

biscotti biscuits

bistecca steak
  bistecca alla fiorentina thickly cut, charcoal-grilled steak
  bistecca alla pizzaiola fried steak in a tomato and herb sauce

bistecchini di cinghiale wild boar steaks in a sweet and sour sauce

bitter non-alcoholic, bitter drink served as an aperitif

bocconcini di vitello little pieces of veal cooked in wine and butter

bollito boiled
  bollito misto different kinds of meat and vegetables cooked together. There are many regional variations

bolognese, ...alla with tomato and minced meat sauce, served with parmesan

bomba doughnut with custard filling

bonet chocolate pudding with caramel

borlotti dried red haricot beans

boscaiola, ...alla with mushroom and ham sauce

bottarga preserved tuna or mullet roes, served in thin slices as a starter (speciality from Sardinia)

brace, ...alla grilled

braciola rib steak/chop
  braciole al ragù chops cooked in tomato sauce

brasato beef stew

bresaola dried cured beef, cut very finely and served with black pepper and olive oil

broccoletti leafy green vegetable similar to turnip tops

broccoli broccoli

brodetto di pesce a substantial fish soup made with different kinds of fish

brodo bouillon or broth often served with meat-stuffed pasta such as ravioli (*in brodo*)

bruschetta thickly-sliced bread rubbed with garlic and olive oil, often served topped with tomato

bucatini a type of pasta like thick spaghetti with a hole running through it

budino a blancmange-type pudding
  budino di ricotta pudding made with ricotta cheese

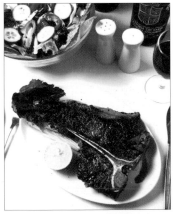

bistecca alla fiorentina

buridda famous Genoese fish soup using a variety of fish

burrini a creamy cheese from Basilicata

burro butter
 burro, ...al fried in butter, usually wih garlic and sage
 burro e salvia butter and sage sauce

busecca rich tripe and cheese soup

C

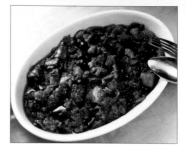

caponata

cacciatora, ...alla meat or game, hunter-style, meaning cooked with tomato, herbs, garlic and wine

cachi persimmons

caciocavallo cow's cheese which is quite strong when mature

caffè coffee – if you ask for *un caffè* you'll be served *un espresso* (small, strong and black)
 caffè americano black filter coffee
 caffè corretto coffee laced with *grappa* (strong spirit)
 caffè doppio a large coffee (twice the normal size)
 caffèllatte milky coffee

calamaretti imbottiti baby squid stuffed with breadcrumbs and anchovies

calamari squid
 calamari fritti squid rings dipped in batter and fried

calzone folded over pizza with filling. There are lots of local variations

camomilla camomile tea

Campari bitter-tasting aperitif made with herbs and fruit

canederli tirolesi Tyrolean dumplings made with bacon and sausage

cannella cinnamon

cannellini small white beans

cannelloni meat-filled tubes of pasta covered with béchamel sauce and baked until golden

brown. Vegetarian options are usually filled with spinach and ricotta

cannoli fried pastries stuffed with ricotta, candied fruit and bitter chocolate from Sicily

cantucci nutty biscuits

capocello smoked salami preserved in olive oil

caponata Sicilian dish of aubergines cooked in a sweet and sour sauce

cappelletti literally 'little hats' filled with ricotta cheese, can be served with bolognese meat sauce

capperi capers

cappon magro an elaborate cold seafood and cooked vegetable salad

cappuccino frothy white coffee

caprese tomato and mozzarella salad with basil

capretto baby goat (kid)
 capretto arrosto kid roasted in the oven with vegetables and wine

caprino soft goat's cheese, usually eaten with a sprinkling of olive oil and freshly ground black pepper

caramelle sweets

carbonade beef cooked in wine; the classic accompaniment is polenta

carbonara, ...alla smoked bacon, egg, cream and parmesan

carciofi globe artichokes

carciofi alla Giudia young globe artichokes, flattened and deep-fried

carciofi alla romana globe artichokes stuffed with breadcrumbs, parsley and anchovies

carciofi ripieni artichokes stuffed with mozarella, parmesan and anchovies

carciofina artichoke hearts

cardi cardoons (vegetable similar to fennel)

carciofo

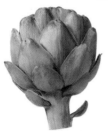

carne meat

carote carrots

carpaccio raw sliced lean beef eaten with lemon juice, olive oil and thickly grated parmesan cheese

carpione carp

carpione, in pickled in vinegar, wine and lemon juice. Fish is often served this way and fried

casalinga, ...alla home-made

cassata layers of ice cream with candied fruits

carpaccio

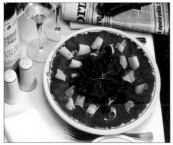

cassata siciliana sponge dessert with ricotta and candied fruits

cassoeula substantial pork and vegetable casserole

castagnaccio chestnut cake

castagne chestnuts

cavolatte rich custard pudding

cavolfiore cauliflower

cavolo cabbage

ceci chickpeas

céfalo grey mullet

cena dinner

Centerbe herbal liqueur

cervelle calves' brains usually fried

cetriolo cucumber

China bitter liqueur

chinotto fizzy soft drink with taste of bitter orange

cialzons alla carnia pasta squares filled with spinach, chocolate and cinnamon

ciambella ring-shaped fruit cake

ciambellini ring-shaped aniseed biscuits

cicoria chicory

ciliege cherries

cinghiale wild boar

Cinzano popular aperitif

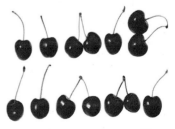

ciliege

cioccolata calda rich hot chocolate, often served with cream

cioccolatini chocolates

cioccolato chocolate

ciociara, ...alla with mushroom, cream and ham sauce

cipolle

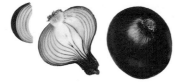

cipolle onions
cipolle ripiene stuffed onions
coccio a yeast cake with dried fruit
cocco coconut
cocomero watermelon
coda di bue oxtail
coda alla vaccinara famous Roman dish, consisting of oxtail stewed with tomatoes and herbs
conchiglie shell-shaped pasta
confetti sugared almonds
congelato frozen
coniglio rabbit
coniglio all'ischiana rabbit stewed in wine
coniglio in umido rabbit stew
contorni vegetable side dishes
cornetto a croissant filled with jam, custard or chocolate
cosciotto d'agnello all'abruzzese braised lamb with garlic, rosemary, tomatoes and wine
cotechino spicy pork sausage usually cooked with lentils
cotoletta cutlet/chop

cotechino

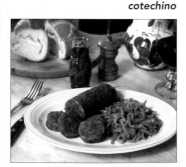

cotoletta al prosciutto veal cutlet with a slice of Parma ham
cotoletta alla bolognese veal cutlet topped with ham and cheese
cotoletta alla milanese veal cutlet dipped in egg and bread-crumbs then fried. Served with lemon wedges
cotoletta alla valdostana breaded veal chop stuffed with cheese
cotoletta di vitello veal cutlet
cotolette di abbacchio lamb chops
cotolette di agnello alla brace marinated, grilled lamb chops
cotto cooked
cozze mussels
cozze arraganate grilled mussels
crema di... cream soup or sauce/custard
crêpe pancake
crespolina stuffed pancake
crocchette di patate potato croquettes
crodino slightly bitter, non-alcoholic aperitif
crostata tart which is usually filled with fruit and glazed
crostata di frutta fruit tart
crostini di fegatini chicken liver pâté on toast
crudo raw
Cynar bitter aperitif (made from artichokes)

D

dente, ...al pasta cooked so that it is still quite firm to the bite
dèntice sea bream
digestivo slightly bitter, herb-flavoured liqueur to help digestion
dolce dessert
dolcelatte soft, creamy blue cheese
dragoncello tarragon

E

entrecote steak

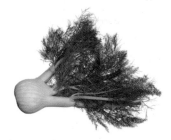

fagiano pheasant
  fagiano con funghi pheasant with porcini mushrooms
  fagiano in salmì pheasant stewed in wine
fagioli type of bean
  fagioli al tonno haricot beans with tuna fish in olive oil
  fagioli con cotiche bean stew with pork
  fagioli nel fiasco haricot beans cooked in a flask
fagiolini runner beans
faraona guinea fowl
farcito stuffed
farfalle butterfly-shaped pasta
farsu magru veal stuffed and rolled up, cooked in wine (Sicilian speciality)
fave broad beans
  fave al guanciale broad beans cooked with bacon and onion
fegatini di pollo chicken livers
fegato liver (mainly calves')
  fegato alla veneziana calves' liver fried in butter and onion
ferri, ...ai grilled without oil
fettuccine fresh ribbon pasta
ficatu all'agru e duci calves' liver in sweet and sour sauce
fichi figs
  fichi d'India prickly pears
filetto fillet steak
  filetto di tacchino alla bolognese turkey breast served with a slice of ham and cheese
Filu Ferru very strong liqueur

from Sardinia
finanziera, ...alla with chicken livers, mushrooms and wine sauce
finocchio fennel
fiori di zucchini courgette flowers fried in batter
focaccia flat bread brushed with garlic, salt and olive oil, sprinkled with herbs or onions. There are many variations
fonduta al parmigiano cheese fondue made with Fontina cheese, eggs, butter and truffles. Eaten with crusty bread

focaccia

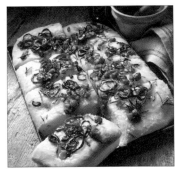

fichi

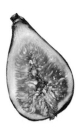

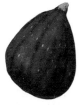

fontina mild to strong cow's milk cheese from northern Italy
formaggio cheese
forno, ...al cooked in the oven
fragole strawberries
frittata omelette, usually with different ingredients

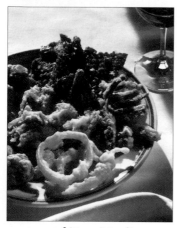

fritto misto di mare

fritto fried
  fritto misto platter of deep-fried food including different kinds of meat and vegetables
  fritto misto di mare fried/grilled selection of seafood
frullato di frutta milk shake made with fruits
frutta fruit
frutti di mare shellfish/seafood
funghi mushrooms – very popular and varied in Italy. In autumn many Italians take to the woods in search of the prized porcini
  funghi trifolati sliced mushrooms fried with garlic and parsley
Fuoco dell'Etna very strong liqueur from Sicily
fusilli spiral-shaped pasta

G

gamberi prawns
gamberoni giant prawns
gazzosa fizzy bottled lemonade
gelato ice cream
  gelato misto a selection of different flavoured ice creams
gioddu yoghurt
girasole sunflower

gnocchi small dumplings made from potato and flour, can be made with spinach. Boiled and served with tomato sauce or ragù
  gnocchi alla romana dumplings made from semolina, butter and parmesan, baked in the oven
  gnocchi verdi spinach and cheeese dumplings, usually cooked in melted butter, garlic and sage
Gorgonzola a strong blue cheese made from cows' milk
granchio crab
grana hard cows' milk cheese; generic name given to Parmesan cheese
granita flavoured crushed ice drink
  granita di caffè coffee drink with crushed ice and cream
  granita di limone lemon drink with crushed ice
granseola large crab
grappa strong spirit from grape pressings, often added to coffee
grattugiato grated
griglia, ...alla grilled
grigliata di cervo grilled venison steaks
grigliata mista mixed grill consisting of various barbecued meats
grissini breadsticks provided along with bread on the table
guanciale streaky bacon made from pig's cheek
gulasch spicy beef stew

I

impepata di cozze peppery mussels
insalata salad
  insalata caprese tomato, basil and mozarella salad
  insalata di mare mixed seafood salad
  insalata di pomodori tomato salad
  insalata di riso rice salad

insalata mista mixed salad
insalata russa cold diced cooked vegetables served with mayonnaise
insalata verde green salad
involtini rolls of veal or pork stuffed with chicken liver, pork sausage and parmesan
italiana, ...alla platters with mixed cured meats/cheeses, olives and savouries like anchovies and pickles

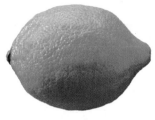

limone

L

lamponi raspberries
lasagne layers of pasta with bolognese and béchamel sauces, baked until golden
lasagne verdi layers of green

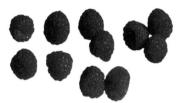

lamponi

(spinach) pasta filled with bolognese and béchamel sauces. May be made with ricotta filling
latte milk
lattuga lettuce
lemonsoda fizzy drink with taste of real lemons
lenticchie lentils usually cooked with pork sausage
lepre hare
lepre in salmì hare stewed in wine
latte milk
lesso boiled
limonata bottled lemon drink
limone lemon
limoncello lemon liqueur
lingua tongue
linguine thin strips of pasta
lombata di maiale pork chop

lonza type of salami
luccio pike
lumache snails

M

maccheroni macaroni
maccheroni ai quattro formaggi pasta with four cheeses
maccheroni alla chitarra square-shaped pasta often served with lamb in chilli and tomato sauce
macedonia (con panna) fresh fruit salad (with cream)
macinata mince
magro, di a meatless dish (often a fish alternative)
maiale pork
maionese mayonnaise
mandorle almonds
manzo beef
marmellata jam
Marsala dark dessert wine from Sicily
Martini famous Italian aperitif
mascarpone rich cream cheese used in desserts such as *tiramisù*
mela apple
melanzane aubergines – found in a great variety of regional dishes
melanzane alla Parmigiana layers of aubergine baked with tomato sauce, parma ham, parmesan and mozzarella

melanzane

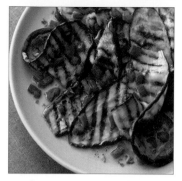

melanzane ripiene stuffed aubergines

melograno pomegranate

melone melon

menta mint

merengata meringue and ice cream dessert

merluzzo cod

miele honey

milanese, ...alla normally applied to veal cutlets which are dipped in egg and breadcrumbs before frying

minestra soup
  minestra calanchina vegetable and rice soup served with cheese

minestrone thick vegetable, bean and pasta soup with many regional variations
  minestrone al pesto minestrone flavoured with pesto

melograno

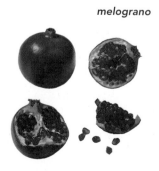

sauce

missultitt grilled dried fish from Lake Como, often eaten with *polenta*

misto di funghi mushroom stew

more blackberries

mortadella type of salami

mostarda fruit pickled in syrup and mustard sauce. Served with *bollito* (boiled meats)

mozzarella cheese traditionally made from buffalo milk but increasingly made from cow's milk. Usually preserved in liquid and used on pizza
  mozzarella in carozza mozarella sandwiched between slices of bread dipped in egg and bread-crumbs and then fried

mugnaia, ...alla usually applies to fish dusted in flour then fried in butter

N

nocciole hazelnuts

nocciole d'agnello noisette of lamb

nocepesca nectarine

noci walnuts

norma, ...alla a sauce from Sicily, with tomatoes and aubergines

O

olio oil
  olio d'oliva olive oil

olive olives

orecchiette ear-shaped pasta
  orecchiette ai broccoli pasta with broccoli

origano oregano

orzata cool, milky drink made from barley

ossobucco marrow-bone veal steak cooked in tomato and wine sauce

ostriche oysters

P

paglia e fieno literally 'straw and grass', a combination of green and plain ribbon pasta cooked

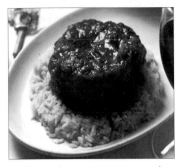

ossobucco

with mushrooms, sausage and cream

pan pepato sweet loaf with mixed nuts

pancetta streaky bacon

pandoro a large yeast cake rich in butter and eggs, traditionally eaten at Christmas

pane bread
  pane e coperto cover charge
  pane integrale wholemeal bread

panettone a large cork-shaped yeast cake with dried fruit, rich in eggs and butter. Traditionally eaten at Christmas

panforte a hard, dried-fruit and

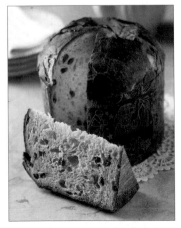

panettone

nut cake

panino bread roll or sandwich

panna cream

pansôti (di Rapallo) literally 'pot-bellied', pasta squares filled with spinach and egg and served in a walnut and parmesan sauce

panzerotti ravioli stuffed with mozzarella, salami and ham, usually fried

paparelle e fegatini chicken livers with pasta

pappardelle wide ribbon-shaped pasta
  pappardelle al sugo di lepre wide ribbon pasta with hare, wine and tomato sauce

parmigiana, ...alla with parmesan cheese

parmigiana di melanzane layers of aubergine cooked in the oven with tomato sauce and parmesan cheese

parmigiano parmesan cheese. A hard cow's milk cheese used extensively in Italian cooking. It is always best to use freshly grated parmesan

pasta the dry variety takes between 10 and 15 minutes to cook. The fresh variety just 3 or 4 minutes
  pasta al forno pasta baked with minced meat, eggs, tomato and cheese
  pasta all'uovo fresh pasta made from flour and eggs
  pasta asciutta pasta served with a sauce such as *spaghetti al sugo* and not in a soup form such as *ravioli in brodo* (ravioli in bouillon)
  pasta con le sarde a baked dish of layers of pasta and fried sardines
  pasta e fagioli pasta with beans
  pasta fresca fresh pasta

pasticcio pie

pastina in brodo pasta pieces in clear broth

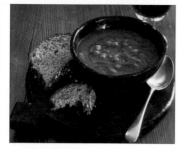

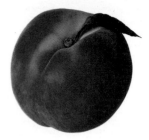

patate potatoes
  patate fritte chips
patatine crisps
  patatine fritte chips
pecorino hard tangy cheese made from ewe's milk, used in *pesto*
penne quill-shaped pasta
  penne rigate ribbed quill-shaped pasta
pepe pepper
peperonata sweet peppers cooked with tomatoes and olive oil
peperoncino hot chilli pepper
peperoni peppers
  peperoni ripieni stuffed peppers (the filling depends on the region)
pere pears
pesca peach
pesce fish
  pesce arrosto baked fish
  pesce persico perch

pesce spada swordfish, often grilled or served in a tomato sauce
  pesce spada alla siciliana swordfish cooked with orange and lemon juice
pesto sauce traditionally made from fresh young basil leaves pounded with garlic, pine-nuts, olive oil and pecorino cheese
petto di pollo chicken breast
pezzenta variety of salad
piatto dish
  piatto del giorno dish of the day
  piatti tipici regional dishes
piccatine al limone tender thinly sliced veal in butter and lemon
pietanze main courses
pinoli pine nuts
piselli peas
pistacchio pistachio
pizza originally from Naples and cooked in wood-burning ovens. The most basic is *pizza margherita* with tomato, basil and mozarella
  pizza ai funghi mushroom pizza
  pizza alla Siciliana pizza with tomato, anchovy, black olives and capers
  pizza capricciosa pizza with baby artichoke, ham and egg
  pizza cardinale pizza with ham and olives
  pizza frutti di mare pizza with seafood

patate

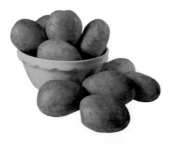

pizza margherita named after the first queen of a united Italy and symbolising the colours of the Italian flag: red (tomatoes), green (basil) and white (mozarella)

pizza marinara tomato and garlic pizza

pizza Napoli/Napoletana pizza with tomato, cheese, anchovy, olive oil and oregano

pizza quattro formaggi a pizza divided into four sections, each with a different type of cheese topping

pizza quattro stagioni literally means four seasons: the pizza is divided into four sections with a selection of toppings on each section

pizzaiola, ...alla cooked with tomatoes, garlic and herbs

pizzetta small cheese and tomato pizza

pizzoccheri pasta noodles made from buckwheat flour and cooked in the oven with cabbage, potatoes and melted cheese

polenta coarse corn or maize meal porridge which solidifies and can be cut into slices. Considered rather bland by those who have not grown up with it, it is a perfect accompaniment to stews. Can be dipped in egg, breadcrumbs, grated parmesan and then fried

polenta e osei polenta with song birds. Not for the squeamish

polenta uncia polenta cooked with butter, garlic and Fontina cheese

pollame poultry/fowl

pollo chicken

pollo alla diavola chicken grilled with herbs and chilli pepper

pollo alla marengo chicken cooked in wine, served with eggs and prawns

pollo alla romana chicken with tomatoes and peppers

pollo arrosto roast chicken

polpette meatballs made from minced lean beef with grated parmesan and parsley

polpo octopus, served in salad (cold) or tomato sauce

polpo affogato octopus cooked in tomato sauce

pomodoro tomato

pomodoro, ...al classic tomato sauce (same as *sugo*)

pomodori da sugo plum tomatoes

polenta e peperoni

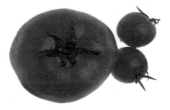

pomodori

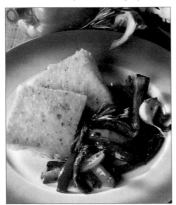

pomodori ripieni stuffed tomatoes

pompelmo grapefruit

porceddu suckling pig

porchetta roast suckling pig

porcini prized cep mushrooms which are often dried

porri leeks

pranzo lunch

prezzemolo parsley

prima colazione breakfast

primo first course

prosciutto ham
  prosciutto cotto boiled ham
  prosciutto crudo cured Parma ham which is sliced off the bone
  prosciutto di cinghiale cured ham made from wild boar
  prosciutto e melone Parma ham and melon slices

Prosecco sparkling dry white wine

provolone creamy cow's milk cheese, mild to strong

prugne plums

puttanesca, ...alla tomato, garlic, hot chilli, anchovies and capers

Q

quaglie quails

R

radicchio red-leaf lettuce

ragù, ...al minced meat, tomato and garlic (same as *bolognese*)

rana pescatrice monkfish

rane frogs' legs

ravioli pasta cushions filled with meat or cheese and spinach

ribes blackcurrants

riccio di mare sea urchin

ricotta soft white cheese used as filling for pasta as well as in desserts

rigatoni ribbed tubes of pasta

ripieno stuffed

risi e bisati rice cooked with eel, a traditional Venetian dish

risi e bisi thick rice and pea soup (almost liquid risotto) cooked with bacon

riso rice
  riso alla pilota rice cooked with sausage, nutmeg and cinnamon

risotto rice cooked in broth with different ingredients added

risotto alla milanese

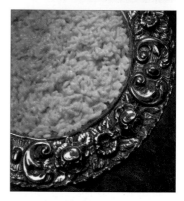

risotto ai funghi risotto with porcini mushrooms

risotto al nero di seppie risotto made with cuttlefish and its ink

risotto alla milanese rich yellow risotto flavoured with saffron, parmesan and butter. It is cooked in meat broth

risotto alla pescatora seafood rice

risotto alle seppie Venetian speciality, risotto cooked with squid. Its ink turns the rice black

risotto con le quaglie quails with risotto

robiola creamy cheese with a mild taste

rognone kidney

rosmarino

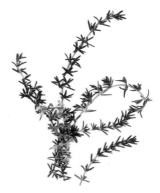

rosmarino rosemary
rospo monkfish

S

salame salami (there are many types)

sale salt

salmone salmon

salsa sauce
  salsa verde sauce made of olive oil, breadcrumbs, anchovies, hard boiled egg and parsley, usually served with boiled meat or fish

salsicce sausages: there are many regional variations but they are mainly thick pork sausages which can be boiled or grilled

saltimbocca alla romana veal cooked in white wine with parma ham

salvia sage

Sambuca aniseed liqueur, served with coffee beans and set alight

sampiero John Dory (type of fish)

sangue, ...al rare

sarde sardines
  sarde e beccafico sardines stuffed with breadcrumbs, anchovies, sultanas and pine-nuts
  sarde in saour sardines marinated in vinegar, sultanas and pine nuts

sartù di riso rice and meat timbale (rather like a pie)

scaloppine veal escalopes
  scaloppine al limone veal escalopes cooked in lemon juice
  scaloppine al marsala veal escalopes cooked in marsala
  scaloppine alla milanese veal escalopes dipped in egg, breadcrumbs and fried in butter, served with wedges of lemon

scamorza a cheese similar to mozzarella but smoked

scampi scampi

secondo main dish, usually meat or fish

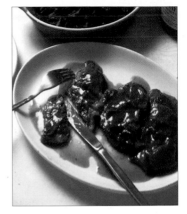

scaloppine al marsala

sedano celery

selz soda water

semifreddo chilled dessert made with ice cream

senape mustard

seppie coi piselli squid cooked with peas

servizio compreso service included

sfogliatelle frolle puff pastry cakes filled with ricotta cheese

sgavecio fried fish served cold with vinegar and seasonings

sgombro mackerel

soffritto pig's offal with tomatoes and spices

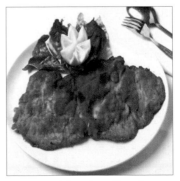

scaloppine alla milanese

sogliola sole

sopa cauda soup made from bread and pigeon meat

soppressata type of salami, with pistachio

sott'olio in olive oil

spaghetti spaghetti

spaghetti aglio, olio e peperoncino spaghetti with garlic, chilli pepper and olive oil sauce

spaghetti all'amatriciana spaghetti with bacon, onion and tomato sauce

spaghetti alle vongole spaghetti with clams

spaghettini aromatici very fine spaghetti cooked in a sauce of anchovies, garlic, black olives and capers

speck bacon

spaghetti alle vongole

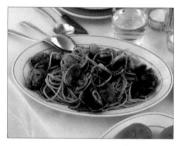

spezzatino stew, usually with tomato sauce

spiedini meat kebabs

spiedo, ...allo spit-roasted, or on skewer, kebab-style

spinaci spinach

spinaci alla piemontese spinach cooked with anchovies and garlic

spremuta freshly squeezed fruit juice

spremuta di pompelmo fresh grapefruit juice

spumante sparkling wine

stoccafisso stoccafisso (*bacalà*, as opposed to *baccalà*) is dried, not

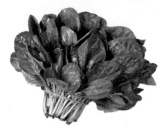

salted cod and needs still more soaking before cooking

stracciatella consommé with egg stirred in and grated parmesan

stracotto braised beef which is cooked with vegetables for over three hours so that the meat becomes very tender. Often served with polenta

Strega strong herb-flavoured liqueur

succo di frutta bottled fruit juice

sugo sauce, often refers to the basic tomato, basil and garlic sauce (same as *al pomodoro*)

surgelato frozen

T

tacchino turkey

tagliatelle ribbon-like pasta often served in cream sauce

Taleggio soft, creamy cheese similar to Camembert

tartine canapés

tartufo truffles: both white (*bianco*) and black (*nero*) used extensively in risotto and game dishes

tartufo di cioccolato a rich chocolate ice cream shaped like a truffle

tè tea. It is not very popular in Italy and normally served with lemon (*al limone*). If you want it with milk you must ask for **tè al latte**

teglia earthenware casserole dish

107 **tiella di sardine** baked sardines
with cheese

timballo a baked dish
timballo di melanzane baked
dish of aubergines, egg, cheese
and parma ham

timo thyme

tinche tench

tiramisù dessert made with
mascarpone, sponge, coffee
and marsala

tónica tonic water

tonno tuna fish
tonno, ...al with a sauce made
of tuna fish and tomatoes
tonno e fagioli tuna and bean
salad

torrone nougat, traditionally
eaten at Christmas

torta cake/flan/tart

tortellini meat-filled pasta
cushions reputedly modelled
on Venus's navel
tortellini panna e prosciutto
tortellini cooked with cream and
ham

tortine al tartufo little savoury
tarts with truffles

tramezzini ready-made sliced
white bread with mixed fillings

trenette long thin strips of pasta,
traditionally served with pesto
sauce

triglie red mullet
triglie alla livornese red mullet
fried with chillies in tomato
sauce
triglie alla siciliana a Sicilian
dish of red mullet cooked
in white wine and orange
peel

trippa tripe, often cooked with
tomatoes and onions

trota trout
trote alla panna acida trout in
soured cream

U

ucelli scappati pork kebabs

umido, in stewed

uova eggs

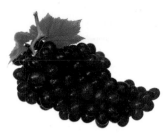

uva

uova alla fiorentina poached
eggs on spinach tarts

uva grapes

uva passa raisins

V

vaniglia vanilla

Vecchia Romagna Italian cognac

verdure vegetables

vermicelli very thin pasta

Vermut very popular aperitif
made from herbs and wine

verza Savoy (green) cabbage

vino wine
vin bianco white wine
vin dulce sweet wine
vin rosato rosé wine
vin rosso red wine
vin secco dry wine

vitello veal

vongole clams
vongole, ...alle clam, parsley,
garlic and olive oil

W

wurstel Frankfurter sausages

Y

yogurt yoghurt

Z

zabaglione frothy dessert made
with egg yolks and sugar
beaten with marsala over heat

zafferano saffron, used in *risotto
alla milanese*

zampone spicy sausage in the
shape of a pig's trotter, sliced
and served hot

zucca marrow
zucchero sugar
zucchini courgettes
zuccotto rich cream and nut pudding in the shape of a pumpkin
zuppa soup
  zuppa di cozze mussel and tomato soup

zuppa di fagioli bean soup
zuppa di pesce seafood soup with many delicious regional variations
zuppa inglese dessert similar to trifle
zuppa pavese a bread soup with broth and poached eggs, topped with grated cheese

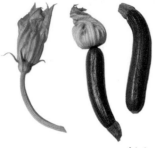

zucchini

DICTIONARY

english–italian

italian–english

A

a(n) un/una/uno
abbey l'abbazia *(f)*
able: to be able (to) essere capace (di)
abortion l'aborto *(m)*
about su ; circa
a book about... un libro su...
about ten o'clock circa le dieci
above sopra
abroad l'estero *(m)*
to go abroad andare all'estero
abscess l'ascesso *(m)*
accelerator l'acceleratore *(m)*
accent l'accento *(m)*
to accept accettare
access l'accesso *(m)*
wheelchair access l'accesso per disabili
accident l'incidente *(m)*
accident & emergency department il pronto soccorso
accommodation l'alloggio *(m)*
to accompany accompagnare
account *(bill)* il conto
(in bank) il conto in banca
account number il numero del conto
to ache fare male
it aches fa male
acid l'acido *(m)*
actor *(m/f)* l'attore/l'attrice
adaptor *(electrical appliance)* il riduttore
address l'indirizzo *(m)*
what is the address? qual è l'indirizzo?
address book la rubrica
admission charge/fee il biglietto d'ingresso
to admit *(to hospital)* ricoverare
adult l'adulto(a)
for adults per adulti
advance: in advance in anticipo
advertisement la pubblicità
(in newspaper) l'annuncio *(m)*
to advise consigliare
A&E il pronto soccorso
aeroplane l'aeroplano *(m)*
aerosol l'aerosol *(m)*
afraid: to be afraid avere paura
after dopo
afternoon il pomeriggio
this afternoon oggi pomeriggio
tomorrow afternoon domani

pomeriggio
in the afternoon di pomeriggio
aftershave il dopobarba
again ancora ; di nuovo
against contro
age l'età *(f)*
agency l'agenzia *(f)*
ago fa
a week ago una settimana fa
to agree essere d'accordo
agreement l'accordo *(m)*
AIDS l'AIDS *(m)*
airbag l'airbag *(m)*
airbed il matarassino gonfiabile
air-conditioning l'aria condizionata *(f)*
air freshener il deodorante per l'ambiente
airline la linea aerea
air mail: by air mail per via aerea
airplane l'aeroplano *(m)*
airport l'aeroporto *(m)*
airport bus l'autobus per l'aeroporto *(m)*
air ticket il biglietto d'aereo *(m)*
aisle il corridoio
alarm l'allarme *(m)*
alarm clock la sveglia
alcohol l'alcool *(m)*
alcohol-free analcolico(a)
alcoholic alcolico(a)
all tutto(a)
allergic to allergico(a) a
I'm allergic to... sono allergico(a) a...
allergy l'allergia *(f)*
to allow permettere
all right *(agreed)* va bene
are you all right? sta bene?
almost quasi
alone solo(a)
Alps le Alpi
already già
also anche
altar l'altare *(m)*
aluminium foil la carta stagnola
always sempre
a.m. del mattino
am: I am sono
amber *(light)* il giallo
ambulance l'ambulanza *(f)*
America l'America *(f)*
American americano(a)
anaesthetic l'anestetico *(m)*
local anaesthetic l'anestetico locale
general anaesthetic l'anestetico generale

anchor l'ancora *(f)*
ancient antico(a)
and e
angina l'angina pectoris *(f)*
angry arrabbiato(a)
animal l'animale *(m)*
ankle la caviglia
anniversary l'anniversario *(m)*
to announce annunciare
announcement l'annuncio *(m)*
annual annuale
another un altro/un'altra
  another beer un'altra birra
  another coffee un altro caffè
answer la risposta
to answer rispondere
answerphone la segreteria telefonica
antacid l'antiacido *(m)*
antibiotic l'antibiotico *(m)*
antifreeze l'antigelo *(m)*
antihistamine l'antistaminico *(m)*
antiques i pezzi d'antiquariato
antique shop il negozio d'antiquariato
antiseptic l'antisettico *(m)*
any dei/delle/degli (di)
  I haven't any money non ho soldi
  have you any apples? ha delle mele?
anyone qualcuno
anything qualcosa
anywhere da qualche parte
apartment l'appartamento *(m)*
appendicitis l'appendicite *(f)*
apple la mela
application form il modulo di domanda
appointment l'appuntamento *(m)*
  I have an appointment ho un appuntamento
approximately circa
April aprile
architect *m/f* l'architetto
architecture l'architettura *(f)*
are sono
arm il braccio
armbands *(swimming)* i braccioli
armchair la poltrona
to arrange sistemare
to arrest arrestare
arrivals *(plane, train)* gli arrivi
to arrive arrivare
art l'arte *(f)*
art gallery la galleria d'arte ; la pinacoteca
arthritis l'artrite *(f)*
artificial finto(a)

artist *m/f* l'artista
ashtray il portacenere
to ask *(question)* domandare
  (for something) chiedere
asleep: he/she is asleep dorme
aspirin l'aspirina *(f)*
asthma l'asma *(f)*
  I have asthma ho l'asma
at a
  at home a casa
  at 8 o'clock alle otto
  at once subito
  at night di notte
to attack aggredire
attractive attraente
auction l'asta *(f)*
audience il pubblico
August agosto
aunt la zia
au pair la ragazza alla pari
Australia l'Australia *(f)*
Australian australiano(a)
author *m/f* l'autore/l'autrice
automatic automatico(a)
automatic car la macchina con cambio automatico
auto-teller *(cashpoint)* il Bancomat®
autumn l'autunno *(m)*
available disponibile
avalanche la valanga
avenue il viale
average medio(a)
to avoid evitare
awake: to be awake essere sveglio(a)
away via
awful terribile
axle *(car)* l'asse *(m)*

B

baby il/la bambino(a)
baby food gli alimenti per bambini
baby milk il latte per bambini
baby wipes le salviettine per bambini
baby's bottle il biberon
babyseat *(in car)* il seggiolino per bambini
babysitter il/la babysitter
back *(of body)* la schiena
backpack lo zaino
bacon la pancetta

bad *(food)* andato(a) a male
  (weather, news) brutto(a)
badminton il badminton
bag la borsa
baggage i bagagli
baggage allowance il peso consentito di bagaglio
baggage reclaim il ritiro bagagli
bait *(for fishing)* l'esca *(m)*
baked al forno
baker's la panetteria ; il panificio
balcony il balcone
bald *(person)* calvo(a)
  (tyre) liscio(a)
ball *(large: football, etc)* il pallone
  (small: golf, tennis, etc) la pallina
ballet il balletto
balloon il palloncino
banana la banana
band *(musical)* la banda
bandage la benda
bank la banca
  (river) la riva
bank account il conto in banca
banknote la banconota
bankrupt fallito(a)
bar il bar
bar of chocolate la tavoletta di cioccolato
barbecue il barbecue
  to have a barbecue fare il barbecue
barber il barbiere
to bark abbaiare
barn il granaio
barrel *(wine/beer)* il barile
basement il seminterrato
basil il basilico
basket il cestino
basketball il basket
bat *(baseball, etc)* la mazza
bath il bagno
  to have a bath fare un bagno
bathing cap la cuffia
bathroom il bagno
  with bathroom con bagno
battery *(radio, camera, etc)* la pila
  (car) la batteria
bay *(along coast)* la baia
B&B la pensione familiare
to be essere
beach la spiaggia
  private beach la spiaggia privata

sandy beach la spiaggia con sabbia
nudist beach la spiaggia di nudisti
beach hut la cabina
bean il fagiolo
beard la barba
beautiful bello(a)
beauty salon l'istituto di bellezza *(m)*
because perché
to become diventare
bed il letto
  double bed il letto matrimoniale
  single bed il letto a una piazza
  sofa bed il divano letto
  twin beds i letti gemelli
bed and breakfast la pensione familiare
bed clothes le coperte e lenzuola
bedroom la camera da letto
bee l'ape *(f)*
beef il manzo
beer la birra
  draught beer la birra alla spina
before prima di
  before breakfast prima di colazione
to begin cominciare
behind dietro di
beige beige
to believe credere
bell *(church)* la campana
  (doorbell) il campanello
to belong to appartenere a
  it belongs to... appartiene a...
below sotto
belt la cintura
bend *(in road)* la curva
berth *(train, ship)* la cuccetta
beside *(next to)* accanto a
  beside the bank accanto alla banca
best: the best il/la migliore
bet la scommessa
to bet scommettere
better (than) meglio (di)
between fra
to beware of stare attento(a) a
beyond oltre
bib *(baby's)* il bavaglino
bicycle la bicicletta ; la bici
  by bicycle in bicicletta
bicycle repair kit il kit per riparare la bici
bidet il bidet
big grande
  bigger (than) più grande (di)
bike *(pushbike)* la bici
  (motorbike) la moto

113 **bike lock** il lucchetto della bici
bikini il bikini
bill (in hotel, restaurant) il conto
(for work done) la fattura
(gas, telephone) la bolletta
bin (dustbin) il bidone
bin liner la borsa della spazzatura
binoculars il binocolo
bird l'uccello (m)
biro la biro
birth la nascita
birth certificate il certificato di nascita
birthday il compleanno
happy birthday! auguri! buon compleanno
my birthday is on... il mio compleanno è il…
birthday card il biglietto d'auguri di compleanno
birthday present il regalo di compleanno
biscuits i biscotti
bit il pezzo
a bit un po'
bite (of insect) la puntura
(of dog) la morsicatura
a bite to eat qualcosa da mangiare
to bite (animal) mordere
(insect) morsicare
bitten morso(a)
(by insect) morsicato(a)
bitter (taste) amaro(a)
black nero(a)
black ice il ghiaccio sulla strada
blanket la coperta
bleach la candeggina
to bleed sanguinare
blender il frullatore
blind (person) cieco(a)
blind (for window) l'avvolgibile (f)
blister la vescica
block of flats il palazzo
blocked (pipe, sink) ingorgato(a)
(road) bloccato(a)
blond (person) biondo(a)
blood il sangue
blood group il gruppo sanguigno
blood pressure la pressione sanguigna
blood test l'analisi del sangue (f)
blouse la camicetta
to blow-dry asciugare con il fon
blue (light) azzurro(a)
dark blue blu scuro
light blue azzurro(a)
blunt (knife, blade) non taglia

eng–italian b

boar il cinghiale
to board (plain, train, etc) imbarcarsi su
boarding card/pass la carta d'imbarco
boarding house la pensione
boat la barca ; il battello
(rowing) la barca a remi
boat trip la gita in battello
body il corpo
(dead) il cadavere
to boil bollire
boiler la caldaia
boiled bollito(a)
bomb la bomba
bone l'osso (m)
fish bone la spina di pesce
bonfire il falò
bonnet (car) il cofano
book il libro
book of tickets il blocchetto di biglietti
to book prenotare
booking la prenotazione
booking office (train) la biglietteria
bookshop la libreria
boot (of car) il bagagliaio
boots (long) gli stivali
(ankle) gli stivaletti
border (of country) la frontiera
boring noioso(a)
born: to be born essere nato(a)
to borrow prendere in prestito
boss il capo
both tutti e due
bottle la bottiglia
a bottle of wine una bottiglia di vino
a half-bottle una mezza bottiglia
bottle opener l'apribottiglie (m)
bowl (for cereal, soup) la scodella
bow tie la cravatta a farfalla
box la scatola
box office il botteghino
boxer shorts i boxer
boy (young child) il bambino
(teenage) il ragazzo
boyfriend il ragazzo
bra il reggiseno
bracelet il braccialetto
brain il cervello
to brake frenare
brake fluid il liquido dei freni
brake light il fanalino dello stop

brake pads le pastiglie dei freni
brakes i freni
branch *(of tree)* il ramo
  (of bank, etc) la succursale
brand *(make)* la marca
brass l'ottone *(m)*
brave coraggioso(a)
bread il pane
  brown bread il pane integrale
  French bread il filoncino
  sliced bread il pancarré
bread roll il panino
to break rompere
breakable fragile
breakdown *(car)* il guasto
  (nervous) l'esaurimento nervoso *(m)*
breakdown van il carro attrezzi
breakfast la (prima) colazione
breast il seno
to breast-feed allattare
to breathe respirare
brick il mattone
bride la sposa
bridegroom lo sposo
bridge il ponte
briefcase la cartella
Brillo-pad la paglietta
to bring portare
Britain la Gran Bretagna
British britannico(a)
broccoli i broccoli
brochure l'opuscolo *(m)*
broken rotto(a)
broken down *(car, etc)* guasto(a)
bronchitis la bronchite
bronze il bronzo
brooch la spilla
broom *(brush)* la scopa
brother il fratello
brother-in-law il cognato
brown marrone
bruise il livido
brush la spazzola
bubble bath il bagnoschiuma
bucket il secchiello
buffet car il vagone ristorante
to build costruire
building l'edificio *(m)*
bulb *(lightbulb)* la lampadina
bumbag il marsupio
bumper *(on car)* il paraurti

bunch *(of flowers)* il mazzo di fiori
  (of grapes) il grappolo d'uva
bungee jumping il bungee jumping
bureau de change l'agenzia di
  cambio *(f)*
burger l'hamburger *(m)*
burglar il/la ladro(a)
burglar alarm l'antifurto *(m)*
to burn bruciare
bus l'autobus *(m)*
bus pass la tessera dell'autobus
bus station la stazione delle autolinee
bus stop la fermata (dell'autobus)
bus ticket il biglietto d'autobus
business gli affari
  on business per affari
business card il biglietto da visita
business class la business class
businessman/woman l'uomo/la donna
  d'affari
business trip il viaggio d'affari
busy occupato(a) ; impegnato(a)
but ma ; però
butcher's il macellaio
butter il burro
button il bottone
to buy comprare
by *(next to)* accanto a
  (via) via
  by bus in autobus
  by car in macchina
  by train in treno
  by ship in battello
bypass *(road)* la circonvallazione

C

cab *(taxi)* il taxi
cabaret il cabaret
cabin *(on boat)* la cabina
cabin crew l'equipaggio di bordo *(m)*
cablecar la funivia
café il bar
  internet café il cyber-café
cafetière la caffettiera
cake *(big)* la torta
  (small) il pasticcino
cake shop la pasticceria
calculator la calcolatrice
calendar il calendario
call *(telephone call)* la chiamata
to call chiamare
  (phone) chiamare per telefono
calm calmo(a)
camcorder la videocamera

camera la macchina fotografica
camera case la custodia della macchina fotografica
to camp campeggiare
camping gas il camping gas
camping stove il fornellino da campeggio
campsite il campeggio
can il barattolo ; la scatola
to can (to be able) potere
I can posso
we can possiamo
I cannot non posso
we cannot non possiamo
can I...? posso...?
can we...? possiamo...?
Canada il Canada
Canadian canadese
canal il canale
to cancel cancellare ; annullare
cancellation la cancellazione
cancer il cancro
candle la candela
canoe la canoa
to canoe andare in canoa
can opener l'apriscatole (m)
cap (hat) il berretto
(diaphragm) il diaframma
capital (city) la capitale
car la macchina
car alarm l'antifurto (m)
car ferry il traghetto
car hire l'autonoleggio (m)
car insurance l'assicurazione della macchina (f)
car keys le chiavi della macchina
car park il parcheggio
car parts i pezzi di ricambio
car radio l'autoradio (f)
car seat (for children) il seggiolino per bambini
carwash l'autolavaggio (m)
carafe la caraffa
caravan la roulotte
carburettor il carburatore
card (greetings) il biglietto d'auguri
(business) il biglietto da visita
(playing cards) le carte da gioco
cardboard il cartone
cardigan il cardigan
careful attento(a)
to be careful fare attenzione
carpet (fitted) la moquette
(rug) il tappeto
carriage (railway) il vagone

carrots le carote
to carry portare
carton il cartone
case (suitcase) la valigia
cash i contanti
to cash (cheque) incassare
cash desk la cassa
cash dispenser (autoteller) il Bancomat®
cashier il/la cassiere(a)
cashpoint il Bancomat®
casino il casinò
casserole dish la casseruola
cassette la cassetta
cassette player il registratore
castle il castello
casualty department il pronto soccorso
cat il gatto
cat food il cibo per gatti
catacombs le catacombe
catalogue il catalogo
to catch (bus, train, etc) prendere
cathedral il duomo
Catholic cattolico(a)
cave la grotta
cavity (in tooth) la cavità
CD il CD
CD player il lettore CD
ceiling il soffitto
cellar la cantina
cellphone il cellulare
cemetery il cimitero
centimetre il centimetro
central centrale
central heating il riscaldamento
central locking (car) la chiusura centralizzata
centre il centro
century il secolo
ceramics la ceramica
cereal (for breakfast) i cereali
certificate il certificato
chain la catena
chair la sedia
chairlift la seggiovia
chalet lo chalet
challenge la sfida
chambermaid la cameriera

C eng–italian

Champagne lo Champagne
change il cambio
   (small coins) gli spiccioli
   (money returned) il resto
to change: *to change money* cambiare
soldi
   to change clothes cambiarsi
   to change train cambiare treno
changing room lo spogliatoio
Channel *(English)* la Manica
chapel la cappella
charcoal il carbone
charge *(fee)* la tariffa
to charge chiedere
   please charge it to my account lo
metta sul mio conto, per favore
charger *(for battery)* il caricabatterie
charter flight il volo charter
cheap economico(a)
   cheaper più economico(a)
cheap rate *(phone)* la tariffa economica
to check controllare
to check in *(airport)* fare il check-in
   (at hotel) firmare il registro
check-in il check-in
cheek la guancia
cheers! salute! ; cin-cin!
cheese il formaggio
chef il cuoco
chemist's la farmacia
cheque l'assegno *(m)*
cheque book il libretto degli assegni
cheque card la carta assegni
cherries le ciliegie
chess gli scacchi
chest *(of body)* il petto
chewing gum la cicca
chicken il pollo
chicken breast il petto di pollo
chickenpox la varicella
child il/la bambino(a)
children *(small)* i bambini
   (older children) i ragazzi
   for chidren per bambini
child safety seat *(car)* il seggiolino di
sicurezza per bambini
chimney il camino
chin il mento
china la porcellana
chips *(french fries)* le patatine fritte
chocolate la cioccolata
chocolates i cioccolatini

choir il coro
choice la scelta
to choose scegliere
chop *(meat)* la costoletta
chopping board il tagliere
christening il battesimo
Christian name il nome di battesimo
Christmas il Natale
   Merry Christmas! Buon Natale!
Christmas card il biglietto d'auguri
natalizi
Christmas Eve la vigilia di Natale
church la chiesa
cigar il sigaro
cigarette la sigaretta
cigarette lighter l'accendino *(m)*
cigarette papers le cartine
cinema il cinema
circle *(theatre)* la galleria
circuit breaker il salvavita
circus il circo
cistern la cisterna
   (of toilet) il serbatoio dell'acqua
city la città
city centre il centro città
class: *first class* prima classe
   second class seconda classe
clean pulito(a)
to clean pulire
cleaner *(person)* l'addetto(a) alle pulizie
cleanser *(for face)* il detergente
clear chiaro(a)
client il/la cliente
cliff *(along coast)* la scogliera
   (mountain) la rupe
to climb scalare
climbing l'alpinismo *(m)*
climbing boots gli scarponi da
montagna
Clingfilm® la pellicola per alimenti
clinic la clinica
cloakroom il guardaroba
clock l'orologio *(m)*
to close chiudere
closed *(shop, etc)* chiuso(a)
cloth il panno
clothes i vestiti
clothes peg la molletta
clothes shop il negozio d'abbigliamento
cloudy nuvoloso(a)
club il club
clutch *(car)* la frizione
coach il pullman

117

coach station la stazione dei pullman
coach trip la gita in pullman
coal il carbone
coast la costa
coastguard il guardacoste
coat il cappotto
coat hanger la gruccia
cockroach lo scarafaggio
cocktail il cocktail
cocoa il cacao
code il codice
coffee *(espresso)* il caffè
  black coffee il caffè americano
  white coffee il caffellatte
  cappuccino il cappuccino
  decaffeinated coffee il decaffeinato
coil *(IUD)* la spirale
coin la moneta
Coke® la Coca®
colander lo scolapasta
cold freddo(a)
  I'm cold ho freddo
  it's cold fa freddo
cold *(illness)* il raffreddore
  I have a cold ho il raffreddore
cold sore l'herpes *(m)*
Coliseum il Colosseo
collar il colletto
collar bone la clavicola
colleague il/la collega
to collect raccogliere
  (to collect someone) andare a prendere
collection *(of stamps)* la collezione
  (of letters) la levata
  (of rubbish) la rimozione
colour il colore
colour-blind daltonico(a)
colour film *(for camera)* la pellicola a
  colori
comb il pettine
to come venire
  (to arrive) arrivare
to come back tornare
to come in entrare
  come in! avanti!
comedy la commedia
comfortable comodo(a)
company *(firm)* la ditta
compartment lo scompartimento
compass la bussola
to complain fare un reclamo
complaint il reclamo
complete completo(a)
to complete *(piece of work)* finire
  (form) riempire

compulsory obbligatorio(a)
computer il computer
computer disk *(floppy)* il dischetto
computer game il videogioco
computer program il programma di
  computer
concert il concerto
concert hall la sala da concerti
concession la riduzione
concussion la commozione cerebrale
condensed milk il latte condensato
conditioner il balsamo
condoms i preservativi
conductor *(on bus)* il bigliettaio
cone il cono
conference il congresso
to confirm confermare
confirmation *(of flight, etc)* la conferma
confused confuso(a)
congratulations le congratulazioni
connection *(train, etc)* la coincidenza
constipated stitico(a)
consulate il consolato
to consult consultare
to contact mettersi in contatto con
contact lens cleaner il liquido per lenti
  a contatto
contact lenses le lenti a contatto
to continue continuare
contraceptive l'anticoncezionale *(m)*
contract il contratto
convenient: is it convenient? va bene?
convulsions le convulsioni
to cook cucinare
cooked cotto(a)
cooker la cucina
cookies i biscotti
cool fresco(a)
cool-box *(picnic)* la borsa termica
copper il rame
copy la copia
to copy copiare
cork il tappo
corkscrew il cavatappi
corner l'angolo *(m)*
cornflakes i cornflakes
corridor il corridoio
cosmetics i cosmetici
to cost costare
  how much does it cost? quanto
  costa?

c/d eng-italian

costume (swimming) il costume da bagno
cot il lettino
cottage il cottage
cotton il cotone
cotton bud il cotton fioc®
cotton wool il cotone idrofilo
couchette la cuccetta
cough la tosse
to cough tossire
cough mixture lo sciroppo per la tosse
cough sweets le pasticche per la tosse
counter (in shop, bar, etc) il banco
country (not town) la campagna (nation) il paese
countryside la campagna
couple (two people) la coppia
 a couple of... un paio di...
courgettes le zucchine
courier service il corriere
course (of meal) il piatto (of study) il corso
cousin il/la cugino(a)
cover charge il coperto
cow la mucca
crafts l'artigianato (m)
craftsperson l'artigiano(a)
cramps i crampi
crash (car) lo scontro
to crash (car) avere un incidente
crash helmet il casco
cream (lotion) la crema (dairy) la panna
 soured cream la panna acida
 whipped cream la panna montata
credit card la carta di credito
crime il reato
crisps le patatine
croissant la brioche
to cross (road) attraversare
cross la croce
cross-country skiing lo sci di fondo
crossing (sea, lake) la traversata
crossroads l'incrocio (m)
crossword puzzle il cruciverba
crowd la folla
crowded affollato(a)
crown la corona
cruise la crociera
crutches le grucce

to cry (weep) piangere
crystal (made of) di cristallo
cucumber il cetriolo
cufflinks i gemelli
cul-de-sac il vicolo cieco
cup la tazza
cupboard l'armadio (m)
curlers i bigodini
currant la sultanina
currency: (foreign) currency la valuta (estera)
current (electric, water) la corrente
curtain la tenda
cushion il cuscino
custom (tradition) il costume
customer il/la cliente
customs (duty) la dogana
cut il taglio
to cut tagliare
cutlery le posate
to cycle andare in bicicletta
cycle track la pista ciclabile
cycling il ciclismo
cyst la cisti
cystitis la cistite

D

daily (each day) ogni giorno ; quotidiano(a)
dairy produce i latticini
dam la diga
damage il danno
damp umido(a)
dance il ballo
to dance ballare
danger il pericolo
dangerous pericoloso(a)
dark (colour) scuro(a) (night) buio(a)
 after dark a notte fatta
date la data
date of birth la data di nascita
daughter la figlia
daughter-in-law la nuora
dawn l'alba (f)
day il giorno
 per day al giorno
 every day ogni giorno
 (span of time la giornata
dead morto(a)
deaf sordo(a)
dear caro(a)

debts i debiti
decaffeinated decaffeinato(a)
  have you decaffeinated coffee? ha
  del decaffeinato?
December dicembre
deckchair la sedia a sdraio
to declare dichiarare
  nothing to declare niente da
  dichiarare
deep profondo(a)
deep freeze il surgelatore
deer il cervo
to defrost scongelare
to de-ice sbrinare
delay il ritardo
  how long is the delay? di quant'è il
  ritardo?
delayed: to be delayed (flight) subire
  un ritardo
delicatessen il negozio di specialità
  gastronomiche
delicious delizioso(a)
demonstration la manifestazione
dental floss il filo interdentale
dentist il/la dentista
dentures la dentiera
deodorant il deodorante
to depart partire
department il reparto
department store il grande magazzino
departure la partenza
departure lounge la sala partenze
deposit il deposito
to describe descrivere
description la descrizione
desk la scrivania
  (information, etc) il banco
dessert il dolce
details i dettagli
detergent il detersivo
detour la deviazione
to develop (photos) sviluppare
diabetes il diabete
diabetic diabetico(a)
  I'm diabetic sono diabetico(a)
to dial fare il numero
dialect il dialetto
dialling code il prefisso telefonico
dialling tone il segnale di libero
diamond il diamante
diapers i pannolini
diaphragm il diaframma
diarrhoea la diarrea
diary l'agenda (f)

dice il dado
dictionary il dizionario ; il vocabolario
to die morire
diesel il gasolio
diet la dieta
  I'm on a diet sono a dieta
  special diet una dieta specifica
different diverso(a)
difficult difficile
to dilute diluire
dinghy (rubber) il canotto
dining room la sala da pranzo
dinner (evening meal) la cena
  to have dinner cenare
dinner jacket lo smoking
direct (train, etc) diretto(a)
directions le indicazioni
  to ask for directions chiedere la
  strada
directory (telephone) l'elenco
  telefonico (m)
directory enquiries il servizio
  informazioni
dirty sporco(a)
disability il handicap
disabled (person) disabile ; handicap-
  pato(a)
to disagree non essere d'accordo
to disappear scomparire
disaster il disastro
disco la discoteca
discount lo sconto
to discover scoprire
disease la malattia
dishtowel lo strofinaccio dei piatti
dishwasher la lavastoviglie
disinfectant il disinfettante
disk (floppy disk) il disco
to dislocate (joint) lussarsi
disposable (camera) usa e getta
distance la distanza
distilled water l'acqua distillata (f)
district (of town) il quartiere
to disturb disturbare
to dive tuffarsi
diversion la deviazione
diving i tuffi
divorced divorziato(a)
DIY shop il negozio di bricolage
dizzy: to be dizzy avere il capogiro
to do fare

doctor il medico/la dottoressa
documents i documenti
dog il cane
dog food il cibo per cani
dog lead il guinzaglio
doll la bambola
dollars i dollari
domestic *(flight)* nazionale
donor card la tessera dell'A.I.D.O.
door la porta
doorbell il campanello
double doppio(a)
double bed il letto matrimoniale
double room la camera doppia
down: *to go down* scendere
downstairs giù ; dabbasso
drain lo scarico
draught *(of air)* la corrente (d'aria)
  there's a draught c'è corrente
draught lager la birra alla spina
drawer il cassetto
drawing il disegno
dress il vestito
to dress *(to get dressed)* vestirsi
dressing *(for food)* il condimento
  (for wound) la fasciatura
dressing gown la vestaglia
drill *(tool)* il trapano
drink *(soft)* la bibita
to drink bere
drinking water l'acqua potabile *(f)*
to drive guidare
driver *(of car)* l'autista *(m/f)*
driving licence la patente
drought la siccità
to drown affogare
drug *(medicine)* il farmaco
  (narcotics) la droga
drunk ubriaco(a)
dry secco(a) ; asciutto(a)
to dry asciugare
dry-cleaner's la tintoria ; il lavasecco
dummy *(for baby)* la tettarella
during durante
dust la polvere
duster lo straccio
dustpan and brush lo scopino e la
  paletta
duty-free esente da dogana
duvet il piumino

duvet cover il copripiumone
dye la tinta
dynamo la dinamo

E

each ogni
ear l'orecchio *(m)*
earache il mal d'orecchi
earlier più presto
early presto
to earn guadagnare
earphones le cuffie
earplugs i tappi per le orecchie
earrings gli orecchini
earth la terra
earthquake il terremoto
east l'est *(m)*
Easter la Pasqua
  Happy Easter! Buona Pasqua!
easy facile
to eat mangiare
economy *(class)* la classe turistica
egg l'uovo *(m)*
  eggs le uova
  fried egg l'uovo fritto
  hard-boiled egg l'uovo sodo
  scrambled eggs le uova strapazzate
  soft-boiled egg l'uovo alla coque
either ... or o ... o
elastic band l'elastico *(m)*
Elastoplast il cerotto
elbow il gomito
electric elettrico(a)
electric blanket la coperta elettrica
electrician *m/f* l'elettricista
electricity l'elettricità *(f)*
electricity meter il contatore
  dell'elettricità
electric razor il rasoio elettrico
electric shock la scossa
elevator l'ascensore *(m)*
e-mail la posta elettronica ; l'e-mail *(m)*
  to e-mail s.o. mandare un e-mail a
  qualcuno
e-mail address l'indirizzo di posta
  elettronica *(m)*
embassy l'ambasciata *(f)*
emergency l'emergenza *(f)*
emergency exit l'uscita d'emergenza *(f)*
emery board la limetta per le unghie
empty vuoto(a)
end la fine
engaged *(to be married)* fidanzato(a)
  (phone, toilet, etc) occupato(a)

engine il motore
England l'Inghilterra *(f)*
English inglese
(language) l'inglese *(m)*
to enjoy divertirsi
(to like) piacere
I enjoyed the trip la gita mi è
piaciuta
I enjoy swimming mi piace nuotare
enjoy your meal! buon appetito!
enough abbastanza
that's enough basta così
enquiry desk il banco informazioni
to enter entrare
entertainment il divertimento
entrance l'entrata *(f)* ; l'ingresso *(m)*
entrance fee il biglietto d'ingresso
envelope la busta
epileptic epilettico(a)
epileptic fit la crisi epilettica
equal uguale ; pari
equipment l'attrezzatura *(f)*
eraser la gomma da cancellare
error l'errore *(m)*
eruption l'eruzione *(f)*
escalator la scala mobile
to escape fuggire
essential essenziale
estate agent's l'agenzia immobiliare *(f)*
euro l'Euro *(m)*
eurocheque l'eurocheque *(m)*
Europe l'Europa *(f)*
European europeo(a)
European Union l'Unione Europea *(f)*
eve la vigilia
evening la sera
this evening stasera
tomorrow evening domani sera
in the evening la sera
evening dress l'abito da sera *(m)*
evening meal la cena
every ogni ; ciascuno ; tutti
everyone tutti
everything tutto
everywhere dappertutto
examination l'esame *(m)*
example: for example per esempio
excellent ottimo(a)
except salvo
excess baggage il bagaglio in eccedenza
to exchange cambiare
exchange rate il cambio
exciting emozionante
excursion l'escursione *(f)*

to excuse scusare
excuse me! *(sorry)* mi scusi!
(when passing) permesso!
exercise l'esercizio *(m)*
exhaust pipe il tubo di scappamento
exhibition la mostra
exit l'uscita *(f)*
expenses le spese
expensive costoso(a) ; caro(a)
expert l'esperto(a)
to expire *(ticket, etc)* scadere
to explain spiegare
explosion l'esplosione *(f)*
to export esportare
express *(train)* l'espresso *(m)*
express *(parcel, etc)* espresso(a)
extension *(electrical)* la prolunga
extra *(spare)* in più
(more) supplementare
an extra bed un letto in più
eye l'occhio *(m)*
eyebrows le sopracciglia
eye drops il collirio
eyelashes le ciglia
eye shadow l'ombretto *(m)*

F

fabric la stoffa
face la faccia
face cloth il guanto di spugna
facial la pulizia del viso
facilities *(leisure facilities)* le atrezzature
factory la fabbrica
to fail fallire
to faint svenire
fainted svenuto(a)
fair *(just)* giusto(a)
(blond) biondo(a)
fair *(trade)* la fiera
(funfair) il luna park
fake falso(a)
fall *(autumn)* l'autunno *(m)*
to fall cadere
he/she has fallen è caduto(a)
false teeth la dentiera
family la famiglia
famous famoso(a)
fan *(hand-held)* il ventaglio
(electric) il ventilatore
(football) il/la tifoso(a)

fan belt la cinghia della ventola
fancy dress in costume ; in maschera
far lontano(a)
  is it far? è lontano?
fare la tariffa
farm la fattoria
farmer l'agricoltore *(m)*
farmhouse la fattoria
fashionable alla moda
fast veloce
  too fast troppo veloce
to fasten *(seatbelt, etc)* allacciare
fat grasso(a)
  (noun) il grasso
  saturated fats i grassi saturi
  unsaturated fats i grassi insaturi
father il padre
father-in-law lo suocero
fault *(defect)* il difetto
  it's not my fault non è colpa mia
favour il favore
favourite preferito(a)
fax il fax
  by fax per fax
to fax mandare un fax
February febbraio
to feed dare da mangiare
to feel sentire ; sentirsi
  I don't feel well non mi sento bene
  I feel sick ho la nausea
feet i piedi
felt-tip pen il pennarello
female femmina ; femminile
ferry il traghetto
festival la festa
to fetch *(bring)* portare
  (to go and get) andare a prendere
fever la febbre
few pochi
  a few alcuni
fiancé(e) il/la fidanzato(a)
field il campo
to fight combattere ; lottare
file *(folder)* il raccoglitore
  (computer) l'archivio *(m)*
to fill riempire
to fill in *(form)* compilare
fill it up! *(petrol)* il pieno!
fillet il filetto
filling *(in tooth)* l'otturazione *(f)*
film *(at cinema)* il film
  (for camera) la pellicola

Filofax® l'agenda *(f)*
filter il filtro
to find trovare
fine *(to be paid)* la multa
finger il dito
to finish finire
finished finito(a)
fire il fuoco ; l'incendio *(m)*
  fire! al fuoco!
fire alarm l'allarme antincendio *(m)*
fire brigade i vigili del fuoco
fire engine l'autopompa *(f)*
fire escape la scala antincendio
fire extinguisher l'estintore *(m)*
fireplace il caminetto
fireworks i fuochi d'artificio
firm *(company)* l'azienda *(f)* ; la ditta
first primo(a)
first aid il pronto soccorso
first aid kit la cassetta di pronto soccorso
first class la prima classe
first name il nome di battesimo
fish il pesce
to fish pescare
fisherman il pescatore
fishing permit la licenza di pesca
fishing rod la canna da pesca
fishmonger's la pescheria
to fit *(clothes)* andare bene
  it doesn't fit non va bene
fit *(seizure)* l'attacco *(m)*
to fix riparare ; sistemare
  can you fix it? può ripararlo?
fizzy gassato(a)
flag la bandiera
flame la fiamma
flash *(for camera)* il flash
flashlight la pila
flask *(thermos)* il thermos
flat l'appartamento *(m)*
flat piatto(a)
  flat battery la batteria scarica
  flat tyre la gomma a terra
flavour il gusto
  what flavour? che gusto?
flaw il difetto
fleas le pulci
flesh la carne
flex il filo flessibile
flight il volo
flip flops gli infradito
flippers le pinne

123 **flood** l'alluvione *(f)*
  flash flood l'inondazione *(f)*
floor *(of building)* il piano
  (of room) il pavimento
  which floor? a che piano?
  on the ground floor al pianterreno
  on the first floor al primo piano
  on the second floor al secondo piano
floorcloth lo straccio per pavimenti
Florence Firenze
florist's shop il fioraio
flour la farina
flowers i fiori
flu l'influenza *(f)*
fly la mosca
to fly volare
flysheet *(tent)* il sopratetto
fog la nebbia
foggy nebbioso(a)
foil *(silver paper)* la carta stagnola
to fold ripiegare
to follow seguire
food il cibo
food poisoning l'intossicazione
  alimentare *(f)*
foot il piede
  on foot a piedi
football il calcio ; il pallone
football match la partita di calcio
football pitch il campo di calcio
football player il calciatore
footpath il sentiero
for per
  for me/us per me/noi
  for him/her per lui/lei
  for you per te/lei/voi
forbidden proibito(a)
forehead la fronte
foreign straniero(a)
foreigner lo/la straniero(a)
forest la foresta
forever per sempre
to forget dimenticare
fork *(for eating)* la forchetta
  (in road) il bivio
form *(document)* il modulo
fortnight quindici giorni
forward avanti
foul *(football)* il fallo
fountain la fontana
four-wheel drive con quattro ruote
  motrici
fox la volpe
fracture la frattura

fragile fragile
fragrance la fragranza
frame *(picture)* la cornice
France la Francia
free *(not occupied)* libero(a)
  (costing nothing) gratis
freezer il congelatore
French francese
  (language) il francese
French fries le patatine fritte
frequent frequente
fresh fresco(a)
fresh water l'acqua dolce *(f)*
Friday il venerdì
fridge il frigorifero
fried fritto(a)
friend l'amico(a)
friendly amichevole
frog la rana
from da
  from Scotland dalla Scozia
  from England dall'Inghilterra
front davanti
  in front of... di fronte a...
front door la porta d'ingresso
frost la brina
frozen *(food)* surgelato(a)
fruit la frutta
  dried fruit la frutta secca
fruit juice il succo di frutta
fruit salad la macedonia
to fry friggere
frying-pan la padella
fuel *(petrol)* la benzina
fuel gauge la spia della benzina
fuel pump la pompa
fuel tank il serbatoio della benzina
full pieno(a)
  (occupied) completo(a)
full board la pensione completa
fumes *(of car)* i gas di scarico
fun il divertimento
funeral il funerale
funfair il luna park
funny *(amusing)* divertente
fur il pelo
furnished ammobiliato(a)
furniture i mobili
fuse il fusibile
fuse box la scatola dei fusibili
future il futuro

G

gallery la galleria
game il gioco
  (meat) la selvaggina
garage *(private)* il garage
  (for repairs) l'autofficina *(f)*
  (for petrol) la stazione di servizio
garden il giardino
garlic l'aglio *(m)*
gas il gas
gas cooker la cucina a gas
gas cylinder la bombola del gas
gastritis la gastrite
gate il cancello
  (airport) l'uscita *(f)*
gay *(person)* gay
gear *(car)* la marcia
  first gear la prima
  second gear la seconda
  third gear la terza
  fourth gear la quarta
  neutral folle
  reverse la retromarcia
gearbox il cambio
generous generoso(a)
gents' *(toilet)* la toilette (per uomini)
genuine *(leather, silver)* vero(a)
  (antique, picture, etc) autentico(a)
German tedesco(a)
  (language) il tedesco
German measles la rosolia
Germany la Germania
to get *(obtain)* ottenere
  (to receive) ricevere
  (to fetch) prendere
to get in/on *(vehicle)* salire in/su
to get off *(bus, etc)* scendere da
gift il regalo
gift shop il negozio di souvenir
girl *(young child)* la bambina
  (teenage) la ragazza
girlfriend la ragazza
to give dare
to give back restituire
glacier il ghiacciaio
glass *(substance)* il vetro
  (for drinking) il bicchiere
  a glass of water un bicchiere d'acqua
  a glass of wine un bicchiere di vino
glasses *(spectacles)* gli occhiali
glasses case la custodia degli occhiali

gloves i guanti
glue la colla
to go andare
  I'm going to... vado a...
  we're going to... andiamo a...
to go back ritornare
to go in entrare in
to go out *(leave)* uscire
goat la capra
God Dio
goggles gli occhialini
  (for skiing) gli occhiali da sci
gold l'oro *(m)*
golf il golf
golf ball la pallina da golf
golf clubs le mazze da golf
golf course il campo di golf
good buono(a)
  (pleasant) bello(a)
  very good ottimo(a)
good afternoon buon giorno
  (after 5pm) buona sera
goodbye arrivederci
good day buon giorno
good evening buona sera
good morning buon giorno
good night buona notte
goose l'oca *(f)*
gram il grammo
grandchild il/la nipote
granddaughter la nipote
grandfather il nonno
grandmother la nonna
grandparents i nonni
grandson il nipote
grapes l'uva *(f)*
grass l'erba *(f)*
grated grattugiato(a)
grater la grattugia
greasy grasso(a)
great *(big)* grande
  (wonderful) fantastico(a)
Great Britain la Gran Bretagna
green verde
green card *(car insurance)* la carta verde
greengrocer's il fruttivendolo
greetings card il biglietto d'auguri
grey grigio(a)
grill la griglia
to grill cuocere alla griglia
grilled alla griglia
grocer's il negozio di alimentari
ground la terra
ground floor il pianterreno

on the ground floor a pianterreno
groundsheet il telone impermeabile
group il gruppo
guarantee la garanzia
guard *(on train)* il capotreno
guest *(house guest)* l'ospite *(m/f)*
  (in hotel) il/la cliente
guesthouse la pensione
guide *(tourist)* la guida
guidebook la guida
guided tour la visita guidata
guitar la chitarra
gun *(pistol)* la pistola
  (rifle) il fucile
gym *(place)* la palestra
gym shoes le scarpe da ginnastica

H

haemorrhoids le emorroidi
hail la grandine
hair i capelli
hairbrush la spazzola per capelli
haircut il taglio di capelli
hairdresser il parrucchiere/la
  parrucchiera
hair dryer il fon
hair dye la tintura per capelli
hair gel il gel per capelli
hairgrip la molletta per capelli
hair mousse la spuma
hair spray la lacca per capelli
half la metà
  a half bottle of... una mezza
    bottiglia di...
  half an hour mezz'ora
half board mezza pensione
half fare il ridotto
half-price metà prezzo
ham *(cooked)* il prosciutto cotto
  (cured) il prosciutto crudo
hamburger l'hamburger *(m)*
hammer il martello
hand la mano
handbag la borsa
handicapped disabile ; handicappato(a)
handkerchief il fazzoletto
handle il manico
handlebars il manubrio
hand luggage il bagaglio a mano
hand-made fatto a mano
hands-free phone il telefono per auto
handsome bello(a)
hanger *(coat hanger)* la gruccia per abiti

hang gliding il volo con deltaplano
hangover i postumi della sbornia
to happen succedere
  what happened? cos'è successo?
happy felice
  happy birthday! buon compleanno!
harbour il porto
hard duro(a)
  (difficult) difficile
hard disk l'hard disk *(m)*
hardware shop il negozio di
  ferramenta
to harm nuocere
harvest il raccolto ; la vendemmia
hat il cappello
to have avere
  I have... ho...
  I don't have... non ho...
  we have... abbiamo...
  we don't have... non abbiamo...
  do you have...? ha...?
to have to dovere
hay fever il raffreddore da fieno
he egli ; lui
head la testa
headache il mal di testa
  I have a headache ho mal di testa
headlights i fari
headphones la cuffia
health la salute
health-food shop l'erboristeria *(f)*
healthy sano(a)
to hear sentire
hearing aid l'apparecchio acustico *(m)*
heart il cuore
heart attack l'infarto *(m)*
heartburn il bruciore di stomaco
to heat up *(food)* riscaldare
heater il termosifone
heating il riscaldamento
heavy pesante
heel il tallone
heel bar il banco del calzolaio
height l'altezza *(f)*
helicopter l'elicottero *(m)*
hello! salve! ; ciao!
  (on telephone) pronto
helmet il casco
help! aiuto!
to help aiutare
  can you help me? può aiutarmi?
hem l'orlo *(m)*

h/i   eng-italian

hepatitis l'epatite (f)

her il/la suo(a)
 her passport il suo passaporto
 her room la sua camera

herb l'erba aromatica (f)

herbal tea la tisana

here qui
 here is... ecco...
 here is my passport ecco il mio
 passaporto

hernia l'ernia (f)

hi! ciao!

to hide nascondere

high (price, number, etc) alto(a)
 (speed) forte

high blood pressure la pressione alta

high chair il seggiolone

hill la collina

hill-walking il trekking

him lui ; lo ; gli

hip l'anca (f)

hip replacement la protesi dell'anca

hire il noleggio
 car hire il noleggio auto
 bike hire il noleggio bici
 boat hire il noleggio barche
 ski hire il noleggio sci

to hire noleggiare

hired car la macchina a noleggio

his il/la suo(a)
 his passport il suo passaporto
 his room la sua camera

historic storico(a)

history la storia

to hit colpire

to hitchhike fare l'autostop

hobby il passatempo

to hold tenere
 (to contain) contenere

hold-up (traffic jam) l'ingorgo (m)

hole il buco

holiday la festa
 on holiday in vacanza

holiday rep il/la rappresentante
 dell'agenzia di viaggio

home la casa
 at home a casa

homesick: to be homesick avere
 nostalgia di casa
 I'm homesick ho nostalgia di casa

homosexual omosessuale

honest onesto(a)

honey il miele

honeymoon la luna di miele

hood (on jacket) il cappuccio

hook (for fishing) l'amo (m)

to hope sperare
 I hope so/not spero di sì/no

hors d'œuvre l'antipasto (m)

horse il cavallo

horse racing l'ippica (f)

to horse-ride andare a cavallo

hosepipe la canna dell'acqua

hospital l'ospedale (m)

hostel l'ostello (m)

hot caldo(a)
 I'm hot ho caldo
 it's hot (weather) fa caldo

hot-water bottle la borsa dell'acqua
 calda

hotel l'albergo (m) ; l'hotel (m)

hour l'ora (f)
 half an hour mezz'ora
 1 hour un'ora
 2 hour due ore

house la casa

housewife la casalinga

house wine il vino della casa

housework i lavori di casa

how? (in what way) come?
 how much? quanto(a)?
 how many? quanti(e)?
 how are you? come sta?

hungry: to be hungry avere fame

hunt la caccia

to hunt andare a caccia

hunting permit la licenza di caccia

hurry: I'm in a hurry ho fretta

to hurt fare male
 that hurts fa male

husband il marito

hut (bathing/beach) la cabina
 (mountain) la baita

hydrofoil l'aliscafo (m)

hypodermic needle l'ago
 ipodermico (m)

I

I io

ice il ghiaccio
 with ice con ghiaccio
 without ice senza ghiaccio

ice box il freezer

ice cream il gelato

iced coffee il caffè freddo

iced tea il tè freddo

ice lolly il ghiacciolo

127 **ice rink** la pista di pattinaggio su
  ghiaccio
to ice skate pattinare sul ghiaccio
ice skates i pattini da ghiaccio
idea l'idea *(f)*
identity card la carta d'identità
if se
ignition l'accensione *(f)*
ignition key la chiave dell'accensione
ill malato(a)
  I'm ill sto male
illness la malattia
immediately subito
immersion heater lo scaldabagno
  elettrico
immigration l'immigrazione *(f)*
immunisation l'immunizzazione *(f)*
to import importare
important importante
impossible impossibile
to improve migliorare
in in
  in 2 hours in due ore
  in London a Londra
in front of davanti a
included compreso(a) ; incluso(a)
inconvenient scomodo(a)
to increase aumentare
  to increase volume alzare il volume
indicator *(in car)* la freccia
indigestion l'indigestione *(f)*
indigestion tablets le compresse per
  digerire
indoors dentro
infection l'infezione *(f)*
infectious contagioso(a)
informal *(clothes)* sportivo(a)
information le informazioni
information office l'ufficio
  informazioni *(m)*
ingredients gli ingredienti
inhaler l'inalatore *(m)*
injection l'iniezione *(f)* ; la puntura
to injure ferire
injured ferito(a)
injury la lesione
ink l'inchiostro *(m)*
inn la locanda
inner tube la camera d'aria
inquiries le informazioni
insect l'insetto *(m)*
insect bite la puntura d'insetto
insect repellent l'insettifugo *(m)*
inside dentro

instant coffee il caffè solubile
instead of invece di
instructor l'istruttore/l'istruttrice
insulin l'insulina *(f)*
insurance l'assicurazione *(f)*
insurance certificate il certificato di
  assicurazione
to insure assicurare
insured: *to be insured* essere
  assicurato(a)
to intend to avere intenzione di
interesting interessante
international internazionale
internet l'Internet *(m)*
internet café il cyber-café
interpreter l'interprete *(m/f)*
interval l'intervallo *(m)*
interview l'intervista *(f)*
into in
  into town in città
  into the centre in centro
to introduce someone to presentare
  qualcuno a
invitation l'invito *(m)*
to invite invitare
invoice la fattura
Ireland l'Irlanda *(f)*
Irish irlandese
iron *(for clothes)* il ferro da stiro
  (metal) il ferro
to iron stirare
ironing board l'asse da stiro *(f)*
ironmonger's il negozio di ferramenta
is è
island l'isola *(f)*
it lo/la
Italian italiano(a)
  (language) l'italiano *(m)*
Italy l'Italia *(f)*
to itch prudere
  my leg itches mi prude la gamba
  my eyes itch mi prudono gli occhi
item *(on bill)* la voce
itemised bill il conto dettagliato

J

jack *(for car)* il cric
jacket la giacca
  waterproof jacket il giaccone
  impermeabile
jam *(food)* la marmellata

j/k/l eng-italian

jammed bloccato(a)
January gennaio
jar (honey, jam, etc) il vaso
jaundice l'itterizia (f)
jaw la mascella
jealous geloso(a) ; invidioso(a)
jeans i blue jeans
jelly (dessert) la gelatina
jellyfish la medusa
jet ski l'acqua-scooter (m)
jetty il molo
jeweller's la gioielleria
jewellery i gioielli
Jewish ebreo(a)
job il lavoro
to jog fare jogging
to join (club) iscriversi a
to join in (game) partecipare a
joint (of body) l'articolazione (f)
joke lo scherzo (m)
to joke scherzare
journalist il/la giornalista
journey il viaggio
judge il/la giudice (m/f)
jug la brocca
juice il succo
  a carton of juice un cartone di succo di frutta
July luglio
to jump saltare
jumper il maglione
jump leads (for car) i cavi per far partire la macchina
junction (road) l'incrocio (m)
June giugno
just: *just two* solamente due
  I've just arrived sono appena arrivato(a)

K

to keep (retain) tenere
  keep the change! tenga il resto
kennel il canile
kettle il bollitore
key la chiave
  card key il passe-partout
keyboard la tastiera
keyring il portachiavi
to kick dare calci a
kid (child) il bambino

kidneys (in body) i reni
to kill uccidere
kilo il chilo
  a kilo of apples un chilo di mele
  2 kilos due chili
kilogram il chilogrammo
kilometre il chilometro
kind (sort) il tipo
kind (person) gentile
king il re
kiosk l'edicola (f)
kiss il bacio
to kiss baciare
kitchen la cucina
kitchen paper la carta assorbente da cucina
kite l'aquilone (m)
knee il ginocchio
knee highs i gambaletti
knickers le mutandine
knife il coltello
to knit lavorare a maglia
to knock (on door) bussare
to knock down (car) investire
to knock over (glass, vase) rovesciare
knot il nodo
to know (facts) sapere
  (to be acquainted with) conoscere
  I don't know non lo so
to know how to sapere
  to know how to swim saper nuotare
kosher kasher

L

label l'etichetta (f)
lace il pizzo
laces (shoe) i lacci
ladder la scala
ladies' (toilet) la toilette (per signore)
lady la signora
lager la birra (bionda)
lake il lago
lamb l'agnello (m)
lame zoppo(a)
lamp la lampada
lamppost il lampione
lampshade il paralume
land la terra
to land (plane) atterrare
landlady la padrona di casa
landlord il padrone di casa
landslide la frana
lane la stradina

(of motorway) la corsia
language la lingua
language school la scuola di lingue
laptop il laptop
large grande
last ultimo(a) ; scorso(a)
  the last bus l'ultimo autobus
  the last train l'ultimo treno
  last night ieri notte
  last week la settimana scorsa
  last year l'anno scorso
  last time l'ultima volta
late tardi
  the train's late il treno è in ritardo
  sorry we're late scusi il ritardo
later più tardi
to laugh ridere
launderette la lavanderia automatica
laundry il bucato
lavatory la toilette
lavender la lavanda
law la legge
lawn il prato inglese
lawyer (m/f) l'avvocato/l'avvocatessa
laxative il lassativo
layby la piazzola di sosta
lazy pigro(a)
lead (electric) il filo
lead (metal) il piombo
lead-free senza piombo
leaf la foglia
leak (of gas, liquid) la perdita
  (in roof) il buco
to leak: *it's leaking* (pipe) perde
to learn imparare
lease (rental) l'affitto (m)
leather il cuoio ; la pelle
to leave (leave behind) lasciare
  (train, bus, etc) partire
  when does the bus leave? quando
  parte l'autobus?
  when does the train leave? quando
  parte il treno?
left la sinistra
  on/to the left a sinistra
left-handed mancino(a)
left-luggage il deposito bagagli
left luggage locker l'armadietto per
  despositare i bagagli (m)
leg la gamba
lemon il limone
lemonade la limonata
to lend prestare
length la lunghezza
lens (camera) l'obiettivo (m)
  (contact lens) la lente a contatto

eng–italian   l

lenses le lenti
lesbian lesbica
less meno
  less than meno di
lesson la lezione
to let (allow) permettere
  (to hire out) affittare
letter la lettera
letterbox la cassetta delle lettere
lettuce la lattuga
level crossing il passaggio a livello
library la biblioteca
licence il permesso
  (driving) la patente
lid il coperchio
lie (untruth) la bugia
to lie down sdraiarsi
life belt il salvagente
lifeboat la scialuppa di salvataggio
lifeguard il bagnino
life insurance l'assicurazione sulla
  vita (f)
life jacket il giubbotto salvagente
life raft la zattera di salvataggio
lift (elevator) l'ascensore (m)
  (in car) il passaggio
lift pass (on ski slopes) lo skipass
light (not heavy) leggero(a)
  (colour) chiaro(a)
light la luce
  have you a light? ha da accendere?
light bulb la lampadina
lighter l'accendino (m)
lighthouse il faro
lightning il fulmine
like come
to like piacere
  I like coffee mi piace il caffè
  I don't like... non mi piace...
  I'd/we'd like... vorrei/vorremmo...
lilo il materassino
lime (fruit) la limetta
line (row, queue) la fila
  (telephone) la linea
linen il lino
lingerie la biancheria intima da donna
lip reading la labiolettura
lips le labbra
lip salve il burro di cacao
lipstick il rossetto
liqueur il liquore
list l'elenco (m) ; la lista

to listen (to) ascoltare
litre il litro
  a litre of milk un litro di latte
litter *(rubbish)* i rifiuti
little *(small)* piccolino(a)
  a little... un po' di...
to live vivere ; abitare
  I live in London vivo a Londra
  he lives in a flat abita in un
  appartamento
liver il fegato
living room il salotto
loaf of bread la pagnotta
local locale
to lock chiudere a chiave
lock la serratura
  the lock is broken la serratura è rotta
locker l'armadietto *(m)*
locksmith il fabbro
log book *(car)* il libretto di circolazione
logs i ceppi
lollipop il lecca lecca
London Londra
  in/to London a Londra
long lungo(a)
  for a long time molto tempo
long-sighted ipermetrope
to look after prendersi cura di
to look at guardare
to look for cercare
loose *(not fastened)* slegato(a)
  it's come loose (knot) si è allentato(a)
lorry il camion
to lose perdere
lost *(object)* perso(a)
  I've lost my... ho perso il/la...
  I'm lost mi sono smarrito(a)
  we're lost ci siamo smarriti(e)
lost property office l'ufficio oggetti
  smarriti *(m)*
lot: a lot molto
lottery la lotteria
loud forte
lounge *(in hotel)* il salone
  (in house) la sala
  (in airport) la sala d'attesa
love l'amore *(m)*
to love *(person)* amare
  I love you ti amo
  I love swimming mi piace nuotare
lovely bellissimo(a)
low basso(a)

(standard, quality) scadente
low-alcohol a basso contenuto alcolico
to lower volume abbassare il volume
low-fat magro(a)
luck la fortuna
lucky fortunato(a)
luggage i bagagli
luggage rack il portabagagli
luggage tag l'etichetta *(f)*
luggage trolley il carrello
lump *(swelling)* il gonfiore
lunch il pranzo
lunch break l'intervallo del pranzo *(m)*
lung il polmone
luxury di lusso

M

machine la macchina
mad *(insane)* matto(a)
  (angry) arrabbiato(a)
magazine la rivista
maggot il baco
magnet la calamita
magnifying glass la lente
  d'ingrandimento
maid *(in hotel)* la cameriera
maiden name il nome da ragazza
mail la posta
main principale
main course *(meal)* il secondo
main road la strada principale
to make *(generally)* fare
  (meal) preparare
make-up il trucco
male maschio ; maschile
mallet la mazza
man l'uomo *(m)*
to manage *(be in charge of)* dirigere
manager il direttore ; il gerente
manual *(gear change)* manuale
many molti(e)
map *(of country)* la carta geografica
  (city) la piantina
marble il marmo
March marzo
margarine la margarina
marina il porticciolo
mark *(stain)* la macchia ; il segno
  (brand) la marca
market il mercato
  where is the market? dov'è il
  mercato?

when is the market? quando c'è il mercato?
marmalade la marmellata d'arance
married sposato(a)
  I'm married sono sposato(a)
  are you married? è sposato(a)?
marry: *to get married* sposarsi
marsh la palude
mascara il mascara
mass *(in church)* la messa
mast l'albero *(m)*
masterpiece il capolavoro
match *(game)* la partita
matches i fiammiferi
material il materiale
  (cloth) il tessuto
to matter importare
  it doesn't matter non importa
  what's the matter? cosa c'è?
mattress il materasso
May maggio
mayonnaise la maionese
mayor il/la sindaco(a)
maximum il massimo
me me ; mi
meal il pasto
to mean *(signify)* voler dire
  what does it mean? cosa vuol dire?
measles il morbillo
to measure misurare
meat la carne
mechanic il/la meccanico(a)
medical insurance l'assicurazione medica *(f)*
medical treatment le cure mediche
medicine la medicina
Mediterranean il Mediterraneo
medium rare *(steak)* poco cotto(a)
to meet incontrare
  pleased to meet you! piacere!
meeting la riunione
  (by chance) l'incontro *(m)*
meeting point il meeting point
to melt sciogliere
member *(of club, etc)* il/la socio(a)
membership card la tessera
memory la memoria
  (memories) i ricordi
men gli uomini
to mend riparare
meningitis la meningite
menu il menù
  set menu il menù a prezzo fisso ; il menù turistico
  à la carte menu il menù alla carta

eng–italian   **m**

message il messaggio
metal il metallo
meter il contatore
metre il metro
metro *(underground)* la metropolitana
metro station la stazione del metrò
microwave oven il forno a microonde
midday il mezzogiorno
  at midday a mezzogiorno
middle il mezzo
middle-aged di mezz'età
midge il moscerino
midnight la mezzanotte
  at midnight a mezzanotte
migraine l'emicrania *(f)*
  I have a migraine ho l'emicrania
Milan Milano
mild dolce ; mite
milk il latte
  fresh milk il latte fresco
  hot milk il latte caldo
  long-life milk il latte a lunga conservazione
  powdered milk il latte in polvere
  whole milk il latte intero
  semi-skimmed milk il latte parzialmente scremato
  soya milk il latte di soia
  with/without milk con/senza latte
milkshake il frappé
millimetre il millimetro
mince *(meat)* la carne macinata
mind: *do you mind?* le dà fastidio?
  I don't mind non mi dà fastidio
mineral water l'acqua minerale *(f)*
minibar il minibar
minimum il minimo
minister *(church)* il sacerdote
  (political) il ministro
minor road la strada secondaria
mint *(herb)* la menta
mint tea il tè alla menta
minute il minuto
mirror lo specchio
to misbehave comportarsi male
miscarriage l'aborto spontaneo *(m)*
to miss *(train, etc)* perdere
Miss Signorina
missing *(thing)* smarrito(a)
  (person) scomparso(a)
mistake l'errore *(m)*
misty nebbioso(a)

misunderstanding il malinteso
to mix mescolare
mobile phone il cellulare
modem il modem
modern moderno(a)
moisturizer l'idratante *(m)*
mole *(on skin)* il neo
moment: *just a moment* un momento
monastery il monastero
Monday il lunedì
money i soldi
 I have no money non ho soldi
money belt il marsupio
money order il vaglia
month il mese
 this month questo mese
 last month il mese scorso
 next month il mese prossimo
monthly mensilmente
monument il monumento
moon la luna
mooring l'ormeggio *(m)*
mop il mocio Vileda
moped il motorino
more (than) più (di)
 more than 3 più di tre
 more wine ancora un po' di vino
morning la mattina
 in the morning di mattina
 this morning stamattina
 tomorrow morning domani mattina
morning-after pill la pillola del giorno
dopo
mosquito la zanzara
mosquito net la zanzariera
mosquito repellent lo zanzarifugo
most il/la più ; il massimo
moth *(clothes)* la tarma
mother la madre
mother-in-law la suocera
motor il motore
motorbike la moto
motorboat il motoscafo
motorway l'autostrada *(f)*
mould la muffa
mountain la montagna
mountain bike la mountain bike
mountain rescue il soccorso alpino
mountaineering l'alpinismo *(m)*
mouse il topo
 (computer) il mouse
moustache i baffi

mouth la bocca
mouthwash il colluttorio
move muoversi
 it isn't moving non si muove
movie il film
Mr Signor
Mrs Signora
Ms Signora
much molto
 too much troppo
muddy *(ground)* fangoso(a)
mugging lo scippo
mumps gli orecchioni
muscle il muscolo
museum il museo
mushrooms i funghi
music la musica
musical il musical
mussels le cozze
must *(to have to)* dovere
 I must devo
 we must dobbiamo
 I mustn't non devo
 we mustn't non dobbiamo
mustard la senape
my il/la mio(a)
 my passport il mio passaporto
 my room la mia camera

N

nail *(metal)* il chiodo
 (fingernail) l'unghia *(f)*
nailbrush lo spazzolino per le unghie
nail clipper il tagliaunghie
nail file la limetta per le unghie
nail polish/varnish lo smalto per le
unghie
nail polish remover l'acetone *(m)*
nail scissors le forbicine
name il nome
 my name is... mi chiamo...
 what is your name? come si chiama?
nanny la bambinaia
napkin il tovagliolo
Naples Napoli
nappies i pannolini
narrow stretto(a)
national nazionale
national park il parco nazionale
nationality la nazionalità
natural naturale
nature la natura
nature reserve la riserva naturale

133 **navy blue** blu marino
near to vicino(a) a
  is it near? è vicino?
  near the bank vicino alla banca
necessary necessario(a)
neck il collo
necklace la collana
nectarine la nocepesca
to need avere bisogno di...
  I need... ho bisogno di...
  we need... abbiamo bisogno di...
needle l'ago (m)
  a needle and thread un ago e filo
negative (photo) il negativo
neighbour il/la vicino(a)
nephew il nipote
net la rete
  the Net l'Internet (m)
never mai
  I never drink wine non bevo mai il vino
new nuovo(a)
news le notizie
  (on television) il telegiornale
newsagent's il giornalaio
newspaper il giornale
newsstand l'edicola (f)
New Year il Capodanno
  happy New Year! buon Anno!
New Year's Eve la notte di San
  Silvestro ; l'ultimo dell'anno (m)
New Zealand la Nuova Zelanda
next prossimo(a)
  next to accanto(a) a
  next week la settimana prossima
  the next bus il prossimo autobus
  the next train il prossimo treno
  the next stop la prossima fermata
nice piacevole
  (person) simpatico(a)
niece la nipote
night la notte
  at night di notte
  last night ieri notte
  per night a notte
  tomorrow night domani sera
  tonight stasera
nightclub il nightclub
nightdress la camicia da notte
night porter il portiere notturno
no no
  no entry vietato l'ingresso
  no smoking vietato fumare
  no thanks no, grazie
  (without) senza
  no sugar senza zucchero
  no ice senza ghiaccio
  no problem non c'è problema

nobody nessuno
noise il rumore
noisy rumoroso(a)
  it's very noisy è molto
  rumoroso(a)
non-alcoholic analcolico(a)
none nessuno(a)
non-smoker non-fumatore
non-smoking per non-fumatori
north il nord
Northern Ireland l'Irlanda del Nord (f)
nose il naso
not non
  I do not know non lo so
note (bank note) la banconota
  (letter) il biglietto
note pad il bloc-notes
nothing niente
  nothing else nient'altro
notice l'avviso (m)
notice board la bacheca
novel il romanzo
November novembre
now adesso
nowhere da nessuna parte
nuclear nucleare
nudist beach la spiaggia nudista
number il numero
number plate (car) la targa
nurse l'infermiera/l'infermiere (f/m)
nursery (for children) l'asilo (m)
  (for plants) il vivaio
nursery slope la pista per principianti
nut (to eat) la noce
  (for bolt) il dado

O

oars i remi
oats l'avena (f)
to obtain ottenere
occupation (work) il lavoro
ocean l'oceano (m)
October ottobre
octopus il polpo
odd (strange) strano(a)
of di
  a bottle of wine una bottiglia di vino
  a glass of water un bicchiere d'acqua
  made of... fatto di...

off *(machine, etc)* spento(a)
(milk, food) andato(a) a male
this meat is off questa carne è
andata a male
office l'ufficio *(m)*
often spesso
how often? ogni quanto?
oil l'olio *(m)*
oil filter il filtro dell'olio
oil gauge l'indicatore del livello
dell'olio *(m)*
ointment la pomata
OK! va bene!
old vecchio(a)
how old are you? quanti anni ha?
I'm ... years old ho ... anni
old age pensioner il/la
pensionato(a)
olive oil l'olio d'oliva *(m)*
olives le olive
on *(light, engine)* acceso(a)
(tap) aperto(a)
on the table sulla tavola
on time in orario
once una volta
at once subito
one-way *(street)* a senso unico
onions le cipolle
only solo(a)
open aperto(a)
to open aprire
opera l'opera *(f)*
operation *(surgical)* l'operazione *(f)*
operator *(telephone)* il/la
centralinista
opposite di fronte a
opposite the hotel di fronte
all'albergo
quite the opposite al contrario
optician's l'ottico *(m)*
or o
orange *(colour)* arancione
orange *(fruit)* l'arancia *(f)*
orange juice il succo d'arancia
orchestra l'orchestra *(f)*
order *(in restaurant)* l'ordine *(f)*
out of order fuori servizio
to order *(in restaurant)* ordinare
oregano l'origano *(m)*
organic biologico(a)
to organize organizzare
ornament il soprammobile

other l'altro(a)
the other one l'altro
have you any others? ce ne sono altri?
our il/la nostro(a)
our car la nostra macchina
our hotel il nostro albergo
out *(light)* spento(a)
he/she's out è fuori
he's gone out è uscito
outdoor *(pool, etc)* all'aperto
outside: *it's outside* è fuori
oven il forno
ovenproof dish la pirofila
over *(on top of)* sopra
to overbook accettare troppe
prenotazioni
to overcharge far pagare troppo
overdone *(food)* troppo cotto(a)
overdose l'overdose *(f)*
to overheat surriscaldare
to overload sovraccaricare
to oversleep non svegliarsi in tempo
to overtake *(in car)* sorpassare
to owe dovere
I owe you... le devo...
you owe me... mi deve
owner il/la proprietario(a)
oxygen l'ossigeno *(m)*

P

pace il passo
pacemaker il pacemaker
to pack *(suitcase)* fare la valigia
package il pacco
package tour il viaggio organizzato
packet il pacchetto
padded envelope la busta imbottita
paddling pool la piscina per bambini
padlock il lucchetto
Padua Padova
page la pagina
paid pagato(a)
I've paid ho pagato
pain il dolore
painful doloroso(a)
painkiller l'analgesico *(m)*
to paint *(wall, house)* verniciare
(picture) dipingere
painting *(picture)* il quadro
pair il paio
palace il palazzo
pale pallido(a)
pan *(saucepan)* la pentola
(frying pan) la padella

pancake la crêpe
panniers *(bike)* le borse per la bici
panties le mutandine
pants le mutande
panty liner il proteggislip
paper la carta
paper hankies i fazzolettini di carta
paper napkins i tovagliolini di carta
paragliding il parapendio
paralysed paralizzato(a)
parcel il pacco
pardon? scusi?
  I beg your pardon mi scusi
parents i genitori
park il parco
to park parcheggiare
parking disk il disco orario
parking meter il parchimetro
parking ticket *(fine)* la multa per sosta vietata
parmesan il parmigiano
  grated parmesan il parmigiano grattugiato
part la parte
partner *(business)* il/la socio(a)
  (boy/girlfriend) il/la compagno(a)
party *(celebration)* la festa
  (political) il partito
pass *(mountain)* il valico
  (bus, train) la tessera
passenger il/la passeggero(a)
passport il passaporto
passport control il controllo passaporti
pasta la pasta
pastry la pasta
  (fancy cake) il pasticcino
path il sentiero
patient *(in hospital)* il/la paziente
pavement il marciapiede
to pay pagare
  I want to pay vorrei pagare
  where do I pay? dove pago?
payment il pagamento
payphone il telefono pubblico
peace la pace
peaches le pesche
peak rate la tariffa ore di punta
peanut allergy l'allergia alle arachidi *(f)*
pearls le perle
pears le pere
peas i piselli
pedal il pedale
pedal boat/pedalo il pedalò
pedestrian il/la pedone(a)

pedestrian crossing il passaggio pedonale
to pee pisciare
to peel *(fruit)* sbucciare
peg *(for clothes)* la molletta
  (for tent) il picchetto
pen la penna
pencil la matita
penfriend l'amico(a) di penna
penicillin la penicillina
penis il pene
penknife il temperino
pension la pensione
pensioner il/la pensionato(a)
people la gente
pepper *(spice)* il pepe
  (vegetable) il peperone
per per
  per day al giorno
  per hour all'ora
  per week alla settimana
  per person a persona
  100 km per hour 100 km all'ora
perfect perfetto(a)
performance la rappresentazione
perfume il profumo
perhaps forse
period *(menstrual)* le mestruazioni
perm la permanente
permit il permesso
person la persona
personal organizer l'agenda elettronica *(f)*
personal stereo il walkman®
pet l'animale domestico *(m)*
pet food il cibo per gli animali domestici
pet shop il negozio di animali domestici
petrol la benzina
  4-star petrol la super
  unleaded petrol la benzina senza piombo
petrol cap il tappo del serbatoio
petrol tank il serbatoio della benzina
petrol pump la pompa della benzina
petrol station la stazione di servizio
pharmacy la farmacia
phone il telefono
  by phone per telefono
to phone telefonare
phonebook l'elenco telefonico *(m)*

phonebox la cabina telefonica
phonecard la scheda telefonica
photocopy la fotocopia
  I need a photocopy mi serve una fotocopia
to photocopy fotocopiare
photograph la foto
  to take a photo fare una foto
phrase book il manuale di conversazione
piano il pianoforte
to pick *(fruit, flowers)* cogliere
  (to choose) scegliere
pickpocket il borseggiatore
pickle i sottaceti
picnic il picnic
  to have a picnic fare un picnic
picnic hamper il cestino per il picnic
picnic rug il plaid
picnic table il tavolo da picnic
picture *(painting)* il quadro
  (photo) la foto
pie *(sweet)* la torta
  (savoury) il pasticcio
piece il pezzo
pier il pontile
pig il maiale
pill la pillola
  to be on the pill prendere la pillola
pillow il guanciale ; il cuscino
pillowcase la federa
pilot il pilota
pin lo spillo
pink rosa
pipe *(water, etc)* il tubo
  (smoker's) la pipa
pity: what a pity! che peccato!
pizza la pizza
place il luogo
place of birth il luogo di nascità
plain *(obvious)* chiaro(a) ; evidente
  (unflavoured) naturale
plait la treccia
plan il piano
to plan progettare
plane l'aereo *(m)*
plant la pianta
plaster *(sticking)* il cerotto
  (for broken limb) l'ingessatura *(f)*
plastic *(made of)* di plastica
plastic bag il sacchetto di plastica
plate il piatto

platform *(railway)* il binario
  from which platform? da quale binario?
play *(theatre)* la commedia
to play *(games)* giocare
play area l'area giochi *(f)*
playground il parco giochi
play park il parco giochi
playroom la stanza dei giochi
pleasant piacevole
please per favore
pleased: pleased to meet you piacere
plenty l'abbondanza *(f)*
pliers le pinze
plug *(electrical)* la spina
  (for sink) il tappo
to plug in *(appliance)* attaccare
plum la prugna ; la susina
plumber l'idraulico *(m)*
plumbing l'impianto idraulico *(m)*
plunger *(to clear sink)* lo sturalavandini
p.m. del pomeriggio
poached *(egg)* in camicia
  (fish) bollito(a)
pocket la tasca
points *(in car)* le puntine
poison il veleno
poisonous velenoso(a)
police la polizia
policeman/woman il poliziotto/la donna poliziotto
police station il commissariato ; la questura
polish *(for shoes)* il lucido
  (for furniture) la cera
pollen il polline
polluted inquinato(a)
pony il pony
pony trekking le escursioni a cavallo
pool *(swimming)* la piscina
pool attendant il bagnino
poor povero(a)
pope il papa
pop socks i gambaletti
popular popolare
pork la carne di maiale
port *(seaport, wine)* il porto
porter il portiere
  (for luggage) il facchino
portion la porzione
Portugal il Portogallo
Portuguese portoghese
possible possibile
post: by post per posta

137 **to post** *(letters, etc)* imbucare
postbox la buca delle lettere
postcard la cartolina
postcode il codice postale
poster il poster
postman/woman il/la postino(a)
post office la posta ; l'ufficio postale *(m)*
to postpone rimandare
pot *(cooking)* la pentola
potato la patata
  baked potato la patata al forno
  boiled potatoes le patate lesse
  fried potatoes le patate fritte
  mashed potatoes il purè di patate
  roast potatoes le patate arrosto
potato masher lo schiacciapatate
potato peeler il pelapatate
potato salad l'insalata di patate *(f)*
pothole la buca
pottery la terracotta
pound *(money)* la sterlina
to pour versare
powder: *in powder form* in polvere
powdered milk il latte in polvere
power *(electricity)* l'elettricità *(f)*
power cut l'interruzione di corrente *(f)*
pram la carrozzina
to pray pregare
to prefer preferire
pregnant incinta
  I'm pregnant sono incinta
to prepare preparare
to prescribe ordinare
prescription la ricetta
present *(gift)* il regalo
preservative il conservante
president il presidente
pressure: *tyre pressure* la pressione dei pneumatici
  blood pressure la pressione del sangue
pretty carino(a)
price il prezzo
price list il listino prezzi
priest il prete
print *(photo)* la foto
printer lo stampante
prison il carcere ; la prigione
private privato(a)
prize il premio
probably probabilmente
problem il problema
professor il professore/la professoressa
programme il programma

eng-italian p/q

prohibited proibito(a)
promise la promessa
to promise promettere
to pronounce pronunciare
  how's it pronounced? come si pronuncia?
protein la proteina
Protestant protestante
to provide fornire
public pubblico(a)
public holiday la festa nazionale
pudding il dessert
to pull tirare
to pull over *(car)* accostare
pullover il pullover
pump la pompa
puncture la gomma a terra
puncture repair kit il kit per riparare le gomme
puppet il burattino
puppet show lo spettacolo di burattini
purple viola
purse il borsellino
to push spingere
pushchair il passeggino
to put *(to place)* mettere
to put back rimettere
pyjamas il pigiama

Q

quality la qualità
quantity la quantità
quarantine la quarantena
to quarrel litigare
quarter: *a quarter* un quarto
quay il molo
queen la regina
question la domanda
queue la coda
to queue fare la coda
quick veloce
quickly velocemente
quiet *(place)* tranquillo(a)
  a quiet room una stanza tranquilla
quilt la trapunta
quite *(rather)* abbastanza
  it's quite expensive è abbastanza caro(a)
  quite the opposite al contrario
quiz show il gioco a quiz

R

rabbit il coniglio
rabies la rabbia
race *(sport)* la gara
race course l'ippodromo *(m)*
racket *(tennis, etc)* la racchetta
radiator *(car)* il radiatore
  (heater) il termosifone
radio la radio
railcard la tessera di riduzione
  ferroviaria
railway station la stazione dei treni
rain la pioggia
to rain piovere
  it's raining piove
raincoat l'impermeabile *(m)*
rake il rastrello
rape lo stupro
raped violentata
  I've been raped sono stata violentata
rare *(unique)* raro(a)
  (steak) al sangue
rash *(skin)* l'orticaria *(f)*
rate *(cost)* la tariffa
rate of exchange il cambio
raw crudo(a)
razor il rasoio
razor blades le lamette
to read leggere
ready pronto(a)
  to get ready prepararsi
real vero(a)
to realize rendersi conto di
rearview mirror lo specchietto
  retrovisore
receipt la ricevuta
receiver *(phone)* il ricevitore
reception *(desk)* la reception
receptionist il/la receptionist
to recharge *(battery)* ricaricare
recipe la ricetta
to recognize riconoscere
to recommend raccomandare
to record *(programme)* registrare
to recover *(from illness)* rimettersi
to recycle riciclare
red rosso(a)
to reduce ridurre
reduction la riduzione

to refer to *(for information)* rivolgersi a
refill *(pen)* il ricambio
  (lighter) la bomboletta di gas
refund il rimborso
to refuse rifiutare
regarding riguardo a
region la regione
register il registro
to register *(letter)* assicurare
  (car) immatricolare
  (for class) iscriversi
registered letter la lettera

registration form il modulo d'iscrizione
to reimburse rimborsare
relation *(family)* il/la parente
relationship il rapporto
to remain restare ; rimanere
to remember ricordare
  I don't remember non mi ricordo
remote control il telecomando
removal firm la ditta di traslochi
to remove togliere
rent l'affitto *(m)*
to rent *(house)* affittare
  (car) noleggiare
rental *(house)* l'affitto *(m)*
  (car) il nolo
repair la riparazione
to repair riparare
to repeat ripetere
to reply rispondere
report il resoconto
to report *(crime)* denunciare
request la richiesta
to request richiedere
to rescue salvare
reservation la prenotazione
to reserve prenotare
reserved prenotato(a)
resident residente
resort la località di vacanza
rest *(repose)* il riposo
  (remainder) il resto
to rest riposarsi
restaurant il ristorante
restaurant car il vagone ristorante
retired: *I'm retired* sono in pensione
to return *(go back)* ritornare
  (to give back) restituire
return ticket il biglietto di andata e
  ritorno
to reverse fare marcia indietro
to reverse the charges fare una
  telefonata al carico del destinatario

reverse charge call la chiamata a carico del destinatario
reverse gear la retromarcia
rheumatism il reumatismo
rib la costola
rice il riso
rich ricco(a)
ride *(in a car)* il giro in macchina
to ride a horse andare a cavallo
right *(correct)* giusto(a)
right la destra
 at/to the right a destra
 on the right sulla destra
right of way la precedenza
to ring *(bell)* suonare
 (phone) squillare
 it's ringing suona
ring l'anello *(m)*
ring road la circonvallazione
ripe maturo(a)
river il fiume
road la strada
road map la carta stradale
road sign il cartello stradale
roadworks i lavori stradali
roast arrosto(a)
roll *(bread)* il panino
rollerblades i pattini in linea
romantic romantico(a)
roof il tetto
roof-rack il portabagagli
room *(hotel)* la camera
 (space) lo spazio
 double room la camera doppia
 family room la camera per famiglia
 single room la camera singola
room number il numero di camera
room service il servizio in camera
root la radice
rope la corda
rose la rosa
rosé wine il vino rosato
rotten *(food)* marcio(a)
rough *(sea)* mosso(a)
round rotondo(a)
roundabout la rotatoria
row *(in theatre, etc)* la fila
to row *(boat)* remare
rowing boat la barca a remi
rubber *(eraser)* la gomma da cancellare
 (material) la gomma
rubber band l'elastico *(m)*
rubber gloves i guanti di gomma
rubbish la spazzatura

rubella la rosolia
rucksack lo zaino
rug *(carpet)* il tappeto
ruins le rovine
ruler *(for measuring)* il righello
to run correre
rush hour l'ora di punta *(f)*
rusty arrugginito(a)

S

sad triste
saddle la sella
safe *(for valuables)* la cassaforte
safe *(medicine, etc)* senza pericolo
 is it safe? è senza pericolo?
safety la sicurezza
safetybelt la cintura di sicurezza
safety pin la spilla di sicurezza
to sail andare in barca
sailboard la tavola da windsurf
sailing la vela
sailing boat la barca a vela
saint il/la santo(a)
salad l'insalata *(f)*
 green salad l'insalata verde
 mixed salad l'insalata mista
 potato salad l'insalata di patate
 tomato salad l'insalata di pomodori
salad dressing il condimento per l'insalata
salami il salame
salary lol stipendio
sales *(reductions)* i saldi
salesman/woman il/la commesso(a)
sales rep il/la rappresentante
salt il sale
salt water l'acqua salata *(f)*
salty salato(a)
same stesso(a)
sample il campione
sand la sabbia
sandals i sandali
sandwich il panino ; il tramezzino
 toasted sandwich il toast
sanitary towels gli assorbenti
Sardinia la Sardegna
satellite dish l'antenna parabolica *(f)*
satellite TV la televisione via satellite
Saturday il sabato

s   eng–italian

sauce la salsa
  tomato sauce la salsa di pomodoro
saucepan la pentola
saucer il piattino
sauna la sauna
sausage la salsiccia
to save *(life)* salvare
  (money) risparmiare
savoury *(not sweet)* salato(a)
to say dire
scales *(weighing)* la bilancia
scarf la sciarpa
  (headscarf) il foulard
scenery il paesaggio
schedule il programma
  (timetable) l'orario *(m)*
school la scuola
  primary school la scuola elementare
  secondary school il liceo
scissors le forbici
score il punteggio
to score *(goal)* segnare
Scot lo/la scozzese
Scotland la Scozia
Scottish scozzese
scouring pad la paglietta
screen *(computer, TV)* lo schermo
screen wash il liquido lavavetri
screw la vite
screwdriver il cacciavite
  phillips screwdriver il cacciavite a stella
scuba diving le immersioni subacquee
sculpture la scultura
sea il mare
seacat il catamarano
seafood i frutti di mare
seam *(of dress)* la cucitura
to search cercare
sea sickness il mal di mare
seaside: *at the seaside* al mare
season *(of year)* la stagione
  (holiday) il periodo delle vacanze
  in season di stagione
seasonal stagionale
seasoning il condimento
season ticket l'abbonamento *(m)*
seat *(chair)* la sedia
  (in theatre, plane, etc) il posto
seatbelt la cintura di sicurezza
seaweed le alghe
second *(time)* il secondo

second secondo(a)
second class la seconda classe
second-hand di seconda mano
secretary la segretaria
security guard la guardia giurata
sedative il sedativo
to see vedere
to seize afferrare
self-catering con uso di cucina
self-employed autonomo(a)
self-service il self-service
to sell vendere
  do you sell...? vende...?
sell-by date la data di scadenza
Sellotape® lo Scotch®
to send mandare ; spedire ; inviare
senior citizen l'anziano(a)
sensible pratico(a)
separated separato(a)
separately: *to pay separately* pagare separatamente
September settembre
septic tank la fossa settica
serious grave
  (not funny) serio(a)
to serve servire
service *(in church)* la funzione
  (in restaurant) il servizio
  is service included? il servizio è incluso?
service charge il servizio
service station la stazione di servizio
set menu il menù turistico
settee il divano
several alcuni(e)
to sew cucire
sewerage la fognatura
sex *(gender)* il sesso
  (intercourse) i rapporti sessuali
shade l'ombra *(f)*
  in the shade all'ombra
to shake *(bottle)* agitare
shallow basso(a)
shampoo lo shampoo
shampoo and set lo shampoo e messa in piega
to share dividere
sharp *(razor, blade)* affilato(a)
to shave farsi la barba
shaving cream la crema da barba
shawl lo scialle
she ella ; lei
sheep la pecora
sheet *(bed)* il lenzuolo

shelf la mensola
shell *(seashell)* la conchiglia
shellfish i frutti di mare
sheltered riparato(a)
to shine brillare
shingles *(illness)* il fuoco di sant'Antonio
ship la nave
shirt la camicia
shock *(mental)* lo shock
  (electric) la scossa
shock absorber l'ammortizzatore *(m)*
shoe la scarpa
shoelaces i lacci delle scarpe
shoe polish il lucido per scarpe
shoe repairer il calzolaio
shoe shop il negozio di calzature
shop il negozio
to shop andare a fare compere
shop assistant il/la commesso(a)
shop window la vetrina
shopping: to go shopping fare
  compere ; fare la spesa
shopping centre il centro commerciale
shore la riva
short corto(a)
  (person) basso(a)
short circuit il corto circuito
short cut la scorciatoia
shortage la carenza
shorts i calzoncini corti
short-sighted miope
shoulder la spalla
to shout gridare
show *(at theatre)* lo spettacolo
to show mostrare
shower la doccia
  (rain) il rovescio
  to take a shower fare la doccia
shower cap la cuffia da doccia
shower gel il bagnoschiuma
to shrink restringersi
shrub l'arbusto *(m)*
shut *(closed)* chiuso(a)
shutter l'imposta *(f)*
shuttle service la navetta
Sicily la Sicilia
sick *(ill)* malato(a)
  (nauseous) nauseato(a)
  I feel sick mi sento male
side il lato
side dish il contorno
sidelight la luce di posizione
sidewalk il marciapiede
sieve il setaccio

sightseeing tour il giro turistico
sign il segno
  (on road) il segnale
to sign firmare
signature la firma
signpost il segnale
silk la seta
silver l'argento *(m)*
similar to simile a
since *(time)* da
to sing cantare
single *(unmarried)* non sposato(a)
  (not double) singolo(a)
  (ticket) di (sola) andata
single bed il letto a una piazza
single room la camera singola
sink il lavandino
sir Signore
sister la sorella
sister-in-law la cognata
to sit sedersi
  please, sit down prego, si accomodi
size *(of clothes)* la taglia
  (of shoes) il numero
to skate *(on ice)* pattinare sul ghiaccio
skateboard lo skateboard
skates *(ice)* i pattini da ghiaccio
  (roller) i pattini a rotelle
to ski sciare
ski lo sci
  skis gli sci
ski boots gli scarponi da sci
ski instructor il/la maestro(a) di sci
ski jump il trampolino
ski lift lo ski-lift
ski pass lo skipass
ski pole/stick la racchetta da sci
ski run la pista
ski suit la tuta da sci
skin la pelle
skirt la gonna
sky il cielo
sledge la slitta
to sleep dormire
to sleep in dormire fino a tardi
sleeper *(on train)* la cuccetta
sleeping bag il sacco a pelo
sleeping car il vagone letto
sleeping pill il sonnifero
slice *(piece of)* la fetta
sliced bread il pancarrè

slide (*photo*) la diapositiva
to slip scivolare
slippers le pantofole
slow lento(a)
to slow down rallentare
slowly lentamente
small piccolo(a)
  smaller (than) più piccolo (di)
smell l'odore (m)
  bad smell il puzzo
  nice smell il profumo
to smell (*bad*) puzzare
  to smell of avere odore di
smile il sorriso
to smile sorridere
smoke il fumo
to smoke fumare
  I don't smoke non fumo
  can I smoke? posso fumare?
smoke alarm l'allarme antincendio (m)
smoked (*food*) affumicato(a)
smokers (*sign*) fumatori
smooth liscio(a)
snack lo spuntino
  to have a snack fare lo spuntino
snake il serpente
  (*grass*) la biscia
snake bite il morso di vipera
to sneeze starnutire
snorkel il boccaglio
snow la neve
to snow: *it's snowing* nevica
snowboard lo snowboard
snowboarding: *to go snowboarding* andare a fare lo snowboard
snow chains le catene da neve
snow tyres i pneumatici da neve
snow plough lo spazzaneve
snowed up isolato(a) a causa della neve
soap il sapone
soap powder il detersivo in polvere
sober sobrio(a)
socket (*electric*) la presa
socks i calzini
soda water l'acqua di selz (f)
sofa il divano
sofa bed il divano letto
soft soffice ; morbido(a)
soft drink la bibita
software lo software

soldier il soldato
sole (*of foot, shoe*) la suola
soluble solubile
some di (del/della)
  (*a few*) alcuni/alcune
someone qualcuno
something qualcosa
sometimes qualche volta
son il figlio
son-in-law il genero
song la canzone
soon presto
  as soon as possible il più presto possibile
sore throat il mal di gola
sorry: *I'm sorry!* mi scusi!
sort il tipo
  what sort? che tipo?
soup la minestra
sour aspro(a) ; agro(a)
soured cream la panna acida
south il sud
souvenir il souvenir
spa la stazione termale
space lo spazio
  (*parking*) il posteggio
spade il badile
Spain la Spagna
Spanish spagnolo(a)
spanner la chiave inglese
spare parts i pezzi di ricambio
spare room la stanza degli ospiti
spare tyre la gomma di scorta
spare wheel la ruota di scorta
sparkling frizzante
  sparkling water l'acqua gassata
  sparkling wine il vino frizzante
spark plugs le candele
to speak parlare
  do you speak English? parla inglese?
special speciale
specialist lo/la specialista
speciality la specialità
speech il discorso
speed la velocità
speedboat il motoscafo
speed limit il limite di velocità
  to exceed the speed limit superare il limite di velocità
speeding l'eccesso di velocità (m)
speeding ticket la multa per eccesso di velocità
speedometer il tachimetro
to spell scrivere
  how is it spelt? come si scrive?

143

to **spend** spendere
spice le spezie
spicy piccante
spider il ragno
to **spill** rovesciare
spin-dryer la centrifuga
spine la spina dorsale
spirits (alcohol) i liquori
splinter la scheggia
spoke (of wheel) il raggio
sponge la spugna
spoon il cucchiaio
sport lo sport
sports centre il centro sportivo
sports shop il negozio di articoli sportivi
spot (stain) la macchia
   (place) il posto
sprain la slogatura
spring (season) la primavera
   (metal) la molla
square (in town) la piazza
squash (game) lo squash
to **squeeze** premere ; stringere
squid il calamaro
stadium lo stadio
staff il personale
stage (theatre) il palcoscenico
stain la macchia
stained glass il vetro colorato
stain remover lo smacchiatore
stairs le scale
stale (bread) raffermo(a)
stalls (in theatre) la platea
stamp il francobollo
to **stand** stare in piedi
star la stella
starfish la stella marina
to **start** cominciare
starter (in meal) l'antipasto (m)
   (in car) il motorino d'avviamento
station la stazione
stationer's la cartoleria
statue la statua
stay il soggiorno
   enjoy your stay! buona permanenza!
to **stay** (remain) rimanere
   I'm staying at the Grand Hotel sono
   al Grand Hotel
steak la bistecca
to **steal** rubare
steamed al vapore
to **steam** cuocere a vapore
steel l'acciaio (m)
steep: *is it steep?* è in salita?

steeple il campanile
steering wheel il volante
step (stair) il gradino
stepdaughter la figliastra
stepfather il patrigno
stepmother la matrigna
stepson il figliastro
stereo lo stereo
sterling la sterlina
steward lo steward
stewardess la hostess
to **stick** (with glue) incollare
   (door) incepparsi
sticking plaster il cerotto
still (motionless) fermo(a)
   (water) naturale
   (yet) ancora
sting la puntura
to **sting** pungere
stitches i punti
stockings le calze
stolen rubato(a)
stomach lo stomaco ; la pancia
stomachache il mal di pancia
stone la pietra
to **stop** (come to a halt) fermarsi
   (stop doing something) smettere
stop sign lo stop
store (shop) il negozio
storey il piano
storm la tempesta ; il temporale
story il racconto
straightaway subito
straight on diritto
strange strano(a)
straw (for drinking) la cannuccia
strawberries le fragole
stream il ruscello
street la strada
street map la piantina
strength (of person) la forza
   (of wine) la gradazione alcolica
stress lo stress
strike (of workers) lo sciopero
string lo spago
striped a strisce
stroke (medical) l'ictus (m)
   to have a stroke avere un ictus
strong forte
   strong coffee il caffè ristretto
   strong tea il tè forte

stuck bloccato(a)
student lo studente/la studentessa
student discount lo sconto per studenti
stuffed farcito(a)
stung punto(a)
stupid stupido(a)
subscription l'abbonamento (m)
subtitles i sottotitoli
subway (train) la metropolitana (passage) il sottopassaggio
suddenly all'improvviso
suede il camoscio
sugar lo zucchero
sugar-free senza zucchero
to suggest proporre
suit (man's) l'abito (m) (woman's) il tailleur
suitcase la valigia
sum (of money) la somma
summer l'estate (f)
summer holidays le vacanze estive
summit il vertice
sun il sole
to sunbathe prendere il sole
sunblock la protezione solare totale
sunburn la scottatura solare
Sunday la domenica
sunglasses gli occhiali da sole
sunny: it's sunny c'è il sole
sunrise l'alba (f)
sunroof (car) il tettuccio apribile
sunscreen la crema solare protettiva
sunset il tramonto
sunshade l'ombrellone (m)
sunstroke l'insolazione (f)
suntan l'abbronzatura (f)
suntan lotion la crema abbronzante
supermarket il supermercato
supper (dinner) la cena
supplement il supplemento
to supply fornire
sure sicuro(a) ; certo(a) I'm sure sono sicuro(a)
to surf fare il surf to surf the net navigare in internet
surfboard la tavola da surf
surgery (surgical treatment) la chirurgia
surname il cognome my surname is... di cognome mi chiamo...

surprise la sorpresa
suspension (in car) la sospensione
to survive sopravvivere
to swallow inghiottire
to swear (bad language) dire le parolacce
to sweat sudare
sweater il maglione
sweatshirt la felpa
sweet (not savoury) dolce
sweetener il dolcificante
sweets le caramelle
to swell gonfiare
to swim nuotare
swimming pool la piscina
swimsuit il costume da bagno
swing (for children) l'altalena (f)
Swiss svizzero(a)
switch l'interruttore (m)
to switch off spegnere
to switch on accendere
Switzerland la Svizzera
swollen gonfio(a)
synagogue la sinagoga
syringe la siringa

T

table la tavola
tablecloth la tovaglia
tablet (pill) la pastiglia
table tennis il ping pong
table wine il vino da tavola
tailor il sarto
to take (carry) portare (to grab, seize) prendere (to take someone to) portare a how long does it take? quanto tempo ci vuole?
take-away (food) da asporto
to take off decollare
to take out (of bag) tirar fuori
talc il borotalco
to talk parlare
tall alto(a)
tampons gli assorbenti interni
tangerine il mandarino
tank la cisterna (car) il serbatoio (fish) l'acquario (m)
tap il rubinetto
tap water l'acqua del rubinetto (f)
tape il nastro
tape measure il metro a nastro

145

tape recorder il registratore
target lo scopo
tart la crostata
taste il sapore
to taste assaggiare ; provare
  can I taste some? ne posso
  assaggiare un pò?
tax la tassa ; l'imposta *(f)*
taxi il taxi
taxi driver il/la tassista
taxi rank il posteggio dei taxi
tea il tè
  herbal tea la tisana
  fruit tea il tè alla frutta
  lemon tea il tè al limone
  tea with milk il tè al latte
tea bag la bustina di tè
tea pot la teiera
to teach insegnare
teacher l'insegnante *(m/f)*
team la squadra
tear *(in material)* lo strappo
teaspoon il cucchiaino
teat *(on bottle)* la tettarella
tea towel lo strofinaccio per i piatti
teenager il/la teenager
teeth i denti
telegram il telegramma
telephone il telefono
to telephone telefonare
telephone box la cabina telefonica
telephone call la telefonata
telephone card la scheda telefonica
telephone directory l'elenco
  telefonico *(m)*
telephone number il numero di
  telefono
television la televisione
to tell dire
temperature la temperatura
  to have a temperature avere la febbre
temporary provvisorio(a)
tenant l'inquilino(a)
tendon il tendine
tennis il tennis
tennis ball la pallina da tennis
tennis court il campo da tennis
tennis racket la racchetta da tennis
tent la tenda
tent peg il picchetto
terminal *(airport)* il terminal
terrace la terrazza
terracotta la terracotta
to test *(try out)* provare

testicles i testicoli
tetanus injection l'antitetanica *(f)*
than di
to thank ringraziare
thank you grazie
  thanks very much molte grazie
that quel/quella/quello
  that one quello là
the *(sing)* il/lo/la
  (plural) i/gli/le
theatre il teatro
theft il furto
their il/la loro
them loro ; li ; le
there *(over there)* lì
there is/there are c'è/ci sono
thermometer il termometro
these questi/queste
  these ones questi qui
they loro ; essi/esse
thick spesso(a)
thief il/la ladro(a)
thigh la coscia
thin sottile
  (person) magro(a)
thing la cosa
  my things la mia roba
to think pensare
thirsty: to be thirsty avere sete
this questo/questa
  this one questo(a)
those quei/quelle/quegli
  those ones quelli(e)
thread il filo
throat la gola
throat lozenges le pastiglie per la gola
through attraverso
to throw away buttare via
thumb il pollice
thunder il tuono
thunderstorm il temporale
Thursday il giovedì
thyme il timo
ticket *(bus, train, etc)* il biglietto
  (entry fee) il biglietto d'ingresso
  a single ticket un biglietto di (sola)
  andata
  a return ticket un biglietto di andata
  e ritorno
  tourist ticket il biglietto turistico
  book of tickets il blocchetto di
  biglietti

ticket inspector il controllore
ticket office la biglietteria
tidy ordinato(a)
to tidy up fare ordine
tie la cravatta
tight stretto(a)
tights i collant ; la calzamaglia
tile *(floor)* la piastrella
till *(cash desk)* la cassa
till *(until)* fino a
  till 2 o'clock fino alle due
time il tempo
  (of day) l'ora *(f)*
  this time questa volta
  what time is it? che ore sono?
  do you have the time? ha l'ora?
timetable l'orario *(m)*
tin *(can)* la scatola ; la lattina
tinfoil la carta stagnola
tin-opener l'apriscatole *(m)*
tip *(to waiter, etc)* la mancia
to tip *(waiter, etc)* dare la mancia
tired stanco(a)
tissues i fazzoletti di carta
to a
  to London a Londra
  to the airport all'aeroporto
toadstool il fungo velenoso
toast *(to eat)* il pane tostato
  (raising glass) il brindisi
tobacco il tabacco
tobacconist's il tabaccaio
today oggi
toe il dito del piede
together insieme
toilet la toilette
  toilet for disabled la toilette per i disabili
toilet brush lo spazzolino del gabinetto
toilet paper la carta igienica
toiletries gli articoli per l'igiene
token *(for phone, etc)* il gettone
toll *(motorway)* il pedaggio
tomato il pomodoro
  tinned tomatoes i pelati
tomato juice il succo di pomodoro
tomato purée il concentrato di pomodoro
tomato sauce la salsa di pomodoro
tomorrow domani
  tomorrow morning domani mattina
  tomorrow afternoon domani pomeriggio
  tomorrow evening domani sera
tongue la lingua
tonic water l'acqua tonica *(f)*
tonight stasera
tonsilitis la tonsillite
too *(also)* anche
  too big troppo grande
  too small troppo piccolo(a)
  too hot troppo caldo(a)
  too noisy troppo rumoroso(a)
tool l'attrezzo *(m)*
toolkit gli attrezzi
tooth il dente
toothache il mal di denti
toothbrush lo spazzolino da denti
toothpaste il dentifricio
toothpick lo stuzzicadenti
top: *the top floor* l'ultimo piano *(m)*
top la cima
  (clothing) la maglietta
  on top of sopra di
topless topless
torch *(flashlight)* la pila
torn strappato(a)
total il totale
to touch toccare
tough *(meat)* duro(a)
tour il giro
  guided tour la visita guidata
tour guide la guida turistica *(m/f)*
tour operator l'operatore turistico *(m)*
tourist il/la turista
tourist information le informazioni turistiche
tourist office l'ufficio turistico *(m)*
tourist route l'itinerario turistico *(m)*
tourist ticket il biglietto turistico
to tow rimorchiare
towbar la barra di rimorchio
tow rope il cavo da rimorchio
towel l'asciugamano *(m)*
tower la torre
town la città
town centre il centro città
town hall il municipio
town plan la piantina
toxic tossico(a)
toy il giocattolo
toy shop il negozio di giocattoli
tracksuit la tuta sportiva
traditional tradizionale
traffic il traffico

traffic jam l'ingorgo *(m)*
traffic lights il semaforo
traffic warden il vigile
trailer il rimorchio
train il treno
  the next train il prossimo treno
  the first train il primo treno
  the last train l'ultimo treno
trainers le scarpe da ginnastica
tram il tram
tranquillizer il tranquillante
to transfer trasferire
to translate tradurre
translation la traduzione
to travel viaggiare
travel agent's l'agenzia di viaggi *(f)*
travel documents i documenti di viaggio
travel guide la guida
travel insurance l'assicurazione di viaggio *(f)*
travel sickness *(sea)* il mal di mare
  (air) il mal d'aria
  (car) il mal d'auto
traveller's cheques i traveller's (cheque)
tray il vassoio
tree l'albero *(m)*
trip la gita ; il viaggio
trolley il carrello
trouble i problemi
  to be in trouble avere qualche problema
trousers i pantaloni
truck il camion
true vero(a)
trunk *(luggage)* il baule
trunks *(swimming)* i calzoncini da bagno
to try provare
to try on *(clothes, shoes)* provare
t-shirt la maglietta
Tuesday il martedì
tumble dryer l'asciugatrice *(f)*
tunnel la galleria
Turin Torino
to turn *(handle, wheel)* girare
  to turn around girarsi
to turn off *(light, etc)* spegnere
  (tap) chiudere
to turn on *(light, etc)* accendere
  (tap) aprire
turquoise *(colour)* turchese
tweezers le pinzette
twice due volte ; il doppio
twin beds i letti gemelli
twins i gemelli

eng–italian t/u

to type battere a macchina
typical tipico(a)
tyre la gomma ; il pneumatico
tyre pressure la pressione delle gomme

U

ugly brutto(a)
ulcer *(stomach)* l'ulcera *(f)*
  (mouth) l'afta *(f)*
umbrella l'ombrello *(m)*
  (sunshade) l'ombrellone *(m)*
uncle lo zio
uncomfortable scomodo(a)
unconscious svenuto(a)
under sotto
undercooked poco cotto(a)
underground *(metro)* la metropolitana
underpants le mutande
underpass il sottopassaggio
to understand capire
  I don't understand non capisco
  do you understand? capisce?
underwear la biancheria intima
to undress spogliarsi
unemployed disoccupato(a)
to unfasten slacciare
United Kingdom il Regno Unito
United States gli Stati Uniti
university l'università *(f)*
unleaded petrol la benzina senza piombo ; la benzina verde
unlikely improbabile
to unlock aprire
to unpack disfare la valigia
unpleasant sgradevole
to unplug staccare
to unscrew svitare
until fino a
unusual raro(a)
up: *to get up* alzarsi
upside down sottosopra
upstairs di sopra
urgent urgente
urine l'orina *(f)*
us ci ; noi
to use usare
useful utile
usual solito(a)
usually di solito
U-turn l'inversione a U *(f)*

V

vacancy *(in hotel)* la camera libera
vacant libero(a)
vacation la vacanza
vaccination la vaccinazione
vacuum cleaner l'aspirapolvere *(m)*
vagina la vagina
valid valido(a)
valley la valle
valuable di valore
valuables gli oggetti di valori
value il valore
valve la valvola
van il furgone
vase il vaso
VAT l'IVA *(f)*
vegan vegetaliano(a)
  I'm vegan sono vegetaliano(a)
vegetables le verdure
vegetarian vegetariano(a)
  I'm vegetarian sono vegetariano(a)
vehicle il veicolo
vein la vena
Velcro® il velcro®
vending machine il distributore
  automatico
venereal disease la malattia venerea
Venice Venezia
ventilator il ventilatore
very molto
vest la canottiera
vet il/la veterinario(a)
via passando per
to video *(from TV)* registrare su
  videocassetta
video il video
video camera la videocamera
video cassette/tape la videocassetta
video game il videogioco
video recorder il videoregistratore
view la vista
villa la villa
village il paese
vinegar l'aceto *(m)*
vineyard la vigna
viper la vipera
virus il virus
visa il visto
visit la visita

to visit visitare
visiting hours l'orario delle visite *(m)*
visitor il visitatore/la visitatrice
vitamin la vitamina
voice la voce
volcano il vulcano
volleyball la pallavolo
voltage il voltaggio
to vomit vomitare
voucher il buono

W

wage il salario
waist la vita
waistcoat il gilè
to wait (for) aspettare
waiter/waitress il cameriere/la
  cameriera
waiting room la sala d'aspetto
to wake up svegliare
Wales il Galles
walk la passeggiata
to walk andare a piedi
walking boots gli scarponcini
walking stick il bastone
Walkman® il walkman®
wall il muro ; la parete
wallet il portafoglio
to want volere
  I want... voglio...
  we want... vogliamo...
war la guerra
ward *(hospital)* il reparto
wardrobe l'armadio *(m)*
warm caldo(a)
  it's warm fa caldo
to warm up *(milk, etc)* riscaldare
warning triangle il triangolo
  d'emergenza
to wash lavare
  (to wash oneself) lavarsi
wash and blow dry lo shampoo e
  messa in piega
washbasin il lavandino
washing machine la lavatrice
washing powder il detersivo in
  polvere
washing-up bowl la bacinella
washing-up liquid il detersivo per i
  piatti
wasp la vespa
wasp sting la puntura di vespa
waste bin il bidone della spazzatura

149 **watch** l'orologio *(m)*
  to watch guardare
  watchstrap il cinturino dell'orologio
  water l'acqua *(f)*
    bottled water l'acqua in bottiglia *(f)*
    drinking water l'acqua potabile
    mineral water l'acqua minerale
    sparkling water l'acqua gassata
    still water l'acqua naturale
  water heater lo scaldabagno
  watermelon l'anguria *(f)*
  waterproof impermeabile
  to water-ski fare lo sci nautico
  watersports gli sport acquatici
  waterwings i braccioli salvagente
  waves *(on sea)* le onde
  waxing *(hair removal)* la ceretta
  way in l'entrata *(f)* ; l'ingresso *(m)*
  way out l'uscita *(f)*
  we noi
  weak *(person)* debole
    (tea, coffee, etc) leggero(a)
  to wear portare
  weather il tempo
  weather forecast le previsioni del
    tempo
  website il sito web
  wedding il matrimonio
  wedding anniversary l'anniversario di
    matrimonio *(m)*
  wedding present il regalo di
    matrimonio
  wedding ring la fede
  Wednesday mercoledì
  week la settimana
    last week la settimana scorsa
    next week la prossima settimana
    per week alla settimana
    this week questa settimana
    during the week durante la settimana
  weekday il giorno feriale
  weekend il fine settimana
    next weekend il prossimo fine
    settimana
    this weekend questo fine settimana
  weekly settimanale
    weekly ticket l'abbonamento
    settimanale *(m)*
  to weigh pesare
  weight il peso
  welcome benvenuto
  well bene
  well *(for water)* il pozzo
  well-done *(steak)* ben cotto(a)
  wellington boots gli stivale di gomma
  Welsh gallese

eng-italian   w

west ovest
wet bagnato(a)
wetsuit la muta
what cosa
  what is it? cos'è?
wheat il grano
wheel la ruota
wheelchair la sedia a rotelle
wheel clamp il ceppo bloccaruote
when quando
where dove
which qual/quale
while mentre
  in a while fra poco
whipped cream la panna montata
whisky l'whisky *(m)*
white bianco(a)
who chi
whole tutto
wholemeal bread il pane integrale
whose: *whose is it?* di chi è?
why perché
wide largo(a) ; ampio(a)
widow la vedova
widower il vedovo
width la larghezza
wife la moglie
wig la parrucca
to win vincere
wind il vento
windbreak *(camping)* il frangivento
windmill il mulino a vento
window la finestra
  (shop) la vetrina
  (car) il finestrino
windscreen il parabrezza
windscreen wiper il tergicristallo
to windsurf fare il windsurf
windy: *it's windy* c'è vento
wine il vino
  red wine il vino rosso
  white wine il vino bianco
  dry wine il vino secco
  sweet wine il vino dolce
  rosé wine il vino rosato
  sparkling wine il vino frizzante
  house wine il vino della casa
wine list la lista dei vini
wing *(of bird)* l'ala *(f)*
  (of car) la fiancata
wing mirror lo specchietto laterale
winter l'inverno *(m)*

w/x/y/z eng–italian

wire il filo
with con
  with ice con ghiaccio
  with milk con latte
  with sugar con zucchero
without senza
  without ice senza ghiaccio
  without milk senza latte
  without sugar senza zucchero
witness il/la testimone
woman la donna
wonderful meraviglioso(a)
wood *(material)* il legno
  (forest) il bosco
wooden di legno
wool la lana
word la parola
work il lavoro
to work *(person)* lavorare
  (machine, car, etc) funzionare
  it doesn't work non funziona
work permit il premesso di lavoro
world il mondo
worried preoccupato(a)
worse peggio
worth *(value)* il valore
  it's worth £5 vale cinque sterline
to wrap up *(parcel)* incartare
wrapping paper la carta di regalo
wrinkles le rughe
wrist il polso
to write scrivere
  please write it down lo scriva per favore
writing paper la carta da lettere
wrong sbagliato(a)
  what's wrong? cosa c'è?
wrought iron il ferro battuto

X

x-ray la radiografia
to x-ray radiografare

Y

yacht lo yacht
year l'anno *(m)*
  this year quest'anno
  next year l'anno prossimo
  last year l'anno scorso
yearly *(every year)* annualmente

yellow giallo(a)
Yellow Pages le pagine gialle®
yes sì
yesterday ieri
yet: *not yet* non ancora
yoghurt lo yogurt
  plain yoghurt lo yogurt naturale
yolk il tuorlo
you lei ; tu ; voi
young giovane
your il/la suo(a) ; il/la tuo(a) ; il/la vostro(a)
  your passport il suo passaporto
  your room la sua camera
youth hostel l'ostello della gioventù *(m)*

Z

zebra crossing le strisce pedonali
zero lo zero
zip la cerniera
zone la zona
zoo lo zoo
zoom lens lo zoom

a at ; in

abbaglianti *mpl* full-beam headlights

abbiamo... we have...
  non abbiamo... we don't have...

abbigliamento *m* clothes

abbonamento *m* subscription ; season ticket

abbronzatura *f* suntan

abito *m* dress ; man's suit

aborto *m* abortion
  aborto spontaneo miscarriage

abuso *m* misuse

a.C. B.C.

accamparsi to camp

accanto (a) beside ; next (to)

acceleratore *m* accelerator

accendere to turn on ; to light
  accendere i fari switch on your headlights

accendino *m* cigarette lighter

accensione *f* ignition

accento *m* accent *(pronunciation)*

acceso(a) on *(light, engine)*

accesso *m* access
  divieto di accesso no access

accettazione *f* reception
  accettazione bagagli check-in

accomodarsi to make oneself comfortable
  si accomodi do take a seat

accompagnare to accompany

accordo *m* agreement

acetone *m* nail polish remover

ACI *m* = Automobile Association

acqua *f* water
  acqua calda hot water
  acqua corrente running water
  acqua distillata distilled water
  acqua gassata sparkling water
  acqua minerale mineral water
  acqua naturale still water
  acqua potabile drinking water

acquisto *m* purchase

addetto(a) authorized

adesso now

adulto(a) adult

aereo *m* plane ; aircraft

aeroplano *m* airplane

aeroporto *m* airport

affari *mpl* business
  per affari on business

affittare to rent ; to let
  affitasi for rent

affitto *m* lease ; rent

affogare to drown

agenda *f* diary

agenzia *f* agency
  agenzia di viaggi travel agent
  agenzia immobiliare estate agent

aggredire to attack

aglio *m* garlic

ago *m* needle
  ago ipodermico hypodermic needle

agosto *m* August

AIDS *m* AIDS

aiutare to help

aiuto! help!

alba *f* dawn

albergo *m* hotel

albero *m* tree ; mast

albicocca *f* apricot

alcolici *mpl* alcoholic drinks

alcolico(a) alcoholic

alcool *m* alcohol

alcuni(e) some ; a few

alcuno(a) any ; some

alimentari *mpl* groceries

allacciare to fasten *(seatbelt, etc)*

allarme *m* alarm
  allarme antincendio fire alarm

allergia *f* allergy

allergico(a) a allergic to

alloggio *m* accommodation

alluvione *f* flood

Alpi *fpl* Alps

alpinismo *m* climbing

alt stop

altezza *f* height

alto(a) high ; tall
  alta stagione high season
  alta marea high tide

altro(a) other
  altri passaporti other passports

alzarsi to get up ; to stand up

amabile sweet *(wine)*

amare to love *(person)*

amarena *f* bitter cherry

amaro(a) bitter *(taste)*

ambasciata *f* embassy

ambiente *m* environment

ambulanza *f* ambulance

ambulatorio *m* surgery ; out-patients

America *f* America

americano(a) American

amico(a) *m/f* friend

ammalato(a) ill

amministratore delegato *m* managing director

ammontare *m* total amount

ammortizzatore *m* shock absorber

amo *m* bait

amore *m* love

analasi del sangue *f* blood test

analcolico *m* soft drink

analcolico(a) non-alcoholic

analgesico *m* painkiller

ananas *m* pineapple

anatra *f* duck

anca *f* hip

anche too ; also ; even

ancora still ; yet ; again
  ancora un po'? a little more?
  non ancora not yet

ancora *f* anchor

andare to go
  andare a cavallo to ride a horse
  andare a piedi to go on foot
  andare bene to fit *(clothes)*
  andare in macchina to go by car

andata: *andata e ritorno* return *(ticket)*
  di (sola) andata single *(ticket)*

andiamo! let's go!
  andiamo a... we're going to...

anestetico *m* anaesthetic

angina pectoris *f* angina

anguria *f* watermelon

anice *m* aniseed

animale *m* animal
  animale domestico pet

annata *f* vintage ; year
  vino d'annata vintage wine

anniversario *m* anniversary

anno *m* year
  buon anno! happy New Year!

annuale annual

annullamento *m* cancellation

annullare to cancel

annuncio *m* announcement ; advert

antibiotico *m* antibiotic

anticipo *m* advance *(loan)*
  in anticipo in advance ; early

anticoncezionale *m* contraceptive

antifurto *m* burglar alarm

antigelo *m* antifreeze ; de-icer

antipasto *m* starter ; hors d'œuvre

antisettico *m* antiseptic

antistaminico *m* anihistamine

anziano(a) *m/f* senior citizen

ape *f* bee

aperitivo *m* apéritif

aperto(a) open
  all'aperto open-air

appartamento *m* flat ; apartment

appendicite *f* appendicitis

appuntamento *m* appointment ; date

apribottiglie *m* bottle opener

aprile *m* April

aprire to open ; to turn on *(tap)*

apriscatole *m* tin-opener

arachide *f* peanut

arancia *f* orange

aranciata *f* orange squash

arancione orange *(colour)*

area *f* area
  area di servizio service area

argento *m* silver

aria condizionata *f* air-conditioning

armadio *m* cupboard ; wardrobe

arrabbiato(a) angry

arredato(a) furnished

arrestare to arrest

arrivare to arrive

arrivederci goodbye

arrivo *m* arrival
  arrivi nazionali domestic arrivals
  arrivi internazionali international arrivals

arrosto *m* roast

arte *f* art ; craft

articolo *m* article
  articoli da dichiarare goods to declare
  articoli da regalo gifts

artigiano(a) *m/f* craftsperson

artista *m/f* artist

artrite *f* arthritis

ascensore *m* lift ; elevator

ascesso *m* abscess

asciugamano *m* towel

asciugare to dry

asciugatrice *f* tumble dryer

ascoltare to listen (to)

asma *f* asthma

aspettare to wait (for) ; to expect

aspirapolvere *m* vacuum cleaner

155

aspirina f aspirin
assaggiare to taste
asse m axle (car)
  asse da stiro ironing board
assegno m cheque
assicurato(a) insured
assicurazione f insurance
assistente m/f assistant
assistenza f assistance ; aid
associazione f society
assorbenti mpl sanitary towels
  assorbenti interni tampons
ATM public transport service
attaccare to attach ; to attack ; to fasten
attacco m fit (seizure)
  attacco cardiaco heart attack
attendere to wait for
attento(a) careful
attenzione f caution
  fare attenzione to be careful
atterraggio m landing (of plane)
atterrare to land (plane)
attestare to declare
attore m actor
attracco m mooring ; berth
attraente attractive
attraversare to cross
attraverso through
attrazione f attraction
attrezzatura f equipment
attrezzo m tool
attrice f actress
auguri! happy birthday! ; best wishes!
aumentare to increase
Australia f Australia
australiano(a) Australian
austriaco(a) Austrian
autentico(a) genuine
autista m/f driver
auto f car
autobus m bus
autofficina f garage (for repairs)
autoforniture fpl car parts and accessories
autonoleggio m car hire
autore m author
autorimessa f garage
autorizzazione f authorization
autostop m hitchhiking
autostrada f motorway
autunno m autumn

avanti in front ; forward(s)
  avanti! come in!
avere to have
  avere bisogno di to need
  avere fame to be hungry
  avere sete to be thirsty
avvertire to warn
avvisare to inform ; to warn
avviso m notice ; advertisement
azienda f business ; firm
  azienda di soggiorno local tourist board
azzardo m risk ; hazard
azzurro(a) light blue

B

babbo m daddy
  Babbo Natale Father Christmas
baciare to kiss
bacinella f washing-up bowl
bacio m kiss
baci! love and kisses (in letter)
baffi mpl moustache
bagagli mpl luggage
bagagliaio m boot (of car)
bagaglio m luggage
  bagaglio a mano hand luggage
bagnarsi to bathe ; to get wet
bagnino m lifeguard
bagno m bath ; bathroom
balcone m balcony
ballare to dance
balletto m ballet
ballo m dance
balneazione f bathing
  divieto di balneazione no swimming
balsamo m hair conditioner
bambino(a) m/f child ; baby
bambini mpl children
  per bambini for children
bambola f doll
banana f banana
banca f bank
bancarella f stall ; stand
banchina f platform ; quay
banco m counter ; desk
  banco informazioni enquiry desk
Bancomat® m cash dispenser
banconota f banknote

bandiera f flag
bar m bar ; café
barattolo m tin ; jar
barba f beard
barbiere m barber
barca f boat
barista m/f barman/barmaid
basso(a) low ; short
  bassa marea low tide
basta that's enough
battello m boat
batteria f battery (car)
  batteria scarica flat battery
baule m trunk (luggage)
bavaglino m bib
bello(a) beautiful ; fine ; lovely
benda f bandage
bene well ; all right ; OK
benvenuto welcome
benzina f petrol
  fare benzina to get petrol
bere to drink
bevanda f drink
biancheria f linen (for beds, table)
  biancheria intima underwear
bianco(a) white ; blank
  lasciate in bianco leave blank
biberon m baby's bottle
bibita f soft drink
  bibite soft drinks
bicchiere m glass (for drinking)
bici f bike (pushbike)
bicicletta f bicycle
bidet m bidet
bidone m bin ; dustbin ; can
biglietteria f ticket office
biglietto m ticket ; note ; card
  biglietto d'auguri greetings card
  biglietto da visita business card
bin. abbreviation of **binario**
binario m platform
biologico(a) organic
biondo(a) blond (person)
biro f biro
birra f beer
  birra alla spina draught beer
  birra bionda lager
  birra chiara lager
birreria f bar ; pub
biscotto m biscuit
bisogno m need

avere bisogno di to need
bistecca f steak
bloccare to block
  bloccare un assegno to stop a cheque
blocchetto di biglietti m book of tickets
blocco m block ; notepad
blu blue
blue jeans mpl jeans
boa f buoy
bocca f mouth
boccaglio m snorkel
bocce fpl bowls (game)
bolletta f bill
bollire to boil
bollitore m kettle
bomba f bomb
bombola del gas f gas cylinder
bombolone m doughnut
borotalco m talc
borsa f bag ; handbag ; briefcase
  borsa della spazzatura bin liner
  borsa termica cool-box (for picnic)
borseggiatore m pickpocket
borsellino m purse
bosco m wood ; forest
bottega f shop
botteghino m box office
bottiglia f bottle
bottone m button
boxer mpl boxer shorts
braccialetto m bracelet
braccio m arm
braccioli mpl armbands (swimming)
braciola f steak ; chop
brindisi m toast (raising glass)
brioche f croissant
britannico(a) f British
bronchite f bronchitis
bruciare to burn
bruciore di stomaco m heartburn
brutto(a) bad (weather, news) ; ugly
buca delle lettere f postbox
bucato m washing ; laundry
  bucato in lavatrice machine wash
  bucato a mano hand washing
buco m hole ; leak
buono(a) good
  buon appetito! enjoy your meal!
  buon compleanno! happy birthday!
  buon giorno good morning/ afternoon
  buona notte good night

buona sera good afternoon/ evening
a buon mercato cheap
buono *m* voucher ; coupon ; token
burattino *m* puppet
burrasca *f* storm
burro *m* butter
burro di cacao *m* lip salve
bussare to knock *(on door)*
busta *f* envelope
bustina di tè *f* tea bag
buttare via to throw away

C

cabina *f* beach hut ; cabin
cabina telefonica phonebox
cacciavite *m* screwdriver
cadere to fall
caffè *m* coffee *(espresso)*
caffè corretto espresso with spirit
such as grappa
caffè macchiato espresso with a
little warm milk
caffè solubile instant coffee
caffellatte milky coffee
caffettiera *f* espresso-maker
calamita *f* magnet
calciatore *m* football player
calcio *m* football ; kick
calcolatrice *f* calculator
caldo(a) hot
calendario *m* calendar
calle *f* street *(in Venice dialect)*
callo *m* corn *(on foot)*
calmante *m* painkiller
calmo(a) calm
calpestare to tread on
calvo(a) bald
calza *f* stocking ; sock
calzamaglia *f* tights
calzature *fpl* shoeshop
calze *fpl* stockings
calzini *mpl* socks
calzolaio *m* shoe mender's
calzoleria *f* shoeshop
calzoncini corti *mpl* shorts
calzoncini da bagno swimming trunks
cambiamento *m* change
cambiare to change
cambiare autobus/treno to change
bus/train
cambiare soldi to change money
cambiarsi to change one's clothes

cambio *m* exchange ; gear
camera *f* room *(in house, hotel)*
camera da letto bedroom
camera doppia double room
camera libera vacancy *(in hotel)*
camera per famiglia family room
camera singola single room
camere vacancies
cameriera *f* chambermaid
cameriere *m* waiter
camiceria *f* shirt shop
camicetta *f* blouse
camicia *f* shirt
camicia da notte nightdress
camion *m* lorry
camminare to walk
camoscio *m* suede
campagna *f* countryside ; campaign
campanello *m* bell
campeggiare to camp
campeggio *m* camping ; campsite
campeggio libero free campsite
camping gas *m* camping gas
campione *m* sample ; champion
campo *m* field ; court
campo da tennis tennis court
campo di calcio football pitch
campo di golf golf course
campo sportivo sports ground
camposanto *m* cemetery
Canada *m* Canada
canadese Canadian
canale *m* canal ; channel
cancellare to erase ; to cancel
cancellazione *f* cancellation
cancro *m* cancer
candeggina *f* bleach
candela *f* candle ; spark plug
candida *f* thrush *(candida)*
cane *m* dog
canile *m* kennel
canna da pesca *f* fishing rod
cannuccia *f* straw *(for drinking)*
canoa *f* canoe
canottaggio *m* rowing
canottiera *f* vest
canotto *m* dinghy *(rubber)*
cantante *m/f* singer
cantare to sing
cantiere *m* building site

cantina f cellar ; wine cellar
canzone f song
capelli mpl hair
capire to understand
  capisce? do you understand?
  non capisco I don't understand
capitale f capital (city)
capitolo m chapter
capo m head ; leader ; boss
Capodanno m New Year's day
capogruppo m group leader
capolavoro m masterpiece
capolinea m terminus
capoluogo m county town
capotreno m guard (on train)
cappella f chapel
cappello m hat
cappotto m overcoat
cappuccino m cappuccino
capra f goat
carabiniere m policeman
caraffa f carafe
caramelle fpl sweets
carbone m coal ; charcoal
carburante m fuel
carburatore m carburettor
carcere m prison
caricare to charge (battery)
carico m load ; shipment ; cargo
carino(a) pretty ; lovely ; nice
carne f meat
carnevale m carnival
caro(a) dear ; expensive
carote fpl carrots
carrello m trolley
carriera f career
carro m cart
  carro attrezzi breakdown van
carrozza f carriage
  carrozze cuccette couchettes
  carrozza letto sleeper
carrozzeria f bodywork
carrozzina f pram
carta f paper ; card ; map
  carta assegni cheque card
  alla carta à la carte
  carta d'argento senior citizen's
  rail card
  carta di credito credit card
  carta famiglia family rail card

  carta d'identità identity card
  carta igienica toilet paper
  carta d'imbarco boarding card
  carta stradale road map
  carta verde green card
carte da gioco fpl playing cards
cartella f briefcase ; folder
cartello m sign ; signpost
cartine fpl cigarette papers
cartoccio m paper bag
cartoleria f stationer's
cartolina f postcard
casa f house ; home
  a casa at home
casalinga f housewife
casalinghi mpl household articles
cascata f waterfall
casco m helmet
casella postale f post-office box
casinò m casino
caso: in caso di in case of
cassa f vacancies
  cassa chiusa position closed
cassaforte f safe (for valuables)
cassetta f cassette
  cassetta delle lettere letterbox
cassetto m drawer
cassiere(a) m/f cashier ; teller
castello m castle
catena f chain ; mountain range
  catene (da neve) snow chains
cattedrale f cathedral
cattivo(a) bad ; nasty ; naughty
cattolico(a) Catholic
causa f cause ; case (lawsuit)
  a causa di because of
cavalcare to ride (horse)
cavallo m horse
cavatappi m corkscrew
cavo m cable
  cavo da rimorchio tow rope
cavolfiore m cauliflower
CD m CD
c'è there is
cedro m cedar ; lime (fruit)
CE f EC
celibe single (not married)
cellulare m mobile phone
cena f dinner (evening meal)
cenare to have dinner
cenone m New Year's Eve dinner
centimetro m centimetre
cento hundred

centrale central
centralino m switchboard
centro m centre
  centro città city centre
  centro commerciale shopping centre
  centro storico old town
ceppo bloccaruote m wheel clamp
cera f wax (for furniture)
ceramica f ceramics ; pottery
cercare to look for
ceretta f waxing (hair removal)
cerini mpl matches
cerniera f zip
cerotto m sticking plaster
certificato m certificate
  certificato di nascita birth
  certificate
cervello m brain
cestino m basket ; waste paper bin
che what ; who ; which
  che gusto? what flavour?
  che ore sono? what time is it?
cherosene m paraffin
chi? who?
  di chi è? whose is it?
chiamare to call
  chiamare per telefono to phone
chiamarsi to be called (name)
  come si chiama? what's your name?
chiamata f call (telephone)
chiave f key
  chiave inglese spanner
chiedere to ask ; to ask for
chiesa f church
chilo m kilo
chilogrammo m kilogram
chilometraggio m mileage (in km)
chilometro m kilometre
chiodo m nail (metal)
chirurgia f surgery (operations)
chitarra f guitar
chiudere to close ; to turn off (tap)
  chiudere a chiave to lock
chiuso(a) closed
  chiuso per turno closed for weekly
  day off
  chiuso per ferie closed for holidays
chiusura centralizzata f central
  locking (car)
ciabatta f flat bread ; slipper
ciao! hi! ; bye!
cibo m food
cielo m sky
ciliegia f cherry

cinghia della ventola f fan belt
cintura f belt
  cintura di sicurezza seatbelt
cinturino dell'orologio m watchstrap
cioccolato m chocolate
cipolla f onion
circo m circus
circolare to move (traffic)
circolazione f traffic
circonvallazione f ring road
cisterna f cistern ; tank
cisti f cyst
cistite f cystitis
CIT f Italian Tourist Agency
citofono m intercom
città f city ; town
cittadino(a) citizen
classe f class
clavicola f collar bone
cliente m/f customer
climatizzato(a) air-conditioned
clinica f clinic
cocco m coconut
cocomero m watermelon
coda f tail ; queue
codice m code
  codice a barra barcode
  codice postale postcode
cofano m bonnet (car)
cognata f sister-in-law
cognato m brother-in-law
cognome m surname
  di cognome mi chiamo... my
  surname is...
coincidenza f connection (train, etc)
colazione f breakfast ; lunch
collana f necklace
collant mpl tights
collega m/f colleague
colletto m collar
collina f hill
collo m neck ; package
colluttorio m mouthwash
colomba f dove ; Easter cake
colore m colour
Colosseo m Coliseum
colpa f fault
  non è colpa mia it's not my fault
coltello m knife

combustibile m fuel

come like ; as ; how
  come? how? *(in what way)*
  come si chiama? what's your name?
  come si pronuncia? how is it
  pronounced?
  come si scrive? how is it spelt?
  come sta? how are you?

cominciare to begin

commesso(a) m/f assistant ; clerk

commissariato m police station

commozione cerebrale f concussion

comodo(a) comfortable

compagnia f company
  compagnia aerea airline

compilare to fill in *(form)*

compleanno m birthday

completo(a) no vacancies ; full

comporre to dial *(number)*

comprare to buy

compreso(a) included

compressa f tablet

computer m computer

comune m town hall ; commune

con with
  con bagno with bathroom
  con filtro filter-tipped
  con ghiaccio with ice

concerto m concert

conchiglia f seashell

condimento m seasoning ;
  dressing *(for food)*

conducente m/f driver *(taxi, bus)*

confermare to confirm

confine m boundary ; border

congelatore m freezer

congratulazioni! congratulations!

congresso m conference

cono m cone
  cono gelato ice-cream cone

conoscere to know *(to be acquainted
  with)*

consegna f consignment ; delivery

conservante m preservative

consigliare to advise

consiglio m advice

consumare to use up
  da consumarsi entro best before

consumazione f drink

contanti mpl cash
  pagare in contanti to pay cash

contatore m electricity meter

contento(a) happy

continuare to continue

conto m account ; bill
  conto dettagliato itemised bill
  conto in banca bank account

contorno m vegetable side dish

contrabbando m smuggling

contratto m contract

contravvenzione f fine

contro against ; versus

controllare to check

controllo m check ; control
  controllo passaporti passport control

controllore m ticket collector

convalida f date stamp

convalidare to validate *(ticket)*

convincere to persuade

coperta f blanket

coperto m place setting ; cover charge

copertura f cover *(insurance)*

coppa gelato f ice cream served in
  goblet/tub

coppia f couple *(two people)*

copriletto m bedspread

coraggioso(a) brave

corda f rope

cornetto m ice cream cone

corpo m body

corrente f current *(electric, water)*
  corrente d'aria draught

correre to run

corridoio m corridor

corriere m courier

corsa f race ; journey
  corsa semplice single fare

corsia f lane ; hospital ward ; route
  corsia di emergenza hard
  shoulder
  corsia di sorpasso outside lane

corso m course ; avenue
  corso dei cambi exchange rates
  corso intensivo crash course

cortile m courtyard

corto(a) short

cos'è? what is it?
  cos'è successo? what happened?

cosa f thing
  cosa? what?

coscia f thigh

così so ; thus *(in this way)*

cosmetici mpl cosmetics

costa f coast
  Costa Azzurra French Riviera

costare to cost
costoletta f chop
costoso(a) expensive
costruire to build
costume m custom ; costume
  costume da bagno swimsuit
cotone m cotton
  cotone idrofilo cotton wool
cotto(a) cooked
  poco cotto(a) medium rare *(steak)*
cotton fioc® m cotton bud
crampi mpl cramps
cravatta f tie
credere to believe
credito m credit
  non si fa credito no credit given
crema f cream ; custard
  crema da barba shaving cream
crescere to grow
crespella f fried pastry twist
cric m jack *(for car)*
crisi epilettica f epileptic fit
cristallo m crystal
  di cristallo made of crystal
croccante f crisp
croce f cross
crocevia m crossroads
crociera f cruise
crollo m collapse
cronaca f news
cruciverba m crossword puzzle
crudo(a) raw
cuccetta f couchette ; sleeper
cucchiaino m teaspoon
cucchiaio m spoon ; tablespoon
cucina f cooker ; kitchen ; cooking
  cucina a gas gas cooker
cucinare to cook
cucire to sew
cuffia f bathing cap
cuffie fpl earphones
cugino(a) m/f cousin
culla f cradle
cuocere to cook
  cuocere a vapore to steam
  cuocere alla griglia to grill
cuoco m chef
cuoio m leather
cuore m heart
cupola f dome
curva f bend ; corner
cuscino m cushion
custode m caretaker

custodia f case ; holder
cyber-café m internet cafe

D

da from ; by ; with
  da asporto take away (food)
  dall'Inghilterra from England
  dalla Scozia from Scotland
danneggiare to spoil ; to damage
danno m damage
dappertutto everywhere
dare to give
  dare su to overlook ; to give onto
  dare la precedenza give way
  dare da mangiare to feed
  dare la mancia to tip *(waiter, etc)*
data f date
  data di nascita date of birth
  data di scadenza sell-by date
dati mpl data
dattero m date *(fruit)*
davanti a in front of ; opposite
dazio m customs duty
d.C. A.D.
debito m debt
decaffeinato(a) decaffeinated
decollare to take-off
decollo m takeoff
delizioso(a) delicious
dente m tooth
dentiera f dentures
dentifricio m toothpaste
dentro in ; indoors ; inside
deodorante m deodorant
  deodorante per ambienti air
  freshener
deposito bagagli m left-luggage
descrivere to describe
descrizione f description
desiderare to want ; to desire
destinazione f destination
destra f right
detergente m cleanser
detersivo m detergent
  detersivo in polvere soap powder
  detersivo per i piatti washing-up
  liquid
detrazione f deduction
dettagli mpl details

deviazione f detour ; diversion
di of ; some
  di cristallo/plastica made of crystal/plastic
  di lusso luxury (hotel, etc)
  di mattina in the morning
  di pomeriggio in the afternoon
  di notte at night
  di stagione in season
  di valore of value ; valuable
diabete m diabetes
diabetico(a) diabetic
diaframma m cap (diaphragm)
dialetto m dialect
diamante m diamond
diapositiva f slide (photo)
diarrea f diarrhoea
dicembre m December
dichiarare to declare
dichiarazione f declaration
dieta f diet
  essere a dieta to be on a diet
dietro behind ; after
  dietro di behind
difetto m fault
difficile difficult
diga f dam ; dyke
digerire to digest
digestivo m after-dinner liqueur
dimenticare to forget
Dio m God
dipinto(a) painted
diramazione f fork (in road)
dire to say ; to tell
diretto(a) direct
  treno diretto through train
direttore m manager ; director
direzione f management ; direction
dirigere to manage (be in charge of)
diritto(a) straight
  sempre diritto straight on
disabile disabled (person)
disastro m disaster
dischetto m floppy disk ; diskette
disco m disk ; record
  disco orario parking disk
discoteca f disco
disdire to cancel
disegno m drawing
disfare la valigia to unpack

disinfettante m disinfectant
disoccupato(a) unemployed
dispiacere: *mi dispiace* I'm sorry
disponibile available
distaccare to detach ; to unplug
distante far ; distant
distanza f distance
distorsione f sprain
distributore m dispenser
  distributore di benzina petrol station
disturbare to disturb
disturbo m trouble
dito m finger
  dito del piede toe
ditta f firm ; company
diurno(a) day(time)
divano m sofa ; divan
  divano letto sofa bed
diversi(e) several ; various
diverso(a) different
divertente funny (amusing)
divertimento m entertainment ; fun
divertirsi to enjoy oneself
dividere to share
divieto forbidden
  divieto di sorpasso no overtaking
  divieto di sosta no parking
divisa f uniform
divorziato(a) divorced
dizionario m dictionary
DOC abbreviation of **denominazione di origine controllata** (guarantee of wine quality)
doccia f shower
docente m/f lecturer
DOCG abbreviation of **denominazione di origine controllata e garantita** (guarantee of wine quality)
documenti mpl papers (passport)
dogana f customs
dolce sweet (not savoury) ; mild
dolce m sweet ; dessert ; cake
dolcelatte m creamy blue cheese
dolcificante m sweetener
dolciumi mpl sweets
dollari mpl dollars
dolore m pain ; grief
doloroso(a) painful
domanda f question
domandare to ask (a question)
domani tomorrow
  domani mattina tomorrow morning
  domani pomeriggio tomorrow

afternoon
domani sera tomorrow evening/night
domattina tomorrow morning
domenica Sunday
donna f woman
donne Ladies
dopo after ; afterward(s)
dopobarba m aftershave
doppio(a) double
dormire to sleep
dove? where?
dovere to have to
droga f drugs *(narcotics)*
drogheria f grocery shop
duepezzi m bikini
duomo m cathedral
durante during
durare to last
duro(a) hard ; tough ; harsh

E

e and
E east *(abbreviation)*
è is (to be)
ebreo(a) Jewish
ecc. etc.
eccedenza f excess ; surplus
eccesso m excess
eccesso di velocità speeding
eccezionale exceptional
eccezione f exception
ecco here is/are
economico(a) cheap
edicola f newsstand ; kiosk
edificio m building
effetto m effect
effetti personali belongings
egregio(a) dear *(in formal letter)*
elastico m rubber band
elenco m list
elenco telefonico phone directory
elettricista m/f electrician
elettricità f electricity
elettrico(a) electric(al)
elettrodomestici mpl electrical goods
emergenza f emergency
emicrania f migraine
emorroidi fpl haemorrhoids
enoteca f stock of vintage wines

ente m corporation ; body
entrambi(e) both
entrare to come/go in ; to enter
entrata f entrance
entrata abbonati season ticket
holders' entrance
entrata libera free admission
epatite f hepatitis
epilessia f epilepsy
epilettico(a) epileptic
equitazione f horse-riding
erba f grass
ernia f hernia
errore m mistake
esame m examination
esatto(a) exact ; accurate
esaurimento nervoso m nervous
breakdown
esaurito(a) exhausted ; out of print
tutto esaurito sold out
esca m fishing bait
escluso(a) excluding
escursione f excursion
esente exempt
esente da dogana duty-free
esempio example
per esempio for example
esercizio m exercise ; business
esigenza f requirement
esperto(a) expert ; experienced
esplosione f explosion
esportare to export
esposto(a) exposed
esposto(a) a nord north-facing
espresso m express train ; coffee
espresso(a) express *(parcel, etc)*
essere to be
essere assicurato(a) to be insured
essere capace (di) to be able (to)
essere d'accordo to agree
essere nato(a) to be born
est m east
estate f summer
esterno(a) outside ; external
estero(a) foreign
all'estero abroad
estintore m fire extinguisher
estivo(a) summer
età f age
etichetta f luggage tag ; label

eurocheque *m* Eurocheque
Europa *f* Europe
eventuale possible
evitare to avoid

F

fa ago
fabbrica *f* factory
fabbricare to manufacture
facchino *m* porter *(for luggage)*
faccia *f* face
facile easy
fagiano *m* pheasant
fallire to fail
fallito(a) bankrupt
fallo *m* foul *(football)*
falso(a) fake
fame *f* hunger
  avere fame to be hungry
famiglia *f* family
familiare family ; familiar
famoso(a) famous
fanale *m* light
fanalino dello stop *m* brake light
fango *m* mud
farcito(a) stuffed ; filled
fare to do ; to make
  fare attenzione to be careful
  fare la spesa to go shopping
farfalla *f* butterfly
fari *mpl* headlights
farina *f* flour
farmacia *f* chemist's ; pharmacy
  farmacie di turno duty chemists
farmaco *m* drug *(medicine)*
faro *m* headlight ; lighthouse
fascia *f* band ; bandage
fastidio: *non mi dà fastidio* I don't
  mind
fatelo da voi *m* DIY
fatto a mano hand-made
fatto di ... made of ...
fattoria *f* farm ; farmhouse
fattura *f* invoice
favore *m* favour
  per favore please
fax *m* fax
fazzoletto *m* handkerchief

  fazzoletto di carta tissue
febbraio February
febbre *f* fever
  avere la febbre to have a
  temperature
  febbre da fieno hay fever
fede *f* wedding ring
federa *f* pillowcase
fegato *m* liver
felice happy
felpa *f* sweatshirt
femmina *f* female
feriale workday *(Monday-Saturday)*
ferie *fpl* holiday(s)
  essere in ferie to be on holiday
ferire to injure
ferita *f* wound ; injury ; cut
ferito(a) injured
fermare to stop
fermata *f* stop
  fermata dell'autobus bus stop
fermo(a) still ; off *(machine)*
  stare fermo to stay still
ferro da stiro *m* iron *(for clothes)*
ferrovia *f* railway
festa *f* festival ; holiday ; party
  festa nazionale public holiday
festivo(a) sundays/public holiday
fetta *f* slice
fiamma *f* flame
fiammifero *m* match
fico *m* fig
fidanzato(a) engaged *(to marry)*
fieno *m* hay
fiera *f* fair *(trade)*
figlia *f* daughter
figlio *m* son
fila *f* line *(row, queue)*
  fare la fila to queue
filiale *f* branch ; subsidiary
film *m* film *(at cinema)*
filo *m* thread ; wire
  filo interdentale dental floss
filtro *m* filter
  filtro dell'olio oil filter
finanza *f* finance
  Guardia di finanza Customs and
  Excise
fine *f* end
  fine settimana weekend
  fine stagione end of season
finestra *f* window
finestrino *m* window *(car, train)*
finire to finish

finito(a) finished
fino(a) fine ; elegant
fino a until ; as far as
  fino alle due till 2 o'clock
fioraio *m* florist's shop
fior di latte *m* cream *(ice cream flavour)*
fiori *mpl* flowers
fiorista *m/f* florist
Firenze Florence
firma *f* signature
firmare to sign
  firmare il registro to sign register
fiume *m* river
focaccia *f* flat salted bread
foglia *f* leaf *(of tree, etc)*
fogna *f* sewer ; drain
folla *f* crowd
folle mad
  in folle in neutral *(car)*
fon *m* hairdryer
fondo *m* back *(of room)* ; bottom
fontana *f* fountain
fonte *f* source
foratura *f* puncture
forbici *fpl* scissors
  forbicine nail scissors
forchetta *f* fork *(for eating)*
foresta *f* forest
forfora *f* dandruff
formaggio *m* cheese
fornaio *m* baker
fornello *m* stove ; hotplate
fornitore *m* supplier
forno *m* oven
  forno a microonde microwave
forse perhaps
forte strong ; loud ; high *(speed)*
fortunato(a) lucky
forza *f* strength ; force
foto *f* photo
fotocopia *f* photocopy
fotocopiare to photocopy
fototessera *f* passport-type photo
foulard *m* headscarf
fra between ; among(st)
  fra 2 giorni in 2 days
  fra poco in a while
fragile breakable
fragola *f* strawberry
frana *f* landslide
francese French
francese *m* French *(language)*
Francia *f* France

francobollo *m* stamp
frappé *m* milk shake
fratello *m* brother
frattura *f* fracture
frazione *f* village
freccia *f* indicator *(car)* ; arrow
freddo(a) cold
frenare to brake
freno *m* brake
  freno a mano handbrake
frequente frequent
fretta *f* hurry
  avere fretta to be in a hurry
friggere to fry
frigorifero *m* refrigerator
frittata *f* omelette
fritto(a) fried
frizione *f* clutch *(car)*
frizzante fizzy ; sparkling
fronte *f* forehead ; front
  di fronte a facing ; opposite
frontiera *f* frontier ; border
frullato *m* milkshake
frutta *f* fruit
  frutta secca dried fruit
frutti di mare *mpl* seafood
fruttivendolo *m* greengrocer
FS Italian State Railways
fuga *f* escape ; leak *(gas)*
fuggire to escape
fulmine *m* lightning
fumare to smoke
  non fumo I don't smoke
fumatori smokers
fumo *m* smoke
funerale *m* funeral
funghi *mpl* mushrooms
  funghi porcini boletus mushrooms
  funghi secchi dried mushrooms
funicolare *f* funicular railway
funzionare to work *(mechanism)*
  non funziona it doesn't work
fuoco *m* fire ; focus
  fuochi d'artificio fireworks
fuori outside ; out
  fuori servizio out of order
furgone *m* van
furto *m* theft
fuseaux *mpl* leggings
fusibile *m* fuse
futuro *m* future

G

gabinetto m lavatory
  gabinetto biologico chemical toilet
  gabinetto medico doctor's surgery
galleria f tunnel ; gallery ; arcade ;
  circle *(theatre)*
  galleria d'arte art gallery
Galles m Wales
gallese Welsh
gamba f leg
gara f race *(sport)*
garanzia f guarantee ; warranty
gas m gas
gasolio m diesel
gassato(a) fizzy
gassosa f lemonade
gastrite f gastritis
gatto m cat
gay gay *(person)*
gel per capelli m hair gel
gelateria f ice-cream shop
gelatina f jelly
gelato m ice cream
gelo m frost
geloso(a) jealous
gemelli mpl twins ; cufflinks
genere m kind *(type)* ; gender
genero m son-in-law
genitori mpl parents
Genova f Genoa
gentile kind *(person)*
Germania f Germany
gesso m chalk ; plaster *(for limb)*
gettare to throw
  non gettare rifiuti no dumping
gettone m token *(for phone)*
ghiaccio m ice
ghiacciolo m ice lolly
giacca f jacket
giallo m thriller *(book or film)*
giallo(a) yellow ; amber *(light)*
giardiniere m gardener
giardino m garden
gilè m waistcoat
gin m gin
  gin tonic gin and tonic
ginocchio m knee
giocare to play ; to gamble

giocattolo m toy
gioco m game
  gioco a quiz quiz show
gioielleria f jeweller's
gioielli mpl jewellery
gioielliere m jeweller
giornalaio m newsagent
giornale m newspaper
giornalista m/f journalist
giornata f day
giorno m day
  giorni feriali Monday-Saturday
  giorni festivi Sundays/holidays
giovane young
giovedì m Thursday
girare to turn ; to spin
  girarsi to turn around
girasole m sunflower
girella f scrunchie
giro m tour ; turn
  fare un giro a piedi to go for a stroll
  giro turistico sightseeing tour
gita f trip ; excursion
  gita in barca boat trip
  gita in pullman coach trip
giù down ; downstairs
giubbotto salvagente m life jacket
giudice m judge
giugno m June
giusto(a) fair ; right *(correct)*
gli the ; to him/it
globale inclusive *(costs)*
goccia f drop *(of liquid)* ; drip
gola f throat ; gorge
golfo m gulf
gomito m elbow
gomma f rubber ; tyre
  gomma a terra flat tyre
  gomma da cancellare eraser
gommone m dinghy *(inflatable)*
gonfiare to inflate
gonfio(a) swollen
gonfiore m lump *(swelling)*
gonna f skirt
gradazione f content *(of alcohol)*
gradevole pleasant
gradino m step ; stair
Gran Bretagna f Great Britain
grana f parmesan cheese
granaio m barn
granchio m crab
grande large ; great ; big
grande magazzino m department store

grandine f hail

granita f water ice *(flavoured)*

grappa f strong spirit *(often drunk with coffee)*

grasso(a) fat ; greasy

gratis free of charge

grattacielo m skyscraper

grattugia f grater

grattugiato(a) grated

gratuito(a) free of charge
  il servizio è gratuito service included

grave serious

grazie thank you

gridare to shout

grigio(a) grey

griglia f grill
  alla griglia grilled

grissini mpl breadsticks

grosso(a) big ; thick

grucce fpl crutches

gruccia f coat hanger

gruppo m group
  gruppo sanguigno blood group

guadagnare to earn

guanciale m pillow

guanto m glove
  guanto da forno oven glove
  guanto di spugna facecloth
  guanti di gomma rubber gloves

guardacoste m coastguard

guardare to look (at) ; to watch

guardaroba m cloakroom

guardia f guard
  Guardia di finanza Customs and Excise

guasto out of order

guerra f war

guida f guide *(person or book)* ; directory
  guida a sinistra left-hand drive
  guida telefonica telephone directory
  guida turistica tour guide

guidare to drive ; to steer

guidatore m driver

guinzaglio m lead *(for dog)*

gustare to taste ; to enjoy

gusto m flavour

H

ha...? do you have...?
  ha l'ora? do you have the time?

hamburger m burger

herpes m cold sore ; herpes

ho... I have...
  ho ... anni I'm ... years old
  ho bisogno di... I need...
  ho fame I'm hungry
  ho fretta I'm in a hurry
  ho sete I'm thirsty

hostess f stewardess

I

i the

identificare to identify

idratante m moisturizer

idraulico m plumber

ieri yesterday

il the

imbarcarsi to embark

imbarcazione f boat

imbarco m boarding
  carta d'imbarco boarding card

imbottigliato(a) bottled

imbucare to post *(letters, etc)*

immediatamente at once

immergere to dip *(into liquid)*

immersioni subacquee fpl scuba diving

immondizie fpl rubbish

immunizzazione f immunisation

impanato coated in breadcrumbs

imparare to learn

impasto m mixture

imperatore m emperor

impermeabile m raincoat

impero m empire

impiego m use ; employment

impiegato(a) m/f employee ; white-collar worker

importante important

importare to import ; to matter
  non importa it doesn't matter

importo m (total) amount

impossibile impossible

imposta f tax *(on income)* ; shutter
  imposta sul valore aggiunto (IVA) value-added tax (VAT)

improbabile unlikely

in in ; to
  in Spagna to Spain
  in vacanza on holiday

inalatore m inhaler

inadempienza f negligence
incantevole charming
incaricarsi di to take charge of
incartare to wrap up (parcel)
incassare to cash (cheque)
incendio m fire
inchiostro m ink
incidente m accident
incinta pregnant
incluso(a) included ; enclosed
incontrare to meet
incontro m meeting (by chance)
incrocio m crossroads ; junction
indicatore m indicator ; gauge
   indicatore del livello dell'olio oil
   gauge
indicazioni fpl directions
indice m index ; contents
indietro backwards ; behind
indirizzo m address
infarto m heart attack
infatti in fact ; actually
infermeria f infirmary
infermiera f nurse
infezione f infection
infiammabile inflammable
infiammazione f inflammation
influenza f flu
informare to inform
   informarsi (di) to inquire (about)
informazioni fpl information
ingessatura f plaster cast
Inghilterra f England
inghiottire to swallow
inglese English
ingorgato(a) blocked (pipe, sink)
ingorgo m blockage ; hold-up
   ingorgo stradale traffic jam
ingresso m entry/entrance
   ingresso gratuito free entry
iniezione f injection
inizio m start
innocuo(a) harmless
inondazione m flood
inoltre besides
inquinato(a) polluted
insalata f salad
   insalata di patate potato salad
   insalata di pomodori tomato salad
   insalata mista mixed salad

insalata verde green salad
insegnante m/f teacher
insegnare to teach
inserire to insert
   inserire le banconote una per volta
   insert banknotes one at a time
insettifugo m insect repellent
insetto m insect
insieme together
insieme m outfit
insolazione f sunstroke
insulina f insulin
interessante interesting
internazionale international
Internet m Internet
interno m inside ; extension (phone)
intero(a) whole
interpretazione f interpretation
interprete m/f interpreter
interruttore m switch
intervallo m half-time ; interval
intervento m operation
inversione f U-turn
intervista f interview
intestato(a) a registered in the
   name of
intimi donna mpl ladies' underwear
intorno around
intossicazione alimentare f food-
   poisoning
introdurre to introduce
inutile unnecessary ; useless
invalido(a) disabled ; invalid
invece di instead of
invernale winter
inverno m winter
investire to knock down (car)
inviare to send
invitare to invite
invito m invitation
io I
ipermercato m hypermarket
ipermetrope long-sighted
Irlanda f Ireland
   Irlanda del Nord Northern Ireland
irlandese Irish
iscritto m member
   per iscritto in writing
iscriversi a to join (club)
iscrizione f inscription ; enrolment
isola f island
istituto m institute

istruttore(trice) *m/f* instructor
istruzioni *fpl* instructions
Italia *f* Italy
italiano(a) Italian
itinerario *m* route
　itinerario turistico scenic route
itterizia *f* jaundice
IVA *f* VAT

J

jolly *m* joker *(cards)*

L

l' the ; him ; her ; it ; you
la the ; her ; it ; you
là there
　per di là that way
labbra *fpl* lips
lacca *f* lacquer ; hair spray
ladro *m* thief
lago *m* lake
lamette *fpl* razor blades
lampada *f* lamp
lampadina *f* lightbulb
lampone *m* raspberry
lana *f* wool
largo(a) wide ; broad
lasciare to leave ; to let *(allow)*
lassativo *m* laxative
lassù up there
latte *m* milk
　latte a lunga conservazione long-life milk
　latte di soia soya milk
　latte fresco fresh milk
　latte in polvere powdered milk
　latte intero whole milk
　latte scremato skimmed milk
　latte parzialmente scremato semi-skimmed milk
lattuga *f* lettuce
lavabile washable
lavaggio *m* washing
　lavaggio auto car wash
　per lavaggi frequenti for frequent use
lavanderia *f* laundry *(place)*
　lavanderia automatica launderette
lavandino *m* sink
lavare to wash
　lavare a secco to dry-clean
lavarsi to wash *(oneself)*

lavasecco *m* dry-cleaner's
lavastoviglie *f* dishwasher
lavatrice *f* washing machine
lavorare to work *(person)*
lavoro *m* job ; occupation ; work
　lavori stradali road works
　lavori in corso road works
le the ; them ; to her/it ; to you
legge *f* law
leggere to read
leggero(a) light (not heavy) ; weak
legno *m* wood *(material)*
lei she ; her ; you
lentamente slowly
lente *f* lens *(of glasses)*
　lente d'ingrandimento magnifying glass
　lenti a contatto contact lenses
lento slow
lenzuolo *m* sheet *(bed)*
lesbica lesbian
lesione *f* injury
lettera *f* letter
　lettera raccomandata registered letter
lettino *m* cot
letto *m* bed
　letto a una piazza single bed
　letto matrimoniale double bed
　letti gemelli twin beds
　letti a castello bunk beds
lettore CD *m* CD player
lì there *(over there)*
libero(a) free/vacant
libreria *f* bookshop
libretto *m* booklet
　libretto degli assegni cheque book
libro *m* book
licenza *f* licence ; permit
　licenza di caccia hunting permit
　licenza di pesca fishing permit
limetta per le unghie *f* nail file
limite *m* limit ; boundary
　limite di velocità speed limit
limone *m* lemon
linea *f* line ; route
　linea aerea airline
lingua *f* language ; tongue
lino *m* linen
liquido *m* liquid
　liquido dei freni brake fluid

liquido lavavetri screen wash
liquido per lenti a contatto contact lens solution
liquore *m* liqueur
liquori *mpl* spirits *(alcohol)*
liscio(a) straight ; smooth
lista *f* list
lista dei vini wine list
listino prezzi *m* price list
litro *m* litre
livello *m* level
lo him ; it
locale local
locale *m* room ; place ; local train
locale notturno nightclub
località di vacanza *f* resort
locanda *f* inn
Londra *f* London
lontano(a) far
lozione *f* lotion
lozione solare suntan lotion
lucchetto *m* padlock
lucchetto della bici bike lock
luce *f* light
lucertola *f* lizard
luglio *m* July
lui him
lumaca *f* snail
luna *f* moon
luna di miele honeymoon
luna park *m* funfair
lunedì *m* Monday
lunghezza *f* length
lungo(a) long
lungo la strada along the street
a lungo for a long time
lungomare *m* promenade ; seafront
luogo *m* place
luogo di nascita place of birth
lupo *m* wolf
lusso *m* luxury
di lusso luxury *(hotel, etc)*

M

ma but
macchia *f* stain ; mark
macchina *f* car ; machine
macchina a noleggio hire car
macchina fotografica camera

macchina sportiva sports car
macedonia *f* fruit salad
macellaio *m* butcher's
macinato(a) ground *(coffee, meat)*
madre *f* mother
magazzino *m* warehouse
maggio *m* May
maggiore larger ; greater ; largest ; older ; oldest
maglietta *f* t-shirt
maglione *m* jumper ; sweater
magro(a) thin *(person)* ; low-fat ; lean *(meat)*
mai never ; ever
maiale *m* pig ; pork
mal *see* **male**
malato(a) ill ; sick
malattia *f* disease
malattia venerea venereal disease
male badly *(not well)*
male *m* pain ; ache
mal d'aria air sickness
mal d'auto car sickness
mal d'orecchi earache
mal di denti toothache
mal di gola sore throat
mal di mare sea sickness
mal di pancia stomachache
mal di testa headache
maltempo *m* bad weather
mamma *f* mum(my)
mancia *f* tip *(to waiter, etc)*
mandare to send
mandare per fax to fax
mangiare to eat
mangiare fuori to eat out
manica *f* sleeve
la Manica the English Channel
mano *f* hand
fatto(a) a mano handmade
Mantova *f* Mantua
manuale di conversazione *m* phrase book
manzo *m* beef
marca *f* brand *(make)*
marcia *f* gear *(car)* ; march
marciapiede *m* pavement
mare *m* sea ; seaside
Mare del Nord North Sea
margarina *f* margarine
margherita *f* daisy
marina *f* navy
marito *m* husband

marmellata f jam
  marmellata d'arance marmalade
marrone m brown ; chestnut
marsupio m bumbag ; money belt
martedì m Tuesday
  martedì grasso Shrove Tuesday
martello m hammer
marzo m March
maschera f mask ; fancy dress
maschile masculine ; male
massimo(a) maximum
masticare to chew
materassino m airbed ; lilo
materasso m mattress
materiale m material
matrigna f stepmother
matrimonio m wedding
mattina f morning
  di mattina in the morning
matto(a) mad
mazza f mallet
  mazze da golf golf clubs
meccanico m mechanic ; repair shop
medicina f medicine
medico m doctor
Mediterraneo m Mediterranean
medusa f jellyfish
meglio better ; best
  meglio di better than
mela f apple
melanzana f aubergine ; eggplant
melone m melon
membro m member
meningite f meningitis
meno less ; minus
mensa f canteen
mensile monthly
mensilmente monthly
mensola f shelf
menta f mint
mento m chin
mentre while ; whereas
menù m menu
  menù alla carta à la carte menu
  menù a prezzo fisso set-price menu
  menù turistico set menu
meraviglioso(a) wonderful
mercatino dell'usato m flea market
mercato m market
merce f goods
merci fpl freight ; goods
mercoledì m Wednesday
merenda f snack

meridionale southern
mese m month
messa f mass (in church)
messaggio m message
mestruazioni fpl period (menstrual)
metà f half
  metà prezzo half-price
metro m metre
  metro a nastro tape measure
metropolitana f underground ; metro
mettere to put ; to put on (clothes)
  mettersi in contatto con to contact
mezzanotte f midnight
mezzi mpl means ; transport
mezzo m middle
mezzo(a) half
  mezza pensione half board
mezzogiorno m midday ; noon
  il Mezzogiorno the south of Italy
mezz'ora f half an hour
mi me ; to me ; myself
mia my
miele m honey
migliorare to improve
migliore better ; best
Milano Milan
miliardo m billion
milione m million
mille thousand
millimetro m millimetre
minestra f soup
minimo m minimum
ministro m minister (political)
minorenne underage
minori mpl minors
minuto m minute
mio my
miscela f blend
misto(a) mixed
mittente m/f sender
MM metro ; underground
mobili mpl furniture
moda f fashion
moderno(a) modern
modo m way ; manner
modulo m form (document)
  modulo d'iscrizione registration form
moglie f wife
molletta f clothes peg
  molletta per capelli hairgrip

molo *m* jetty ; quay ; pier
molti(e) many
  molte grazie thanks very much
molto much ; a lot ; very
  molto tempo for a long time
  molta gente lots of people
monastero *m* monastery
moneta *f* coin ; currency
montagna *f* mountain
monumento *m* monument
mordere to bite *(animal)*
morire to die
morsicare to bite *(insect)*
morsicato(a) bite *(from insect)*
morso(a) bitten
morto(a) dead
mosca *f* fly
moscerino *m* midge ; gnat
moschea *f* mosque
mosso(a) rough *(sea)* ; ruffled
mostra *f* exhibition
mostrare to show
moto *f* motorbike
motore *m* engine ; motor
motorino *m* moped
motorino d'avviamento *m*
  starter motor
multa *f* fine *(to be paid)*
municipio *m* town hall
muro *m* wall
museo *m* museum
musica *f* music
muta *f* wetsuit
mutande *fpl* underpants
mutandine *fpl* knickers ; panties

N

N north *(abbreviation)*
nafta *f* diesel
Napoli Naples
nascita *f* birth
naso *m* nose
nastro *m* tape ; ribbon
nato(a) born
nauseato(a) nauseous
nave *f* ship
nave-traghetto *f* ferry
nazionale national ; domestic *(flight)*

nazionalità *f* nationality
nazione *f* nation
né ... né neither ... nor
nebbia *f* fog
necessario(a) necessary
negativo *m* negative *(photo)*
negozio *m* shop
nero(a) black
nessuno(a) no ; nobody ; none
netto *m* net
  al netto di IVA net of VAT
neve *f* snow
nevicare to snow
niente nothing
  niente da dichiarare nothing to
  declare
nipote *f* granddaughter ; niece
nipote *m* grandson ; nephew
noce *f* walnut
nocivo(a) harmful
nodo *m* knot ; bow
  nodo ferroviario junction *(railway)*
noi we
noleggiare to hire
noleggio *m* hire
  noleggio auto car hire
  noleggio barche boat hire
  noleggio bici bike hire
  noleggio sci ski hire
nolo *m* hire
nome *m* name ; first name ;
  nome da ragazza maiden name
non not
  non ancora not yet
  non funziona it doesn't work
  non capisco I don't understand
  non pericoloso(a) safe
non-fumatore *m/f* non-smoker
nonna *f* grandmother
nonno *m* grandfather
nord *m* north
nostro(a) our
notare to notice
notizie *fpl* news
notte *f* night
  notte di San Silvestro New Year's Eve
  di notte at night
novembre *m* November
nubile single *(woman)*
nulla nothing ; anything
nullo(a) void *(contract)*
numero *m* number ; size *(of shoe)*
  numero di camera room number
  numero del conto account number
  numero di telefono phone number

nuora f daughter-in-law
nuotare to swim
Nuova Zelanda f New Zealand
nuovo(a) new
  di nuovo again
nuvoloso(a) cloudy

O

o or
O west (*abbreviation*)
obbligatorio(a) compulsory
oceano m ocean
occasione f opportunity ; bargain
occhiali mpl glasses
  occhiali da sci skiing goggles
  occhiali da sole sunglasses
occhio m eye
occupato(a) busy/engaged
odore m smell
offerta f offer
officina f workshop ; repair shop
oggetto m object
oggi today
ogni each ; every
  ogni giorno every day ; daily
  ogni quanto? how often?
  ogni tanto occasionally
olio m oil
  olio solare suntan oil
  olio di girasole sunflower oil
  olio d'oliva olive oil
olive fpl olives
oltre beyond ; besides
ombra f shade
  all'ombra in the shade
ombrello m umbrella
ombrellone m sun umbrella
ombretto m eye shadow
omogemeizzati mpl baby food
omosessuale homosexual
onde fpl waves
onestà f honesty
onesto(a) honest
opera f opera
operatore turistico m tour operator
operazione f operation (*surgical*)
opuscolo m brochure
ora now
ora f hour
  ora di punta rush hour
  che ore sono? what's the time?
orario m timetable

  in orario on time
  orario di apertura opening hours
  orario di cassa banking hours
  orario visite visiting hours
ordinare to order ; to prescribe
ordine f order (*in restaurant*)
ordinato(a) tidy
orecchini mpl earrings
orecchio m ear
orecchioni mpl mumps
oreficeria f jeweller's
orina f urine
ormeggiare to moor
ormeggio m mooring
oro m gold
  placcato oro gold-plated
orologeria m watchmaker's
orologio m clock ; watch
orticaria f rash (*skin*)
ortografia f spelling
ospedale m hospital
ospite m/f guest ; host/hostess
osso m bone
ostello m hostel
  ostello della gioventù youth hostel
osteria f inn
ottenere to get ; obtain
  ottenere la linea to get through (*on phone*)
ottimo(a) excellent
ottobre m October
otturazione f filling (*in tooth*)
ovest m west

P

pacchetto m packet
pacco m package ; parcel
padella f frying-pan
Padova Padua
padre m father
padrone(a) m/f owner
paesaggio m scenery ; countryside
paese m country (*nation*) ; village
pagare to pay ; to pay for
pagato(a) paid
pagina f page
paio m pair
palazzo m building ; block of flats ; palace

palestra f gym

palla f ball

pallina f ball *(small)*
  pallina da golf golf ball
  pallina da tennis tennis ball

pallone m football

pandoro m Italian Christmas cake

pane m bread ; loaf
  pane integrale wholemeal bread
  pane carré sandwich bread
  pane e coperto cover charge
  pane di segale rye bread

pannettone m Italian Christmas cake

panetteria f baker's

pangrattato m breadcrumbs

panificio m bakery

panino m bread roll
  panino imbottito sandwich

paninoteca f sandwich bar

panna f cream

panno m cloth ; fabric

pannolini mpl nappies

pantaloni mpl trousers
  pantaloni corti shorts

pantofole fpl slippers

papa m pope

papà m daddy

parabrezza m windscreen

paraurti m bumper *(on car)*

parcheggiare to park

parcheggio m car park
  parcheggio custodito supervised car-park
  parcheggio libero free parking
  parcheggio sotterraneo underground car park

parchimetro m parking meter

parco m park
  parco nazionale national park

parente m/f relation ; relative

Parigi f Paris

parlare to speak ; to talk

parmigiano m parmesan
  parmigiano grattugiato grated parmesan

parola f word

parolaccia f swear word

parrucchiere(a) m/f hairdresser

parte f share ; part ; side

partenza f departures
  partenze internazionali international departures
  partenze nazionali domestic departures

partire to depart ; to leave

partita f match ; game
  partita di calcio football match

passaggio m passage ; lift *(in car)*
  dare un passaggio to give a lift

passaporto m passport

passeggiata f walk ; stroll

passeggino m pushchair

passo m pace ; pass *(mountain)*
  passo carrabile keep clear
  passo chiuso pass closed

pasticcino m cake *(small, fancy)*

pastiglia f tablet *(pill)*

pasto m meal

pastorizzato pasteurised

patata f potato

patatine fpl crisps
  patatine frite chips

patente f permit ; driving licence

patrigno m stepfather

pavimento m floor

paziente m/f patient

pecora f sheep

pedaggio m toll *(motorway)*

pedale m pedal

pedalò m pedalboat

pedicure m chiropodist

pedoni mpl pedestrians

peggio worse

pelati mpl tinned tomatoes

pelle f skin ; hide ; leather

pellegrino m pilgrim

pelletterie fpl leather goods

pellicola f film *(for camera)*
  pellicola a colori colour film
  pellicola in bianco e nero black and white film

pelo m fur

pene m penis

penicillina f penicillin

penisola f peninsula

penna f pen

pensare to think

pensione f guesthouse
  pensione completa full board
  mezza pensione half board
  pensione familiare bed and breakfast

pentola f saucepan

pepe m pepper *(spice)*

per for ; per ; in order to
  per esempio for example
  per favore please
  per via aerea air mail

pera f pear

perché why ; because ; so that
percorso *m* walk ; journey ; route
  percorso panoramico scenic route
perdere to lose ; to miss (train, etc)
perdita *f* leak (of gas, liquid)
pericolante unsafe
pericolo *m* danger
pericoloso(a) dangerous
  non pericoloso(a) safe
periferia *f* outskirts ; suburbs
permanente continua parking
  restrictions still apply
permanenza *f* stay ; residency
permesso *m* licence ; permit
  permesso! excuse me! (to get by)
  permesso di soggiorno
  residence permit
permettere to allow
perso(a) lost (object) ; missed (train,
  plane, etc)
persona *f* person
personale *m* staff
pesante heavy
pesare to weigh
pesca *f* angling ; fishing ; peach
  divieto di pesca no fishing
pescare to fish
pesce *m* fish
pescivendolo *m* fishmonger's
peso *m* weight
pettine *m* comb
petto *m* chest ; breast
  petto di pollo chicken breast
pezzo *m* piece ; bit ; cut (of meat)
piacere to please
  le piace? do you like it?
  piacere! pleased to meet you!
piangere to cry (weep)
piano slowly ; quietly
piano *m* floor (of building) ; plan
pianta *f* map ; plan ; plant
pianterreno *m* ground floor
piantina *f* street map
piatto *m* dish ; course ; plate
  primo piatto first course
piazza *f* square (in town)
piazzale *m* large square
piazzola (di sosta) *f* lay-by
piccante spicy ; hot
picchetto *m* tent peg
piccolo(a) little ; small
piede *m* foot
  a piedi on foot

pieno(a) full
pietra *f* stone
pigiama *m* pyjamas
pigro(a) lazy
pila *f* battery ; torch
pillola *f* pill
pinne *fpl* flippers
pino *m* pine
pinze *fpl* pliers
pinzette *fpl* tweezers
pioggia *f* rain
piombo *m* lead (metal)
piovere to rain
piscina *f* swimming pool
  piscina per bambini paddling pool
pista *f* track ; race track
  pista da ballo dance floor
  pista da sci ski run
più more ; most ; plus
  più di more than
  più economico(a) cheaper
  più tardi later
piumino *m* duvet
pizzeria *m* pizza restaurant
pizzico *m* pinch ; sting
pizzo *m* lace
plastica *f* plastic
  di plastica made of plastic
pneumatico *m* tyre
po' a little (shortened form of **poco**)
pochi(e) few
poco(a) little ; not much
  un po' a little
poi then
polizia *f* police
  polizia stradale traffic police
poliziotto *m* policeman
polizza *f* policy
pollo *m* chicken
polmone *m* lung
poltrona *f* armchair ; seat in stalls
pomata *f* ointment
pomeriggio *m* afternoon
  di pomeriggio in the afternoon
pomodoro *m* tomato
pompa *f* pump
pompelmo *m* grapefruit
ponte *m* bridge ; deck
  ponte macchine car deck
pontile *m* jetty ; pier

porcellana f china

porta f door ; gate ; goal
porta di sicurezza emergency exit

portabagagli m luggage rack ;
porter *(at airport, station, etc)*

portacenere m ashtray

portafoglio m wallet

portare to carry/bring ; to wear

portiere m porter *(doorkeeper)* ; goal-
keeper

portineria f caretaker's lodge

porto m port ; harbour
porto di scalo port of call

Portogallo m Portugal

porzione f portion ; helping

posate fpl cutlery

posologia f dosage

possiamo we can
non possiamo we cannot

posso I can
non posso I cannot

posta f post office ; mail
posta elettronica e-mail
posta raccomandata registered mail

posteggio m car park
posteggio taxi taxi rank

posto m place ; job ; seat
posti in piedi standing room
posti a sedere seating capacity
posti prenotati reserved seats

potabile ok to drink

potere to be able

pranzo m lunch

pré-maman m maternity dress

preavviso m advance notice

precotto(a) ready-cooked

predeterminare l'importo desiderato
select required amount

preferire to prefer

preferito(a) favourite

prefisso m prefix ; area code
prefisso telefonico dialling code

pregare to pray
si prega... please...

prego don't mention it!

prelievo m collection ; sample

premere to push ; to press

premio m prize

prendere to take ; to catch *(bus, etc)*
prendere il sole to sunbathe
prendere in prestito to borrow

prenome m first name

prenotare to book ; to reserve

prenotato(a) reserved

prenotazione f reservation

preoccupato(a) worried

preparare to prepare ; to get ready

presa f socket *(electric)*

preservativo m condom

pressione del sangue f blood pressure

prestare to lend

presto early ; soon

prete m priest

previsione f forecast
previsioni del tempo weather
forecast

previsto(a) scheduled ; expected
come previsto as expected

prezzo m price
prezzo al dettaglio retail price
prezzo fisso set price
prezzo di catalogo list price
prezzo al minuto retail price
prezzo d'ingresso entrance fee

prima di before

primavera f spring *(season)*

primo(a) first ; top ; early
primo piano first floor
primo piatto first course

principale main

principiante m/f beginner

privato(a) private

problema m problem

professione f profession

professore m/f teacher ; professor

profondità f depth

profondo(a) deep

profumeria f perfume shop

progettare to plan

programma m programme ;
syllabus ; schedule

proibire to ban ; to prohibit

proibito(a) forbidden ; prohibited

prolunga f extension *(electrical)*

promettere to promise

pronto(a) ready
pronto! hello! *(on telephone)*
pronto soccorso casualty

proprietario(a) m/f owner

proprio(a) own

prossimamente coming soon

prossimo(a) next

proteggislip m panty liner

protesi dell'anca f hip replacement

177 **protestante** Protestant
provare to try ; to test *(try out)* ; to try on *(clothes)*
provvisorio(a) temporary
prugna *f* plum
PTP *abbreviation of* **Posto Telefonico Pubblico**
pubblicità *f* advertisement
pubblico *m* audience ; public
pulce *f* flea
pulito(a) clean
pulizia *f* cleaning
  pulizia del viso facial
pullman *m* coach
pulmino *m* minibus
punteggio *m* score
puntine *fpl* points
punto *m* point ; stitch ; full stop
  punto d'incontro meeting place
puntura *f* bite ; sting ; injection
puzzle *m* jigsaw
puzzo *m* bad smell

Q

qua here
quaderno *m* exercise book
quadro *m* picture ; painting
qual(e) what ; which ; which one
qualche some
  qualche volta sometimes
qualcosa something ; anything
qualcuno someone ; somebody
qualificato(a) qualified
qualità *f* quality
qualsiasi any
qualunque any
quando? when?
quanto(a)? how much?
  quanti(e)? how many?
quartiere *m* district
quarto *m* quarter
  quarto d'ora quarter of an hour
quattro four
quei those ; those ones
quel(la) that ; that one
quelli(e) those ; those ones
quello(a) that ; that one
questi(e) these ; these ones
questo(a) this ; this one
questura *f* police station
qui here

italian–eng p/q/r

quindi then ; therefore
quindici giorni fortnight
quotidiano *m* daily (paper)
quotidiano(a) daily

R

rabarbaro *m* rhubarb
rabbia *f* anger ; rabies
racchetta *f* racket ; bat
  racchetta da neve snowshoe
  racchetta da sci ski pole
raccomandare to recommend
racconto *m* story
radiatore *m* radiator
radio *f* radio
radiografia *f* x-ray
raffreddore *m* cold *(illness)*
  raffreddore da fieno hay fever
ragazza *f* girl ; girlfriend
  ragazza alla pari au pair
ragazzo *m* boy ; boyfriend
RAI *f* Italian State Broadcasting
rallentare to slow down
rapido *m* express train
rapido(a) high-speed ; quick
rasoio *m* razor
  rasoio elettrico electric razor
reato *m* crime
recarsi alla cassa pay at cash desk
recentemente recently
reclamo *m* complaint
recupero monete returned coins
regalo *m* present ; gift
reggiseno *m* bra
regione *f* region ; district ; area
registrare to record
registratore *m* cassette player
registro *m* register
Regno Unito *m* United Kingdom
regolamento *m* regulation
regolare regular ; steady
remare to row *(boat)*
rendersi conto di to realize
rene *m* kidney
reparto *m* department ; ward
restare to stay ; to remain
restituire to return ; to give back
restituzione *f* return ; repayment

resto m remainder ; change *(money)*
restringersi to shrink
rete f net ; goal
  rete portabagagli rack *(luggage)*
retro m back
  vedi retro please turn over
retromarcia f reverse gear
reumatismo m rheumatism
ricambio m spare part ; refill
ricaricare to recharge *(battery)*
ricetta f prescription ; recipe
ricevere to receive ; to welcome
ricevitore m receiver *(phone)*
ricevuta f receipt
richiedere to require
richiesta f request
riciclare to recycle
riconoscere to recognize
riconoscimento m identification
ricordare to remember
  non mi ricordo I don't remember
ricordo m souvenir ; memory
ricorrere a to resort to
ricoverare to admit *(to hospital)*
ridere to laugh
ridurre to reduce
riduttore m adaptor
riduzione f reduction
riempire to fill
rientro m return ; return home
rifare to do again ; to repair
rifiutare to refuse
rifiuti mpl rubbish ; waste
rifugio m mountain inn ; shelter
righello m ruler *(for measuring)*
rigore m penalty *(football)*
riguardo m care ; respect
  riguardo a... regarding...
rilasciato(a) a issued at
rimandare to postpone
rimanere to stay ; to remain
rimborsare to reimburse
rimborso m refund
rimessa f remittance ; garage
rimettere to put back
rimettersi to recover *(from illness)*
rimorchiare to tow
rimorchio m trailer
  a rimorchio on tow

rimozione f removal ; towing away
Rinascimento m Renaissance
rinfreschi mpl refreshments
ringraziare to thank
rinnovare to renew
rinunciare to give up
riparare to repair
riparato(a) sheltered
riparazione f repair
ripetere to repeat
ripido(a) abrupt ; steep
ripiegare to fold
ripieno m stuffing
riposarsi to rest
riposo m rest *(repose)*
risalita f reascent
risarcimento m compensation
riscaldamento m heating
riscaldare to heat up *(food)*
rischio m risk
risciacquare to rinse
riscuotere to collect ; to cash
riserva f reserve ; reservation
  riserva di caccia private hunting
  riserva naturale nature reserve
riservare to reserve
riservato(a) reserved
riso m rice ; laugh
risotto m rice cooked in stock
risparmiare to save *(money)*
rispondere to answer ; to reply
risposta f answer
ristorante m restaurant
ritardo m delay
ritirare to withdraw
ritiro m retirement ; withdrawal
  ritiro bagagli baggage reclaim
ritornare to return *(go back)*
ritorno m return
riunione f meeting
riuscita f result ; outcome
riva f bank ; shore
riviera f riviera
rivista f magazine ; revue
rivolgersi a to refer to *(for info)*
roba f stuff ; belongings
roccia f rock
rognoni mpl kidneys
romanico(a) Romanesque
romanzo m novel
  romanzo rosa romantic novel
rompere to break

rondine f swallow (bird)
rosa pink
rosa f rose
rosmarino m rosemary
rosolia f German measles ; rubella
rossetto m lipstick
rosso(a) red
rosticceria f shop selling cooked food
rotonda f roundabout
rotondo(a) round
rotto(a) broken
roulotte f caravan
rovesciare to spill ; to knock over
rovine fpl ruins
rtd delay
rubare to steal
rubinetto m tap
rubrica f address book
ruggine f rust
rughe fpl wrinkles
rullino m roll of film
rum m rum
rumore m noise
rumoroso(a) noisy
ruota f wheel
  ruota di scorta spare wheel
rupe f mountain cliff
ruscello m stream
russare to snore

S

S south (abbreviation)
sabato Saturday
sabbia f sand
saccarina f saccharin
sacchetto m small bag
  sacchetto di carta paper bag
  sacchetto di plastica plastic bag
sacco a pelo m sleeping bag
sacerdote m priest
sagra f local food festival
sala f hall ; auditorium
  sala da pranzo dining room
  sala d'aspetto waiting room
  sala partenze departure lounge
salame m salami
salario m wage
salato(a) salted ; savoury
saldare to settle (bill) ; to weld
saldi sale
saldo m payment ; balance

sale m salt
salire to rise ; to go up
  salire in to get in (vehicle)
salita f climb ; slope
  in salita uphill
salmone m salmon
  salmone affumicato smoked salmon
salone m lounge ; salon
salotto m living room ; lounge
salsa f sauce
salsiccia f sausage
saltare to jump
saltato(a) sautéed
salumeria f delicatessen
salumi mpl cured pork meats
salute f health
  salute! cheers!
saluto m greeting
salvagente m life belt
salvare to rescue ; to save (life)
salvavita m circuit breaker
salve! hello!
salvia f sage (herb)
salvietta f serviette
salviettine per bambini fpl baby wipes
salvo except ; unless
sandali mpl sandals
sangue m blood
  al sangue rare (steak)
sanguinare to bleed
sapere to know
sapone m soap
sapore m flavour ; taste
saporito(a) tasty
Sardegna f Sardinia
sarto m tailor
sartoria f tailor's ; dressmaker's
sasso m stone
sauna f sauna
sbagliato(a) wrong
sbaglio m mistake
sbarco m landing (boat)
sbrigare to hurry
scadente low (standard, quality)
scadenza f expiry
scadere to expire (ticket, etc)
scaduto(a) out-of-date ; expired
scala f scale ; ladder ; staircase
  scala antincendio fire escape
  scala mobile escalator

scalare to climb
scaldabagno m water heater
scaldare to heat up
scale fpl stairs
scalino m step
scalo m stopover
scaloppina f veal escalope
scarico(a) flat (battery)
scarpa f shoe
  scarpe da ginnastica trainers
scarponcini mpl walking boots
scarponi da sci mpl ski boots
scatola f box ; tin
scegliere to choose
scelta f range ; selection ; choice
scendere to go down
  scendere da to get off (bus, etc)
scheda f slip (of paper) ; card
  scheda telefonica phonecard
schiena f back (of body)
sci m ski ; skiing
  sci di fondo cross-country skiing
  sci nautico water-skiing
scialuppa di salvataggio f lifeboat
sciare to ski
sciarpa f scarf
sciogliere to melt
sciopero m strike
sciovia f ski-lift
scivolare to slip
scomodo(a) inconvenient ; uncomfortable
scomparire to disappear
scompartimento m compartment
scongelare to defrost
sconto m discount
  sconti reductions
scontrino m ticket ; receipt ; chit
scopa f broom (brush)
scorso(a) last
scossa f shock (electric)
scottatura f burn
  scottatura solare sunburn
Scozia f Scotland
scozzese Scottish
scrivania f desk
scrivere to write ; to spell
scultura f sculpture
scuola f school
  scuola di sci ski school
  scuola materna nursery school

scuro(a) dark (colour)
scusare to excuse ; to forgive
scusarsi to apologise
scusi? pardon?
se if ; whether
sé oneself
seconda f second gear
secondo m second (time) ; main course (meal)
secondo(a) second ; according to
  seconda classe second class
  di seconda mano secondhand
sede f seat ; head office
sedersi to sit down
sedia f chair
  sedia a rotelle wheelchair
  sedia a sdraio deckchair
sedile per bambini m babyseat (car)
seggiolone m highchair
seggiovia f chair-lift
segnale m signal ; road sign
segnare to score (goal)
segreteria telefonica f answering machine
seguente following
seguire to follow ; to continue
sella f saddle
selvatico(a) wild
semaforo m traffic lights
semifreddo m dessert made with ice cream
seminterrato basement
semplice plain ; simple
sempre always ; ever
senso unico one-way street
  senso vietato no entry
sentiero m path ; footpath
sentire to hear
sentirsi to feel
senza without
separato(a) separated
sera f evening
serbatoio m tank (car)
  serbatoio dell'acqua cistern
serio serious (not funny)
serpente m snake
serratura f lock
servire to serve
servizio m service ; report (in press)
  servizio al tavolo waiter service
  servizio compreso service included
servizi mpl facilities ; bathroom
sesso m sex

seta f silk
sete f thirst
  avere sete to be thirsty
settembre m September
settentrionale northern
settimana f week
  settimana bianca week's skiing holiday
settimanale weekly
sfida f challenge
sfuso(a) loose ; on tap *(wine)*
sganciare to lift receiver
sì yes
Sicilia f Sicily
sicurezza f safety ; security
sicuro(a) sure
sidro m cider
Sig. Mr *abbreviation of* **Signor**
Sig.a Mrs/Ms *abbreviation of* **Signora**
sigaretta f cigarette
sigaro m cigar
Sig.na Miss *abbreviation. of* **Signorina**
Signor: *il Signor Grandi* Mr Grandi
signora f lady ; madam ; Mrs ; Ms
  signore ladies
signore m gentleman ; sir
  signori gents
signorina f young woman ; Miss
silenzio m silence
simile a similar to
simpatico(a) pleasant ; nice
sindaco m mayor
singolo(a) single
sinistra f loft
sistemare to arrange
sito m site
  sito web website
skipass m skipass
slacciare to unfasten ; to undo
slavina f snowslide ; landslide
slegato(a) loose *(not fastened)*
slogatura f sprain
smarrito(a) missing *(thing)*
smettere to stop doing something
soccorso m assistance ; help
  soccorso alpino mountain rescue
socio m associate ; member
soggiorno m stay ; sitting room
soldi mpl money
sole m sun ; sunshine
solito: *di solito* usually
sollevare to raise ; to relieve
sollievo m relief

solo(a) alone ; only
solubile soluble
  caffè solubile instant coffee
sonnifero m sleeping pill
sono I am (to be)
sopra on ; above ; over
  di sopra upstairs
sopracciglia fpl eyebrows
sopravvivere to survive
sorella f sister
sorpassare to overtake *(in car)*
sorpresa f surprise
sorridere to smile
sorriso m smile
sospeso(a) suspended ; postponed
sosta f stop
  divieto di sosta no parking
sott'acqua underwater
sotterraneo(a) underground
sotto underneath ; under ; below
Spagna f Spain
spagnolo(a) Spanish
spalla f shoulder
sparire to disappear
spazzatura f rubbish
spazzola f brush
  spazzola per capelli hairbrush
  spazzolino da denti toothbrush
speciale special
specialità f speciality
specialmente especially
spedire to send ; to dispatch
spegnere to turn off ; to put out
spendere to spend *(money)*
spento(a) turned off ; out *(light, etc)*
sperare to hope
spese fpl shopping ; expenses
spesso often
spettacolo m show ; performance
spezzatino m stew
spiaggia f beach ; shore
  spiaggia privata private beach
spiccioli mpl small coins ; change
  non ho spiccioli I've no change
spiegare to explain
spina f bone *(of fish)* ; plug *(electric)*
spingere to push
spirale f coil *(IUD)*
spogliatoio m dressing room
sporco(a) dirty

sportello *m* counter ; window

sportivo(a) informal *(clothes)*

sposarsi to get married

sposato(a) married
 non sposato(a) single

spugna *f* sponge

spuma *f* hair mousse

spumante *m* sparkling wine

spuntino *m* snack

squadra *f* team

squillare to ring *(phone)*

Srl Ltd

stabilimento *m* factory

stadio *m* stadium

stagione *f* season
 di stagione in season

stalla *f* stable

stampatello *m* block letters

stanco(a) tired

stanza *f* room
 stanza da bagno bathroom
 stanza dei giochi playroom

stare to be
 stare attento(a) a... beware of..
 stare in piedi to stand

stasera tonight ; this evening

Stati Uniti *mpl* United States

stazione *f* station ; resort
 stazione balneare seaside resort
 stazione dell'autobus bus station
 stazione di servizio petrol station
 stazione ferroviaria train station

stella *f* star

sterlina *f* sterling ; pound

stesso(a) same

stirare to iron

stitichezza *f* constipation

stitico(a) constipated

stivali *mpl* boots

storia *f* history

storico(a) historic(al)
 centro storico old town

strada *f* road ; street
 strada chiusa road closed
 strada panoramica scenic route
 strada sbarrata road closed
 strada statale main road
 strada senza uscita no through road

stradina *f* lane

straniero(a) foreign ; foreigner

strano(a) strange

stupido(a) stupid

su on ; onto ; over ; about ; up

sua his ; her(s) ; its ; your(s)

subito at once ; immediately

succedere to happen

succo *m* juice
 succo d'arancia orange juice
 succo di frutta fruit juice
 succo di mela apple juice
 succo di pomodoro tomato juice

succursale *m* branch *(of bank, etc)*

sud *m* south

sue his ; her(s) ; its ; your(s)

suo(i) his ; her(s) ; its ; your(s)

suocera *f* mother-in-law

suocero *m* father-in-law

suola *f* sole *(of foot, shoe)*

suonare to ring ; to play

suono *m* sound

superare to exceed ; to overtake

supermercato *m* supermarket

supplemento *m* supplement

supposta *f* suppository

surf *m* surf

surgelato(a) frozen

sveglia *f* alarm clock

svegliare to wake up

svenire to faint

sviluppare to develop *(photos)*

Svizzera *f* Switzerland

svizzero(a) Swiss

svolta *f* turn

T

tabaccaio *m* tobacconist's

tacco *m* heel

tachimetro *m* speedometer

taglia *f* size *(of clothes)*

tagliare to cut

tailleur *m* women's suit

tallone *m* heel

tangenziale *f* by-pass

tanti(e) so many

tanto(a) so much ; so

tappo *m* cork ; plug ; cap
 tappo del serbatoio petrol cap

tardi late

targa *f* numberplate *(car)*

tariffa *f* tariff ; rate
 tariffa economica cheap rate
 tariffa festiva rate on holidays
 tariffa ore di punta peak rate

tartuffo m truffle
tasca f pocket
tassa f tax
tasso m rate
  tasso di cambio exchange rate
tavola f table ; plank ; board
  tavola calda hot snacks
  tavola da surf surfboard
  tavola a vela windsurfing board
taxi m taxi
tazza f cup
tè m tea
  tè al latte tea with milk
  tè al limone lemon tea
  tè freddo iced tea
teatro m theatre ; drama
tedesco(a) German
telecomando m remote control
telefonare to (tele)phone
telefonata f phone call
telefonino m mobile phone
telefono m telephone
  telefono pubblico payphone
televisione f television
telone impermeabile m groundsheet
temperatura f temperature
temperino m penknife
tempesta f storm
tempio m temple
tempo m weather ; time
temporale m thunderstorm
tenda f curtain ; tent
tendine m tendon
tenere to keep ; to hold
tenore m tenor (singer)
tenore alcolico m alcohol content
tergicristallo m windscreen wiper
terminal m terminal (airport)
termometro m thermometer
termosifone m heater
terra f earth ; ground
terrazza f terrace
terremoto m earthquake
terza f third gear
terzi mpl third party
terzo(a) third
tessera f pass ; season ticket
tesserino m pass (bus, train)
tessuto m fabric
testa f head
testicoli mpl testicles
tettarella f dummy (for baby)
tetto m roof

tettuccio apribile m sunroof (car)
Tevere m Tiber
thermos m thermos flask
thriller m thriller
timone m rudder
tirare to pull
toccare to touch ; to feel
  non toccare do not touch
togliere to remove ; to take away
toilette f toilet
tonno m tuna
topo m mouse
Torino f Turin
tornare to return ; to come/go back
torneo m tournament
toro m bull
torre f tower
torrone m nougat
torta f cake ; tart ; pie
Toscana f Tuscany
tosse f cough
tossico(a) toxic
tossire to cough
totale m total (amount)
tovaglia f tablecloth
tovagliolo m napkin
tra between ; among(st) ; in
tradizionale traditional
tradurre to translate
traduzione f translation
traffico m traffic
traghetto m ferry
tramezzino m sandwich
trampolino m diving board ; ski jump
tranquillante m tranquillizer
tranquillo(a) quiet (place)
trasferire to transfer
trasporto m transport
trattoria f restaurant
traveller's cheque mpl traveller's cheque
traversata f crossing ; flight
treno m train
  treno merci goods train
triangolo d'emergenza m warning triangle
tribuna f stand (stadium)
tribunale m law court
trimestre m term (school)

triste sad
tritare to mince ; to chop
troppi(e) too many
troppo too much ; too
trovare to find
trucco *m* make-up
tu you *(familiar)*
tubo *m* pipe ; tube
  tubo di scappamento exhaust
tuffarsi to dive
turno *m* turn ; shift
  di turno on duty
tuta sportiva *f* tracksuit
tutti (e) all ; everybody
  tutte le direzioni all routes
tutto everything ; all

U

ubriaco(a) drunk
uccello *m* bird
uccidere to kill
UE European Union
ufficio *m* office ; church service
  ufficio informazioni information
  bureau
  ufficio oggetti smarriti lost
  property office
  ufficio postale post office
ufficio turistico tourist office
uguale equal ; even
ulcera *f* ulcer
ultimo(a) last
un a ; an ; one
unghia *f* nail *(finger, toe)*
unione *f* union
  Unione Europea European Union
Unità Sanitaria Locale local health
  centre
università *f* university
uno(a) a ; an ; one
uomo *m* man
  uomini gents
uova *mpl* eggs
uovo *m* egg
  uovo di Pasqua Easter egg
  uovo sodo hard-boiled egg
uragano *m* hurricane
urgente urgent
usare to use

uscire to go/come out
uscita *f* exit/gate
  uscita di sicurezza emergency exit
USL *abbreviation of* **Unità Sanitaria
  Locale**
uso *m* use
utile useful
uva *f* grapes

V

va bene all right *(agreed)*
vacanza *f* holiday(s)
  vacanze estive summer holidays
vaccinazione *f* vaccination
vagina *f* vagina
vaglia *m* money order
vagone *m* carriage ; wagon
  vagone letto sleeper
  vagone ristorante restaurant car
valanga *f* avalanche
valico *m* pass *(mountain)*
valido(a) valid
  valido fino a... valid until...
valigia *f* suitcase
valore *m* value; worth
  di valore valuable
valuta *f* currency
valvola *f* valve
varicella *f* chickenpox
vasetto *m* jar
vaso *m* vase
vassoio *m* tray
vecchio(a) old
vedere to see
vedova *f* widow
vedovo *m* widower
vegetaliano(a) vegan
vegetariano(a) vegetarian
veicolo *m* vehicle
vela *f* sail ; sailing
veleno *m* poison
velenoso(a) poisonous
veloce quick
velocemente quickly
velocità *f* speed
vena *f* vein
vendere to sell
  vendesi for sale
vendita *f* sale
  vendita al minuto retail
  vendita a rate hire purchase
venerdì *m* Friday

185 **venerdì santo** *m* Good Friday
Venezia *f* Venice
venire to come
ventaglio *m* fan *(hand-held)*
ventilatore *m* electric fan
vento *m* wind
verde green
verdura *f* vegetables
verità *f* truth
vermut *m* vermouth
vernice *f* paint
verniciare to paint
vero(a) true ; real ; genuine
versamento *m* payment ; deposit
versare to pour
vertice *m* summit
vescica *f* blister
vespa *f* wasp
vestaglia *f* dressing gown
vestirsi to get dressed
vestiti *mpl* clothes
vestito *m* dress
vetrina *f* shop window
vetro *m* glass *(substance)*
via *f* street ; by *(via)*
  per via aerea by air mail
viaggiare to travel
viaggiatore *m* traveller
viaggio *m* journey ; trip ; drive
  viaggio d'affari business trip
  viaggio organizzato package tour
viale *m* avenue
vicino (a) near ; close by
vicolo *m* alley ; lane
  vicolo cieco cul-de-sac
videocamera *f* videocamera
videocassetta *f* videocassette
videogioco *m* computer game
videoregistratore *m* video recorder
vietato forbidden
  vietato accendere fuocchi do not light fires
  vietato fumare no smoking
  vietato l'ingresso no entry
  vietato ingresso veicoli no entry for vehicles
  vietato scendere no exit
vigili del fuoco fire brigade
vigilia *f* eve
  Vigilia di Natale Christmas Eve
vigna *f* vineyard
vincere to win
vino *m* wine

  vino bianco white wine
  vini da pasto table wines
  vino da tavola table wine
  vini pregiati quality wines
  vino rosso red wine
violentare to rape
virus *m* virus
visita *f* visit
  visite guidate guided tours
visitare to visit
vista *f* view
visto *m* visa
vita *f* life ; waist
  vita notturna night life
vitamina *f* vitamin
vite *f* vine ; screw
vivere to live
vivo(a) live ; alive
voce *f* voice
volante *m* steering wheel
volare to fly
voler dire to mean *(signify)*
volere to want
volo *m* flight
  volo di linea scheduled flight
  volo charter charter flight
volta *f* time
  una volta once
  due volte twice
voltaggio *m* voltage
vomitare to vomit
vongola *f* clam
vostro(a) your ; yours
vulcano *m* volcano
vuoto(a) empty

Z

zanzara *f* mosquito
zanzaria *f* mosquito net
zia *f* aunt
zio *m* uncle
zona *f* zone
  zona blu restricted parking zone
  zona pedonale pedestrian
zucchero *m* sugar
zucchini *mpl* courgettes
zuppa *f* soup
  zuppa inglese type of trifle

HOW ITALIAN WORKS

NOUNS

*A **noun** is a word such as car, horse or Mary which is used to refer to a person or thing.*

Unlike English, Italian nouns have a gender: they are either *masculine* (**il**) or *feminine* (**la**). Therefore words for *the* and *a(n)* must agree with the noun they accompany – whether *masculine, feminine* or *plural*:

	masculine/plural	*feminine/plural*
the	**il gatto/i gatti**	**la strada/le strade**
	l'anno/gli anni	**l'alba/le albe**
a(n)/some	**un gatto/dei gatti**	**una strada/delle strade**
	un anno/degli anni	**un'alba/delle albe**

NOTE: you will come across the articles **lo** and **gli** for masculine nouns beginning with s+consonant

	masculine/plural
the	**lo stato/gli stati**
a(n)/some	**uno stato/degli stati**

PLURALS

For most nouns, the singular ending changes as follows:

masc. sing.	*masc. plur.*	*example*
-o	**-i**	**il libro → i libri**
-e	**-i**	**il padre → i padri**
fem. sing.	*fem. plur.*	*example*
-a	**-e**	**la mela → le mele**
-e	**-i**	**la madre → le madri**

NOTE: nouns ending in **e** can be either *masculine* or *feminine*. In the plural they all end in -i, e.g.

la televisione	**le televisioni**
il mare	**i mari**

NOTE: most nouns ending in **-co** and **-go** become **-chi** and **-ghi** in the plural to keep the **c** and **g** hard sounding. Some exceptions occur in the masculine, e.g. **amico – amici**

NOTE: nouns ending in **-ca** and **-ga** become **-che** and **-ghe** in the plural to keep the **c** and **g** hard sounding. Nouns ending in **-cia** and **-gia** often becomes **-ce** and **ge** to keep the **c** and **g** soft sounding, e.g.

la barca	**le barche**
la boccia	**le bocce**

NOTE: definite articles (**il**, **la**, **i**, **le**, *etc.*) used after the prepositions **a** (**to, at**), **da**
(**by, from**), **su** (**on**), **di** (**of, some**) and **in** (**in, into**)
contract as follows:

a + il = **al**	**da + il** = **dal**	**su + il** = **sul**
a + lo = **allo**	**da + lo** = **dallo**	**su + lo** = **sullo**
a + l' = **all'**	**da + l'** = **dall'**	**su + l'** = **sull'**
a + la = **alla**	**da + la** = **dalla**	**su + la** = **sulla**
a + i = **ai**	**da + i** = **dai**	**su + i** = **sui**
a + gli = **agli**	**da + gli** = **dagli**	**su + gli** = **sugli**
a + le = **alle**	**da + le** = **dalle**	**su + le** = **sulle**
di + il = **del**	**in + il** = **nel**	
di + lo = **dello**	**in + lo** = **nello**	
di + l' = **dell'**	**in + l'** = **nell'**	
di + la = **della**	**in + la** = **nella**	
di + i = **dei**	**in + i** = **nei**	
di + gli = **degli**	**in + gli** = **negli**	
di + le = **delle**	**in + le** = **nelle**	

e.g. **alla** casa (**to the** house) **sul** tavolo (**on the** table)

ADJECTIVES

*An **adjective** is a word such as **small**, **pretty** or **practical** that describes a person or thing, or gives extra information about them.*

Adjectives normally follow the noun they describe in Italian,
e.g. la mela **rossa** (the red apple)
Some common exceptions which go before the noun are:
bello beautiful, **breve** short, **brutto** ugly, **buono** good, **cattivo** bad, **giovane** young, **grande** big, **lungo** long, **nuovo** new, **piccolo** small, **vecchio** old
e.g. una **bella** giornata (a beautiful day)

Italian adjectives have to reflect the gender of the noun they describe. To make an adjective feminine, an **a** replaces the **o** of the masculine, e.g. ross**o** – ross**a**. Adjectives ending in **e**, e.g. **giovane**, can be either masculine or feminine. The plural forms of the adjective change in the way described for nouns (above).

MY, YOUR, HIS, HER, OUR, THEIR

These words also depend on the gender and number of the noun they accompany, and not on the sex of the 'owner'.

	with masc. sing. noun	with fem. sing. noun	with masc. plur. noun	with fem. plur. noun
my	**il mio**	**la mia**	**i miei**	**le mie**
your (polite)	**il suo**	**la sua**	**i suoi**	**le sue**
your (familiar)	**il tuo**	**la tua**	**i tuoi**	**le tue**
your (plural)	**il vostro**	**la vostra**	**i vostri**	**le vostre**
his/her	**il suo**	**la sua**	**i suoi**	**le sue**
our	**il nostro**	**la nostra**	**i nostri**	**le nostre**
their	**il loro**	**la loro**	**i loro**	**le loro**

*A **pronoun** is a word that you use to refer to someone or something when you do not need to use a noun, often because the person or thing has been mentioned earlier. Examples are **it**, **she**, **something** and **myself**.*

SUBJECT		OBJECT	
I	**io**	me	**mi**
you	**lei**	you	**la**
he	**lui/egli**	him	**lo/l'** *(+vowel)*
she	**lei/ella**	her	**la/l'** *(+vowel)*
it *(masc.)*	**esso**	it *(masc.)*	**lo/l'** *(+vowel)*
it *(fem.)*	**essa**	it *(fem.)*	**la/l'** *(+vowel)*
we	**noi**	us	**ci**
you	**voi**	you	**vi**
they	**loro**	them *(masc.)*	**li**
(things:masc)	**essi**	them *(fem.)*	**le**
(things:fem.)	**esse**		

The object pronouns shown above are also used to mean **to me**, **to us**, etc., except:

to him/to it	= **gli**
to her/to it/to you	= **le**
to them	= **loro**

Object pronouns (other than **loro**) usually go before the verb:

lo vedo	but	**scriverò loro**
I see him		I will write to them

When used with an infinitive (the verb form given in the dictionary), the pronoun follows and is attached to the infinitive less its final *e*:

voglio comprarlo   I want to buy it

Subject pronouns (**io**, **tu**, **egli**, etc.) are often omitted in Italian, since the verb ending generally distinguishes the person:

parlo	I speak
parliamo	we speak
parlano	they speak

In Italian there are two forms for *you* – **Lei** (singular) and **voi** (plural). **Tu**, the familiar form for **you**, should only be used with people you know well, or children.

*A **verb** is a word such as **sing**, **walk** or **cry** which is used with a subject to say what someone or something does or what happens to them. **Regular verbs** follow the same pattern of endings. **Irregular verbs** do not follow a regular pattern so you need to learn the different endings.*

There are three main patterns of endings for verbs in Italian – those ending **-are**, **-ere** and **-ire** in the dictionary. Two examples of the **-ire** verbs are shown, since two distinct groups of endings exist. Subject pronouns are shown in brackets because these are often not used:

	PARL<u>ARE</u>	
(io)	**parlo**	I speak
(tu)	**parli**	you speak
(lui/lei)	**parla**	(s)he speaks
(noi)	**parliamo**	we speak
(voi)	**parlate**	you speak
(loro)	**parlano**	they speak

past participle: **parlato** (with **avere**)

	VEND<u>ERE</u>	
(io)	**vendo**	I sell
(tu)	**vendi**	you sell
(lui/lei)	**vende**	(s)he sells
(noi)	**vendiamo**	we sell
(voi)	**vendete**	you sell
(loro)	**vendono**	they sell

past participle: **venduto** (with **avere**)

	DORM<u>IRE</u>	
(io)	**dormo**	I sleep
(tu)	**dormi**	you sleep
(lui/lei)	**dorme**	(s)he sleeps
(noi)	**dormiamo**	we sleep
(voi)	**dormite**	you sleep
(loro)	**dormono**	they sleep

past participle: **dormito** (with **avere**)

	FIN<u>IRE</u>	
(io)	**finisco**	I finish
(tu)	**finisci**	you finish
(lui/lei)	**finisce**	(s)he finishes
(noi)	**finiamo**	we finish
(voi)	**finite**	you finish
(loro)	**finiscono**	they finish

past participle: **finito** (with **avere**)

Among the most important irregular verbs are the following:

	ESSERE	TO BE		AVERE	TO HAVE
(io)	**sono**	I am		**ho**	I have
(tu)	**sei**	you are		**hai**	you have
(lui/lei)	**è**	(s)he is		**ha**	(s)he has
(noi)	**siamo**	we are		**abbiamo**	we have
(voi)	**siete**	you are		**avete**	you have
(loro)	**sono**	they are		**hanno**	they have

past participle: **stato** (with **essere**)   past participle: **avuto** (with **avere**)

	ANDARE	TO GO		FARE	TO DO
(io)	**vado**	I go		**faccio**	I do
(tu)	**vai**	you go		**fai**	you do
(lui/lei)	**va**	(s)he goes		**fa**	(s)he does
(noi)	**andiamo**	we go		**facciamo**	we do
(voi)	**andate**	you go		**fate**	you do
(loro)	**vanno**	they go		**fanno**	they do

past participle: **andato** (with **essere**)   past participle: **fatto** (with **avere**)

	POTERE	TO BE ABLE		VOLERE	TO WANT
(io)	**posso**	I can		**voglio**	I want
(tu)	**puoi**	you can		**vuoi**	you want
(lui/lei)	**può**	(s)he can		**vuole**	(s)he wants
(noi)	**possiamo**	we can		**vogliamo**	we want
(voi)	**potete**	you can		**volete**	you want
(loro)	**possono**	they can		**vogliono**	they want

past participle: **potuto** (with **avere**)   past participle: **voluto** (with **avere**)

	DOVERE	TO HAVE TO (MUST)
(io)	**devo**	I must
(tu)	**devi**	you must
(lui/lei)	**deve**	he/she must
(noi)	**dobbiamo**	we must
(voi)	**dovete**	you must
(loro)	**devono**	they must

past participle: **dovuto** (with **avere**)

PAST TENSE

*To make a simple past tense you need an **auxiliary verb** with the past participle of the main verb, e.g. **I have** (auxiliary) **been** (past participle), **I have** (auxiliary) **eaten** (past participle). In Italian the basic auxiliary verbs are **avere** (to have) and **essere** (to be). A **reflexive verb** is one where the subject and object are the same e.g. **to enjoy yourself, to dress yourself**. These verbs take **essere** as their auxiliary verb.*

To form the simple past tense, I spoke/I have spoken, I sold/I have sold, etc. combine the present tense of the verb **avere** – to have with the past participle of the verb, e.g.

ho parlato	I spoke/I have spoken
ho venduto	I sold/I have sold

PARL<u>ARE</u> (past)		VEND<u>ERE</u> (past)	
ho parlato	I spoke	**ho venduto**	I sold
hai parlato	you spoke	**hai venduto**	you sold
ha parlato	(s)he spoke	**ha venduto**	(s)he sold
abbiamo parlato	we spoke	**abbiamo venduto**	we sold
avete parlato	you spoke	**avete venduto**	you sold
hanno parlato	they spoke	**hanno venduto**	they sold

DORM<u>IRE</u> (past)		FIN<u>IRE</u> (past)	
ho dormito	I slept	**ho finito**	I finished
hai dormito	you slept	**hai finito**	you finished
ha dormito	(s)he slept	**ha finito**	(s)he finished
abbiamo dormito	we slept	**abbiamo finito**	we finished
avete dormito	you slept	**avete finito**	you finished
hanno dormito	they slept	**hanno finito**	they finished

NOTE: not all verbs take **avere** (**ho**, **hai**, etc.) as their auxiliary verb, some take **essere** (**sono**, **sei**, etc.). These are mainly verbs of motion or staying, e.g. **andare–to go**, **stare–to be** (located at):

e.g. **sono andato**   I went
       sono stato a Roma   I was in Rome

When the auxiliary verb **essere** is used, the past particple (**andato**, **stato**) becomes an adjective and should agree with the subject of the verb, e.g.

sono andat<u>a</u>	I went *(fem. sing.)*
siamo stat<u>i</u>	we went *(masc. plural)*

To make a sentence negative e. g. I am not eating, you use **non** before the verb.

e.g.	**non mangio**	I am not eating
	non sono andato	I did not go